An Introduct
Building and
Renovating Houses

Volume 1 – hiring contractors, managing construction and finishing your home

"Expert tips and advice to help you make the right decisions. Support to ensure that construction of your new house is a success."

Paul Netscher

Published by Panet Publications
PO Box 2119, Subiaco, 6904, Australia

ISBN: 9781070735955

Available from Amazon.com and other retail outlets

For information on the author and his other books visit www.pn-projectmanagement.com

Legal Notices

It should be noted that houses are varied, using different materials and employing diverse construction methods. Countries, states, counties and cities have different regulations, restrictions, codes and laws. To complicate matters further these laws, acts and restrictions are continually evolving and changing. Even terminologies vary between countries and contracts, and may not be the same as those included in this publication. Technology is continually moving. In addition, we're all different and what I might think is a perfect home, or an item I think is important in my house, may not be something you would consider. It's therefore important that readers use the information in this publication, taking cognisance of the particular rules that apply in their region and to their project, and adjust to suit their own personal requirements.

Each house has its own sets of challenges and no one book can cover all the steps and processes in every project. Some of the author's personal opinions may not be pertinent to you, your contract or your house. Readers should undertake further research and reading on the topics particularly relevant to them, even requesting expert advice when required.

Therefore, the author, publisher and distributor assume no responsibility or liability for any loss or damage of any kind arising from the purchaser or reader using the information or advice contained herein.

The examples used in the book should not be seen as a criticism of people or companies, but, should rather be viewed as cases which we can all learn from. After all we've all made mistakes. Any perceived slights are unintentional.

Cover layout by Clark Kenyon, www.camppope.com
Construction schedule in chapter 6 prepared by Gavin Chalmers

Preface

Most of us would like to live in a nice family home where we can be happy and carefree. A home that's just right for us and our family. That has all the space and some of the luxuries and convenience we desire. How do we reach this goal? Why not renovate our house, or maybe build a new home from scratch? Home makeover shows and do-it-yourself magazines make it all look so easy.

With these thoughts in mind many excited homeowners leap straight into their home renovation and home construction projects. It seems so simple – what could go wrong? Unfortunately all too frequently things do go wrong. Projects don't turn out as expected – why doesn't our new house look like the images we envisaged before we embarked on the process. The project takes for ever to finish and we live in a building site for months – even years. Then there're the family arguments over paint colours, types of light fixtures, carpet styles and colours – there seem to be an endless range of choices. Furthermore, there are frequently arguments with the builders when things don't work, roofs leak, damp appears in the house, cracks in the walls, and more. Budgets are blown – often causing financial stresses, family fights, and even the project remaining unfinished. In the worst case banks may repossess the house. How can our dream home turn into this nightmare?

But building or renovating a house doesn't have to be a nightmare. Sure, it can be stressful sometimes, it can involve hard work, but if planned properly it should be a very rewarding process, one that provides your family with a wonderful home for many years. A final result that enhances your financial situation. A home that's the envy of your friends, family and neighbours.

I want to make your building project a success. The path to success starts long before construction work begins on your house. Let me help you as I take you on the exciting journey through the various stages in the process that ends with a renovated home, or a new house, that you and your family will love and enjoy for many years without having broken the bank.

I'm not going to make the decisions for you, nor am I going to tell you what you must do, but I'm going to give you all the information so that you can make informed decisions which are best for you.

Acknowledgements

A special thanks to the readers of my previous books who continue to inspire me to write with their great reviews and comments.

I've been fortunate to have had a successful career in construction thanks to the support of my team and the help and advice I received from numerous colleagues. My experiences have inspired me to pass on my knowledge and experience to others. Thanks to everyone that has taught and helped me over the years.

Thanks to Sandra for her patience and support.

CONTENTS AT A GLANCE

"Building or renovating a house should be exciting. You can make it a success, whether you do everything yourself, outsource some of the work to experts, or leave everything to the experts. But, even experts need to be managed – and of course, make sure that they really are experts! How much you do and how much work you leave to experts will depend on your expertise, confidence, means and time."

Contents

CHAPTER 6 – DOING THE WORK YOURSELF ---77

CHAPTER 7 – FINDING CONTRACTORS ---97

Introduction

You've probably all heard some horror story of a home renovation or a new house build that's gone wrong. The project has gone over budget, it's been finished late, there's been protracted legal arguments with the builder, or the house has been a nightmare of things that needed repair soon after it's finished. Indeed I recently read that someone won a case against their contractor and they were awarded $150,000 in damages to fix a job the builder botched – the only problem is the contractor has since been declared bankrupt and closed their doors so it's doubtful the homeowner will get any of the $150,000.

Several years ago we bought a brand new house – we were the first to live there. It was a lovely house and seemed perfect with good quality but we had no sooner moved in than a waterpipe burst in the upstairs bathroom sending water cascading in a waterfall down the stairs. This resulted in the cupboards in the bathroom having to be replaced. Then soon after this we discovered that the toilet in one bathroom was blocked. Only after several attempts and finally chopping up the bathroom did the builder find concrete in the toilet pipe. After the first heavy rainstorm water flooded into the study ruining the cupboards and carpet. It took the builder several attempts to find the leak which was caused by the roof not being properly sealed around the chimney. But the tale of woes wasn't ended there, we later found water leaking into our enclosed veranda which we finally tracked to a pipe within a wall which wasn't correctly joined. Then the render on the retaining wall in the garden started bubbling and peeling off because the back of the wall against the ground wasn't waterproofed properly. Finally, as I describe later in the book, we discovered tons of building rubble buried in the garden. Many of these issues the builder fixed, but some we eventually gave up on and just repaired them ourselves.

Now you've probably also watched home renovation and construction shows on television and you're become all excited about building your own designer home. It all looks so easy. Sure, some people made mistakes on the show, but it all ended up fine in the end! What could go wrong if you do everything yourself? Of course what we don't see are the experts providing advice and help in the background.

Building a house, or renovating your home, isn't as simple as it looks on a home make-over show. Maybe a few do-it-yourself books can help, but it's more than just construction. It's about planning the project from the beginning – doing your homework properly. You must decide what you need, where you want it, and how much it will cost. If you can afford the project, then you require the right team and you have to manage the process right to the end of the construction phase. Then when construction is complete you should understand your rights and obligations. A wrong step along the way could result in additional costs, delays and possibly even a house that you're not happy with.

So you could decide to do all the work yourself, but this will depend on your expertise, time and budget. Alternatively you could employ a contractor to do everything for you, possibly even completing the design. Then there are various options in between, which could be that you do some of the work yourself and employ contractors to do some of the specialist trades. You may select to appoint a number of specialist contractors to do parts of the project and you then manage and coordinate these various contractors.

Unfortunately many contractors are unreliable, they deliver poor quality work, they charge exorbitant fees, they don't fix their problems, they drag out the job and inevitably there are a litany of excuses. But there are also many good contractors who deliver quality projects on time. It's therefore imperative to do proper research to employ the right team for your project. Don't be swayed only by the cheapest price, rather understand the contractor's abilities and their current resources. Indeed, even good contractors can deliver a bad project when they're under resourced or have too much work. But also, not every building project is suited to every contractor, so it's important to find a contractor that can do your job, and of course a contractor that you can work with.

But even the best contractors usually have to be managed and checked on. If you don't have the skills and knowledge to check on your contractor and project then consider employing a project manager or a clerk of works. This may sound costly, but at the end of the day trying to save costs in the construction process could end up costing you more later, apart from the frustration caused by faulty workmanship or a project that's finished late. Think of my own experiences described above of the problems in our new house, problems which should all have been picked up during the construction phase if there was proper supervision.

Then when your house or renovation is finally finished can you move right in? What needs to be done to make it habitable? What should you check before moving in? What are your rights and obligations if something does go wrong?

There are different rules, national, state, county, local government, and in some cases even estate rules, that could dictate what you can build, what materials you use and even the construction methods that should be used. Frequently these rules are changed and updated and what was allowed previously is now unacceptable. There're sometimes endless permits and permissions that are required, and these vary from region to region and city to city. Failing to get these, or to comply, can lead to expensive mistakes and delays.

I'm not going to tell you what you should do because every project is different and each of us is different. For some of you who have the time, knowledge and energy, building or renovating your own home may be very rewarding and the best option. For others, employing a reputable project manager, architect and contractor could be the correct choice. This book isn't going to give you the 'blueprint', or a step-by-step system to constructing or renovating your new home, rather I intend to equip you with general construction knowledge and advice on avoiding many of the common pitfalls.

Constructing a new house involves hundreds of decisions. Each of these decisions could have a time and a cost associated with them. You'll have to live with many of the decisions for years. So make your decisions wisely, considering all the information at hand. Of course this doesn't mean you should procrastinate, which could be as costly as making the wrong decision. Rather take a steady logical approach.

Never hesitate to engage experts for advice or when you need help. The costs of using an expert may seem big, but that cost must be viewed in the context of the overall project cost, and the risk of getting something wrong without their advice. But if you're confident in your own knowledge, expertise and abilities, then by all means go it alone.

A final word of advice – always double check everything, whether it's a measurement, your budget, an invoice, a contract document, a planning submission, a material quantity, an order, a quote, calculation or a drawing. A simple arithmetic error or missed item could be a very expensive mistake which could jeopardise the success of your project.

Good luck, may your new home be everything that you hoped it would be.

Notes on using this book

Terminologies vary between countries. Please refer to the glossary at the end of this book for the meaning of the terms I've used.

This book doesn't refer to specific permits, licenses or permissions. These vary between countries, states and even districts. But furthermore, they're also revised from time to time. It's important that you refer to local legislation and ask for expert advice to understand the requirements that apply in your district at the present time. Even if you've previously been involved with construction in your area it always pays to check the current rules, ensuring they haven't been recently revised.

I've included a few simple stylised sketches which aren't to scale to illustrate some concepts which I wasn't able to adequately explain in words. I've exaggerated some items on the sketch to highlight particular points.

It should be noted that this is not a detailed guide on how to construct your home, rather it's a guide to what steps you need to take, including some of the more important considerations. There are other excellent guides which will show you specific construction details, materials and construction methods.

In my book *'An Introduction to 'Building and Renovating Houses – Finding Your Ideal Property and Designing Your Dream Home'* I discuss things you should consider when deciding what you need in your new house. Then there's a chapter on finding the right property for you and your family. There are considerations for renovating or remodelling an existing house. I also discuss numerous factors which will influence the design of your house and important considerations when planning your new home. Finally there's a chapter on simple changes you could make to your existing home, changes which can be made at a modest cost and which will transform your home without it being necessary to embark on an extensive renovation project.

Who am I

I have 30 years construction experience, which includes multimillion dollar projects such as stadiums, shopping malls, casinos, roads, reservoirs, bridges and houses. But. importantly, I've owned and lived in several houses. I've employed contractors to renovate and repair some of these. In this time I've seen many mistakes which should have been avoided. Yet, I've also been exposed to many good ideas and excellent construction work. I've also made my own errors and learnt from them.

I hate seeing bad construction projects, those of poor quality, where people have been injured, which were over budget and in some cases didn't satisfy the owner's requirements. I want to make every construction project successful – as they all should be. To pass on my experience and knowledge I've written several construction management books. *'Successful Construction Project Management: The Practical Guide'* is aimed at contractors. *'Construction Management: From Project Concept to Completion'* is for project clients and owners. *'Building a Successful Construction Company: The Practical Guide'* is for owners and senior managers of construction companies. These practical easy to read books have received good reviews from readers, including:

"Great reading. It's a real case of where, what and how to construct, integrated with why, when, where. An easy manner of writing is making content understandable for construction managers..."

"Excellent writing, very useful and all round good read."

"This book is fun to read and full of examples of what to be aware of with project management. His stories are insightful and educational. His style of writing is fun and useful."

"It's also good to learn from someone who made mistakes, takes blame, which made the book real. He presents the information to cover everything in an easy flowing read."

"Really a good practical guide"

"Great book, offers excellent insight"

" Well written and easy to read!"

I want to empower you to make the right decisions – right for you. I want to ensure your building and renovation project is a success. I hope this book gives you the knowledge to successfully build or renovate your house.

Chapter 1 – Who's Who and What They Do

You may choose to do everything yourself, from construction work to planning and design, as well as obtaining all the permits and permissions. Depending on the type of work and your skills this is often possible. But, for most of us, particularly with larger projects such as constructing a new house or major renovations, we usually require some expert advice, guidance and help.

Often renovations are minor, like repainting the inside of the house, small repairs, installing new cupboards, even installing new light fixtures, recarpeting rooms and replacing tiles, or even remodelling kitchens. This work usually doesn't require planning permissions or permits, however any work that requires altering of the electrical, gas or plumbing installations must be done by certified licensed contractors, and in most cases they should submit a certificate to confirm the work is compliant.

Larger projects require approvals from the local authorities, and sometimes other bodies. It must comply with building standards and codes, which could be, national codes, state codes, local town or city codes, and even specific estate rules. Complying with these requires an understanding of them, and often involves particular licenses. Submissions must be made to these authorities, including plans and drawings. Failure to understand the submission requirements and the various codes can result in delays with issuing the permissions, often requiring redesign and rework to bring the submission up to the requirements before it can be approved.

Construction work that doesn't meet the specifications and codes will have to be redone. Substandard work may cause the house to be deemed unsafe, and it will certainly fail inspection should you try and sell the house. Work that doesn't meet the regulatory codes and standards may also result in insurers refusing to insure the building, or it could be reason for them to refute insurance claims. Should someone be injured because of substandard work, or work that doesn't meet codes then that person can institute legal action against you and most courts would find in their favour, and invariably insurance policies wouldn't protect you against the claim.

Architects

Architects prepare plans for building renovations, new houses and apartments. Employing a local architect should provide assurance that they understand the local codes and specifications and that their design will conform to these. Sometimes people employ architects from another state or country to design their house. These architects may be unfamiliar with the local codes and specifications, available building materials, usual building methods and the available construction skills. This could result in them specifying products that aren't compliant, or stipulating materials which aren't available locally, or requiring construction methods which local contractors aren't familiar with. This will result in additional costs and delays to your house.

Architects prepare construction drawings which you or a contractor will use to build the house. Usually these drawings should be approved by you before work starts, and they generally need to be submitted and approved by the local authorities before building work begins.

Depending on the contract with the architect they may have to engage other professionals such as engineers to assist with the design (see next section). They may also be contracted to manage the contractor and monitor the construction quality. In some cases, it's possible to include in their scope of work that they prepare the contract documentation for contractors to price, and then that they also formalise the contract documents and the agreement between you and the contractor.

Architects should be able to provide advice and make recommendations of the types of finishes and products to be incorporated into the house.

Architects should first receive your ideas, requirements, budgets and expectations, then propose a design that satisfies most of these. They should advise you when your expectations are unreasonable, when budgets could be too low, when requirements can't be met and when ideas are poor or could be improved upon. However, in general they shouldn't go against your wishes if you are adamant you want to stick to your original concept ideas despite their warnings and advice, unless these wishes are totally impractical, or where they don't meet the code and specifications.

It should be noted, that should you change your mind, or add additional items into your brief after the architect has started preparing the design then they could charge for their time spent on amending the drawings as a result of these changes.

Engineers

There are various engineers that may be involved with the design of houses. These include structural engineers (they design structural elements of the house such as foundations, beams, slabs and sometimes roofs), ventilation or air-conditioning engineers (design air-conditioning systems), civil engineers or road engineers (design roads, parking and stormwater), electrical engineers (responsible for the design of high voltage electrical installations, or more complex electrical systems), and geotechnical engineers are usually required for buildings located in an area of complex ground conditions or poor founding conditions.

It should be noted that most houses don't require complex engineering design work. In general the location and type of electrical switches, fittings and plug points are shown on the architect's drawings. Most licensed electricians are capable of installing the required electrical systems so electrical engineers aren't usually required.

So to with the air-conditioning and minor mechanical equipment, where it's usually sufficient for the architect to specify the requirements for air-conditioning and then a reliable contractor is capable of designing and installing the system. However, for larger systems for peace of mind it may pay to hire a mechanical engineer to review the drawings of the system as proposed by the contractor and then to check the completed installation to ensure that it's compliant. Unfortunately, there are sometimes 'cowboys' in the air-conditioning business who do a poor job, installing a system which is inadequate and doesn't work efficiently.

Structural engineers design structural elements of the building, particularly foundations, and for multistorey dwellings the supporting structures which include loadbearing walls, columns, beams and suspended floor slabs. Structural engineers are usually required to design buildings in areas prone to tornedoes, hurricanes, typhoons and cyclones, since these have to meet additional more stringent design criteria. Structural engineers are also required to design earth retaining walls where these exceed a specified height (usually above a metre (three feet)).

In general, for average houses, civil or road engineers aren't required, although sometimes they're required to design the intersection of the driveway from the property where it meets the public road and they may be required to design the stormwater drainage on the property.

Usually architects and engineers should be registered with a national or state body representing their professions.

Clerk of works (quality inspector)

A clerk of works, or quality inspector, could be employed by you to check the quality of the construction work as it progresses. Depending on the terms of their contract this inspection could be daily, weekly, or timed to coincide with important milestones of the project, which could be before concrete is poured into foundations or suspended slabs, before services in the ground are covered over, and before services within wall and ceiling spaces are closed. They usually would also prepare a snag or punch list with you when construction is complete and check that all items on the list are satisfactorily completed by the contractor.

Having a clerk of works, or quality inspector, provides you with peace of mind that the work complies with the quality standards and requirements.

In some cases the clerk of works or quality inspector might not have sufficient knowledge to check all elements of construction and it may be necessary to have one person who, say, inspects the electrical systems, another for the air-conditioning and another for the structural elements.

The contractor could employ a clerk of works to ensure the work satisfies the quality requirements. A clerk of works should be honest and impartial, but it's pertinent to understand that a clerk of works employed by the contractor will usually be loyal to the contractor, protecting their interests first.

Project managers

You may elect to appoint a project manager. Depending on your requirements and what's specified in the contract the project manager could be responsible for all or some of the following:

➢ Monitoring and managing the designers and ensuring the construction drawings are received in time so that they don't delay construction.

➢ Coordinating work between the various designers and contractors.

➢ Managing the contractors.

➢ Ensuring that all work achieves the desired quality standards and meets all specifications. (If you employ a project manager it's probably not necessary to have a clerk of works, provided checking quality is part of the project manager's duties.)

➢ Preparing tender documents (request for pricing) and overseeing that suitable contractors price the work, then adjudicating the contractors' prices and making recommendations to you as to which contractor should be appointed to do the work.

➢ Providing a suitable contract document to appoint the contractor.

➢ Assessing all variation claims from designers and contractors, then recommending the required action from you.

➢ Assessing all interim valuation claims from contractors and recommending what amounts you should pay. They should refer any problems with the claims back to the contractor.

➢ Checking the final work and together with you prepare a punch (snag) list. See Chapter 11.

➢ Ensuring that all approvals and permits are in place.

➢ Checking that the completed building is suitable for occupation.

Often a project manager isn't required and the architect could be appointed (at additional cost) to carry out many of the above tasks. Alternatively you may elect to carry out many of these functions.

Quantity surveyors (cost consultant, cost estimator)

Quantity surveyors are primarily involved with costs. They should be able to prepare budgets and indicative costings for your project. They can also prepare pricing documentation and arrange for contractors to price your house. Depending on what you've asked them to do they can also adjudicate contractors' quotes, make recommendations to you as to which contractor to appoint, then prepare contract documentation for you to appoint the selected contractor.

They could also be employed by you to check the contractor's progress claims, their final invoice and any variation claims. Quantity surveyors can also be asked to prepare cash flow forecasts for the project.

Building surveyors (chartered building surveyors)

Building surveyors assess buildings to ensure that they're compliant and structurally sound. If they aren't, they can make recommendations as to the rectification work that should be done. So, if you are unhappy with your contractor's work you can call a building surveyor to inspect the work and make an independent assessment of the quality. Building surveyors can be employed to prepare the final punch or snag list as well as monitor the quality of the work as construction progresses. Building surveyors may also be able to help with preparing and lodging planning submissions.

In some instances the authorities and lending institutions may employ building surveyors to assess your project is compliant and issue permits as required.

Interior designers (decorator)

Interior designers usually look at the complete styling of the house from internal finishes through to helping you select furniture. But, they can be used to only assist with choosing paint colours, floor and wall tiles, light fixtures, and general finishing details. Often the architect is able to fulfil this function, or larger reputable building contractors may have resident interior designers that can assist. Also, many paint manufacturers and tile suppliers have experts who are willing to assist for no fee providing their company's materials are selected.

However, in some cases expert and impartial opinions and ideas may well be worth the additional cost of using an interior designer.

Interior designers usually consider the finished room, including the window dressings (curtains, blinds or shutters), the floor finishes and the furniture. Architects usually don't provide advice on the furniture and the window dressings and they stop at the bare room.

Land surveyors

Land surveyors are used to mark out the property boundaries, or check that they are located in the correct position. In addition, they may be required to locate the position of trees, existing buildings and infrastructure and plot these on a drawing. They can also produce contour plans of the property which indicates the existing ground elevations. This information is often essential for architects and engineers so that they can design the new buildings to tie-in with the existing buildings and infrastructure. So the building takes cognisance of the existing ground levels, thus minimising the amount or earthworks required to form a level platform for the new buildings and that, where possible, large trees can be retained on the property.

They also mark out (set-out) the position of structures where they should be built.

Landscape architect

Landscape architects are primarily involved with designing the external areas of the property. This could include the gardens, water features, locations and design of swimming pools, the positioning of driveways, the creation of patios and external living areas, the type and location of retaining walls and the property boundary fencing or walls. They will provide a plan of the external areas and recommendations of what types of plants and trees to plant and where. They'll structure this plan around the proposed new home taking account of the terrain, existing trees, the climate, the soil conditions and your preferences for the amount of open space, types of plants and the amount of continuing care that you're prepared to invest in the garden.

Employing a landscape architect familiar with the growing conditions of the area and the materials and plants available can be invaluable, especially for larger properties. The alternative is to employ a reputable landscape contractor who has a similar knowledge and who will prepare a similar garden plan. However, the landscaper as part of the deal will require you to employ them to make the garden. Employing a landscape architect to prepare the garden plan provides you the flexibility to employ whichever contractor you decide is the best (price and service) for the project, or you may choose to do some or all of the garden yourself, even doing it in stages as time and budget allows.

Most of us see employing a landscape architect, or a landscaping contractor as an unnecessary expense. After all how hard can it be to plant a few trees and plants and get some grass growing. I've had reasonable success with managing and planting gardens, but it does depend on the growing conditions since I've also battled to get decent gardens growing in other areas. Planning your own garden is often a process of trial and error and some plants will die, some will be in the wrong place, and some may eventually outgrow their location. This trial and error process can yield rewarding results, but it may also be frustrating and costly and you could end with a garden made up of a random mixture of the plants that survived. Sometimes the extra cost of obtaining a plan for your garden may be well worth it, even if you decide not to follow the plan to the letter.

Main contractor (prime contractor, general contractor)

The main contractor is the contractor appointed to complete the full scope of construction work. This usually doesn't include the window dressings and furniture. In some cases it may also include the external landscaping.

The main contractor can have people within the company for the construction work, or they employ and manage subcontractors to execute the work, or they have a combination of their own workers for some trades while engaging specialist subcontractors for other tasks.

Some contractors offer the full service of providing the design for the house. This design may be in the form of standard plans from which you can select the one that best fits the property and your requirements and budget. Alternatively, they could employ an architect, either inhouse or externally, to prepare unique building plans to suit your requirements. They would usually also employ engineers as required to complete any specialist design work. Their service would also generally include obtaining all permits and permissions from the authorities.

The contractor manages all construction processes, including monitoring quality.

You could manage the contractor to ensure they deliver your project on time and to the required quality and safety standards, or you could employ a project manager or clerk of works to fulfil this role.

The contractor will usually have a team of people who could include:

> Project manager or construction manager (not to be confused with the project manager you may appoint to manage the project). The contractor's project manager is their representative appointed to manage the project on their behalf. Often this person should be licensed to work in the state. The contractor's project manager is normally your point of contact and all communications should be addressed to them.

> Supervisor or foreman who directs the contractor's team and subcontractors. In some cases this is your designated point of contact with the contractor.

> Concreters, carpenters, labourers, etc. Basically the team that does the work for the contractor on site.

> Subcontractors appointed by them.

> Office personnel, which could include administrators, planners and designers.

Subcontractors

Subcontractors are employed to execute specific trades. These could include, plumbing, roofing, joinery, electrical work, air-conditioning, bricklaying, tiling, concreting, etc. Subcontractors may be employed by the main contractor. However, should you decide not to employ a main contractor you could employ and manage all the subcontractors for your project. Indeed, you might do some of the work yourself and only employ subcontractors for specialist trades, and for items you don't have the required skills, time, or muscle to execute.

Some subcontractors also carry out design of their work. For instance, air-conditioning contractors would plan the size of air-conditioner to suite your requirements, planning where it should be installed, and where the ducting and pipework should go. Electrical and plumbing contractors will also usually plan where their pipes and cables should go and what sizes they should be. However, the architect who planned the house should have allowed a suitable place for the electrical board, and should have allowed sufficient space in ceiling voids for the air-conditioning ducting and place for plumbing pipes.

Some subcontractors however have additional requirements which need to be considered in the overall design and often have to be provided by another contractor. For instance, the air-conditioning subcontractor will need a place for the external unit, usually a concrete slab, and the unit will require a power point nearby.

Suppliers

Suppliers provide a range of building materials. Contractors and subcontractors procure their materials from their preferred suppliers, and they'll be responsible for ensuring that these materials are of the right quality and meet the project specifications. The contractors must ensure that the materials arrive on time and that they offload and safely store the materials. They normally procure additional materials to take account of the expected wastage, breakages and cutting on the project. If the contractor orders insufficient stock they'll have to ensure more material is delivered to avoid delays to the project. But, contractors normally add a mark-up to the cost of materials they purchase. Alternatively you may have elected to purchase some materials and then you will have to accept many of these responsibilities. See Chapter 8 on materials supplied by you.

Many suppliers have showrooms where their products can be viewed. These include bathroom fixtures, ceramic tiles, carpets, lights, doors and windows. Some have experts who can advise on what products are best for different situations, the best colour combinations to select, as well as installation tips. However beware, since many salespeople at these suppliers may have little construction or product knowledge, and some may be paid incentives to push particular products. It pays to visit various suppliers and search the internet for recommendations.

The developer or landowner

The person or company that you purchase land from. Sometimes they impose particular conditions on the sale of the land which could be included in the sale agreement or the property title deeds.

Utility providers

Utility providers are the gas, electrical, water and communication suppliers who may be a company or could be a government provider. Normally these providers have to provide connection points to the property. These are usually only supplied when an application is received. Often these providers require an application fee as well as a deposit for what they estimate the first few months consumption will be.

In addition, some utility providers won't allow permanent connections to be made to their system unless they inspect the completed installation in the house, or unless they receive the licenses and paperwork from the installers that verifies that the systems connecting to their pipes and power cables are safe and installed to code. See also Chapter 3 for more on getting connected.

Lending institutions

If you're borrowing money for your project you've probably taken out a loan from a bank or a lending institution. This loan normally comes with conditions, which may include when money will be released by the bank, which is usually in tranches as work is completed, and what conditions are attached to the release of funds. Usually certain milestones have to be met before the money is released and the bank will send out inspectors to check that the conditions have been met, or they may require a certificate from a registered building surveyor to confirm that the milestone has been achieved and that the quality of construction is acceptable. Failure to meet these conditions will mean that the money isn't released which could result in you incurring cash flow problems and even being unable to pay contractors and suppliers.

In addition, banks usually want to see supporting documentation, which may include permits and permissions from the local authorities, certified engineer's designs for all structural elements, licenses and registrations of contractors and proof of ownership of the land.

You may deal with a mortgage broker, loans officer, and an appraiser who might visit your current home to assess its value if it's to be used for collateral for the loan. The appraiser might also visit the building works to assess the value of the completed work (which would also include checking the quality and ensuring all required inspections and testing has been done) before another tranche of the loan is paid out.

The authorities

The local authorities (city, town, county, shire) usually have to grant permits, permissions and planning approvals before construction can begin. Some local authorities may also require that their inspectors regular carry out inspections of the work, or that they inspect various elements of the work, which could include all pipework below ground before it's covered up, the foundations and structural elements before concrete is poured, roof structures before roof coverings are added, etc. It's wise to familiarise yourself with these inspections and the notifications required so that inspections aren't missed, which could delay the project or even prevent a certificate of occupancy being issued. Usually these processes are overseen by a planning department at the town or city offices.

Sometimes the local authorities don't inspect the construction progress but demand that a certified building surveyor certifies that the work has been checked at specific milestones and that it's compliant.

In some jurisdictions the local fire department may also have to inspect the property to ensure it complies with fire regulations and that they're able to access the property in the event of a fire.

Where you're planning to use new building materials or construction methods which haven't been approved by the national and state regulators then these bodies will have to be approached to certify the materials or methods you propose using. It should be noted that this could be a lengthy procedure with no guarantee of success. Some authorities are slow to adapt to new methods and technologies.

Testing services

There are various companies that perform specific testing services. These could include testing materials and products in an existing house to determine if they contain asbestos or lead, pressure testing drain and water pipes to ensure there're no leaks, testing the strength of concrete incorporated in your new house (usually taking test samples of the fresh concrete when it's being delivered or mixed on the project and compacting it into cylinders or cubes which are then stored in set conditions (usually water at a specified temperature) before they're crushed, usually at 7 and 28 days to determine whether the concrete has the required strength), and soils tests which determine the suitability of the ground under your house and then also to check that the soil has been compacted to the required density.

Usually the contractor will arrange for testing to be done as per the specifications and according to good practice. However, you should review the results.

Summary

Now that you know who's who and what they do you should be better equipped to decide what help you need and who to call.

Having a united team of professionals working on your home from concept to completion, all working to a shared vision will assist in delivering your home with a uniform style, one that's cohesive through the whole house, where costly mistakes and redoes are limited.

Working with design professionals also means that they'll share their contacts for suppliers and contractors. This can be particularly useful when you're looking for a niche or scarce item. Of course, always check that these suppliers and contractors are actually the best value, even if the recommendation comes with a discount for mentioning the professional's name to the supplier. Regrettably, occasionally professionals will act unprofessionally, only providing contacts for businesses which give them a 'kickback' or commission on sales emanating from their recommendations.

Chapter 2 – Decide What You Do and What Help You Need

Will you be planning the work, or will you ask for expert opinions, or even hand the preparation of the complete design to experts?

Will you be doing all the construction work, maybe some of the work with contractors doing some of the specialised work, or will you employ one contractor to execute all the construction?

Will you manage the construction process, or will you employ a project manager to manage the construction work, or perhaps the project manager will organise the entire project from start to finish, including supervising the designers?

Do you want the project completed as a turnkey project where you'll literally be handed the keys to a completed house, including a fully completed landscaped garden, boundary walls and driveways?

Maybe you even want a complete house including all the furniture, carpets and window fixtures (curtains, blinds, shutters)?

How much work you do yourself, and how much work is executed by others will depend on:

> The size of the project. If the project is simply repainting the interior of the house or a few rooms you could choose to undertake the painting yourself. However, building a house from scratch is often beyond most of our capabilities.

> How much time you have – don't underestimate the time that even minor renovations take. Do you want to come home after a hard day at work and then have to work another few hours every night on your building project? Are you prepared to commit every weekend to working on your house? Or, maybe you intend to take time off work to work on it?

> How quickly you want to finish the project – doing all, or most, of the work yourself will often take much longer than employing a contractor who usually has a team of workers and is able to work full eight hour days on the project. Do you want to be living in a building site for months, even years?

> What skills you have – some of you may be good working with your hands, indeed you may even be carpenters, plumbers or tilers by trade.

Unfortunately many of us aren't as skilled so we take longer to complete even simple construction tasks than the experts require, and inevitably others can see the amateur finished product. Many people have no experience of house construction or managing a project.

➤ Your understanding of construction processes, methods, materials and details. Making mistakes can be costly and add more time to the project.

➤ Your project management skills.

➤ Your understanding of contracts, codes and specifications.

➤ Your physical strength – most construction work requires physical activity. Someone who sits at a desk all day, partaking in little physical activity will find construction hard, and certainly the first few weeks will be exhausting.

➤ Your budget – doing the work yourself may be cheaper, but sometimes it's not. If your cash flow is limited you may need to do the work in stages, even spreading it our over a longer period to suit the pace of your earnings.

➤ How much help you have – it's helpful if your family can assist on occasion, not only adding an extra pair of hands or two to speed up the job, but also helping when heavy lifting is involved. But also, don't underestimate how lonely it will get if you're working on your own on a construction site every night and weekend. In fact working alone is dangerous since if anything goes wrong and you injure yourself there may be nobody to help.

➤ The equipment you have – contractors have the right tools for the job, or when they don't they hire specialist items. There's a cost to purchasing and hiring tools which many home renovators underestimate. Not having the right equipment can be frustrating and it often slows progress, impacts quality and can even lead to accidents. Of course operating some equipment requires specialist licenses. Using construction equipment can be hazardous for the inexperienced.

➤ Your patience and endurance.

➤ Your family's patience and endurance. Will they be happy if you spend large amounts of time on the project? Will they be happy waiting for the house to be finished – even when it seems to be taking forever?

Alternative forms of contracting – who does what

There are many ways of tackling your construction project. You can:

➤ Plan and design the project, and then execute all the construction work.

➤ Plan and design the project, then execute some of the construction work, and employ subcontractors for some of the specialist trades, such as electrical and plumbing work.

➤ Employ architects to prepare the architectural drawings and, if required, an engineer to design the structural elements. Then do all the construction work yourself, or do some yourself and employ specialist subcontractors.

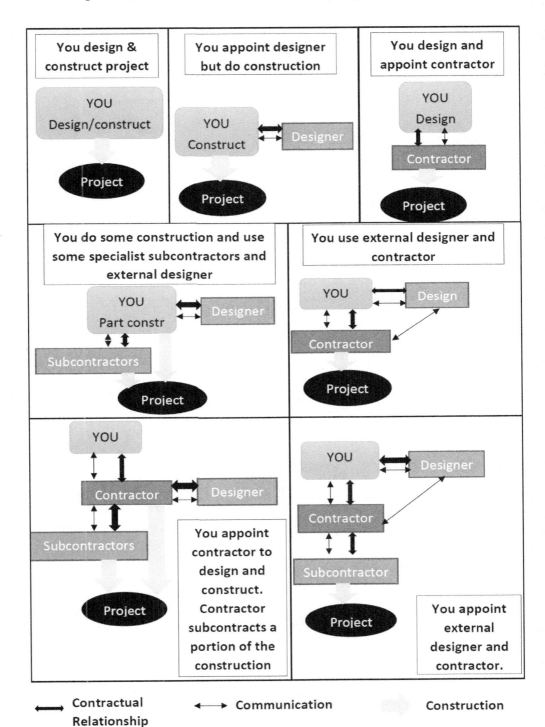

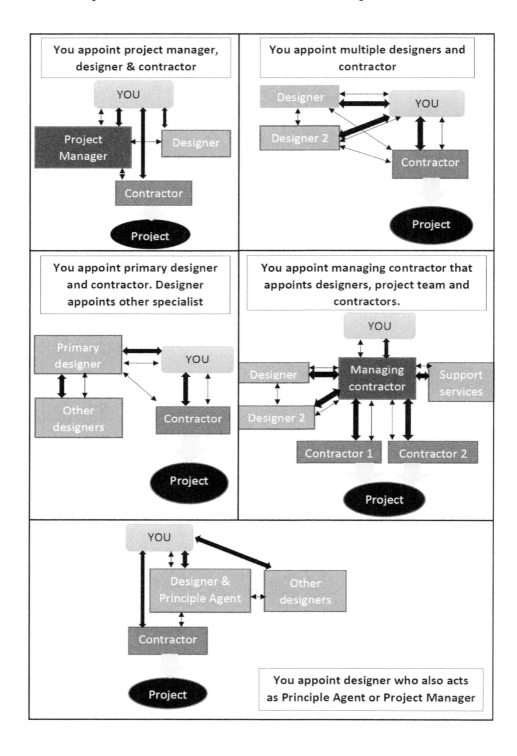

➤ Employ a designer, usually an architect, who prepares all the drawings for the project, including the design for the structural elements which they'll obtain from an engineer. Then you do all, or some of the construction work and employ specialist subcontractors for the remaining work.

➤ Employ a designer to prepare the design, then employ and manage subcontractors to execute all of the construction work.

➤ Employ a designer to prepare the design and a contractor to carry out all of the construction work.

➤ Employ a contractor who is responsible for designing the project as well as completing all construction work.

➤ Employ the designers and contractor, and also employ a project manager to manage the process.

There are many variations on the above. Who is responsible for applying for building permits and permissions will depend on the contractual relationships and could be delegated to you, the designer, the contractor or the project manager.

The risks of doing the construction work yourself

Construction seems so easy, yet for the inexperienced there are many pitfalls, which include:

➤ Accidents which could result in serious injury.

➤ Poor workmanship, which results in aesthetically displeasing defects which can detract from the value of the house.

➤ Poor workmanship can lead to ongoing maintenance issues, including leaks, cracking, etc.

➤ Structural defects could make the building unsafe.

➤ The project takes many long hours, which may cause family feuds and even marriage breakups because you're always working.

➤ Working extended hours on construction activities can result in tiredness, which detracts from your day job. Those who are self-employed may neglect their job that brings in the money, which results in a reduction in income.

➤ Using the wrong materials. For instance some materials shouldn't be used in wet areas such as bathrooms, some materials aren't fire resistant, or aren't treated for pests, while other materials shouldn't be used outside.

➤ Progress is often slow, and for those renovating it could feel like you're living on a building site for years. If you're building a house to live in it could mean there're added costs of renting a house for an extended period before your new home is completed.

➤ The work doesn't comply with codes and specifications.

➤ Mistakes are made which cost additional money to rectify.

But knowing the pitfalls and with some training and help there are many that successfully build their own houses.

Employing and managing subcontractors – will it save money?

In an effort to save money you could choose to appoint a number of subcontractors to complete the different trades. You then manage the subcontractors instead of the main contractor. This strategy can have financial benefits because you're not paying the main contractor's profits and overheads on the subcontractors' work. However there are risks which include:

> It's easy to overlook one trade. Organising a subcontractor at late notice could cause delays to the other following subcontractors, which delays the project and could lead to variation claims from the subcontractors.

> Missing a trade, or not organising the sequence of activities correctly, could mean that completed work is damaged, or has to be redone to accommodate trades that should have been completed beforehand.

> Managing subcontractors takes time. If you're working you aren't always available to monitor that the subcontractor arrived that day and completed everything they were supposed to do. Checking the work after hours (sometimes in the dark) means that problems aren't detected straight away.

Case study: A few years ago a demolition company demolished the wrong house in Sydney Australia. You might think this sounds stupid, but it can easily happen when contractors aren't managed properly. In this case the contractor arrived at what they thought was the correct address, but it turned out that the post-box with the house number was actually for the house next door, the one that should have been demolished and not for the house they actually demolished.

However, if you know what you are doing and plan the work carefully and have time to manage the process there's no reason you can't get this right.

Can you manage the construction process?

Managing the construction process yourself if you don't have the right knowledge could result in:

> The wrong contractor being used.

> Flawed contracts being used which offer you little protection should things go wrong.

> Poor workmanship going unnoticed.

> Building permits and permissions not being in place, which could delay the project, or should construction proceed before they're in place result in the work being stopped, and even the completed work having to be demolished.

> ➤ Claims and variations arising from the contractor which an experienced project manager could have avoided.
> ➤ Overpayments to the contractor and other entities.
> ➤ Delays to the project.
> ➤ Budget problems because of inadequate financial controls or a flawed budget.
> ➤ Failure to ensure that the contractor complies with all the codes and specification.

However, using a reputable contractor can allay many of these concerns and lead to a successful project. Learning about construction processes and being aware of what to check will be an added advantage.

Selecting a project manager – looking after your project

You should consider the following when selecting a project manager:
> ➤ What duties you want them to perform. See Chapter 9.
> ➤ What their experience is with managing similar projects.
> ➤ Talk to them and see if they are someone you could work with.
> ➤ Ask for references. Questions to ask their references include:
>   - Were you happy with the services provided by the project manager?
>   - What did they do for you?
>   - Do you think they looked after your interests?
>   - Were there problems on the project? How were these resolved?
>   - Did the final price for their services differ substantially from their original price? If so, why?
>   - Did they have a good understanding of house construction, including financial and contractual knowledge?
> ➤ Obtain a price for the scope of work you wish them to undertake. Check:
>   - How often they'll be on site.
>   - That the price includes maintaining all records and documentation.
>   - That they'll undertake all quality inspections.
> ➤ If you're happy with their price appoint the project manager. The contract should clearly state:
>   - The price.
>   - The duration of the project.
>   - The full scope of what the project manager must do.
>   - Their responsibilities.
>   - Their level of authority. You don't want the project manager making decisions on your behalf which could increase the cost of the project. On the other hand you also don't want to be called every time there's a decision involving a few dollars because this will slow down decision making processes and ultimately the project.

- A schedule of rates for additional work.

Sometimes you can employ the designer (architect or engineer) to act as the project manager. The only risk may be that they're aren't entirely impartial when it comes to assessing problems caused by their design or late information. But, if this becomes a problem you could seek additional impartial advice.

Purchasing materials – what could go wrong?

Many people decide to purchase some of the items for the contractor to install. This's often done because if the contractor purchases the material you pay for the material plus the contractor's profit and mark-up. However, there are pitfalls for purchasing the materials which the contractor will incorporate into the building.

➢ If the materials arrive late it will delay the contractor and result in a variation claim from them.

➢ If the quantity you order is insufficient the contractor will run short of materials, resulting in them standing waiting for the missing items, incurring additional costs and delaying the project which will be for your account.

➢ If you order too much material this's a wasted cost. In some cases you may be able to return unused material for a refund but you'll have to arrange this.

➢ You may have to offload and store the product until the contractor needs it, unless you've previously negotiated that this's their responsibility, in which case you must timeously warn them of when the material will be delivered.

➢ If a problem later occurs with the product it's your responsibility to fix it. The problem may be as a result of poor installation, but you're going to have to argue the case with the contractor whether it's the product you supplied or their installation.

➢ Often, when ordering products like floor and wall tiles and timber, an extra quantity must be ordered to allow for wastages, breakages and offcuts. You need to find out what the norm is for this and allow for it. However, there's little incentive for the contractor to take care with the product, or to plan their cutting to minimise waste because they haven't paid for the material. This could result in materials running out with the consequent costs and delays. It should be noted, that some products such as ceramic tiles and bricks can have colour variations between batches, so you should try and order the full quantity and not part quantities as required. When placing the order it may be possible to request that the material is delivered in batches at a time to suite the construction progress.

➢ Usually contractors can purchase materials at cheaper rates than you can, or they get preferential discounts from their regular suppliers.

➢ When purchasing materials on sales or at a discount, make enquiries to understand if the item is on sale because it has a defect or been damaged, or perhaps because it's the end of the range. Particular care must be taken when purchasing tiles which are the end of the range because if you need more of that product later it may no longer be available. There's nothing worse than the tiler running out of tiles before the job is complete. There could only be a couple of tiles short, but if there are no tiles that are exactly the same the tiler may end up ripping up all the tiles and replacing them with other available tiles at great cost and inconvenience. The alternative is that you'll be left with mismatched tiles to fill the gaps.

Unfortunately purchasing materials to save the contractor adding their mark-up to the items doesn't mean that the contractor won't add this lost mark-up and profit elsewhere. As a contractor, for each project we executed we had overheads which had to be recouped in our price, and we also had an amount of profit we needed, which was usually based on the amount of effort we had to put into the project. If these overheads and the profit couldn't be added to the cost of materials because our client elected to purchase them then we had to add them elsewhere – so ultimately the client didn't always save much by purchasing the materials themselves.

See Chapter 6 for more on ordering materials.

The advantages of doing things yourself

Of course successfully building your own home with your hands can be tremendously satisfying. Those with the proper skills, with careful planning, sufficient time and with a supporting and helping family can renovate their home or build their new family home. Doing things yourself means that it's possible to progress construction in stages which suits your budget and cash flow. It also means that you can finish one part of the project, take a break in construction while you see how it works, before embarking on the next stage of the project.

Doing everything yourself, and doing it properly, means that you're sure that the quality is right.

Many people construct their houses themselves because it's possible to save money if you know what you're doing. Not only are you saving the cost of employing someone to do the work, but there's the saving of not paying a contractor's overheads and profits. But, if you're savvy, it's even possible to purchase building materials from merchants having sales, even from second-hand suppliers, and on occasion you may even be able to salvage products for nothing from buildings being demolished.

The devil is in the detail

Doing the construction yourself seems so simple, and can be simple if you know what you're doing. Unfortunately many aren't experts. Even leaving out small details could result in a house that leaks, or one that has structural problems. Employing an architect or draughtsperson can ensure that the house is properly designed and that all the little details are shown, such as where waterproof membranes should go, heights of doors and windows, floor levels, and details around windows.

But the detail also goes in making sure that the paper trail is all completed. Even filling in a form incorrectly could delay your project by weeks.

Understand the detail in contracts, insurances, sureties and warranties. Failure to do so could cost you lots of money.

Pessimism kills projects, but optimism is also an enemy

You need to take a realistic and logical approach to your project. Expecting the worst, allowing for the worst, and seeing problems and difficulties on every corner is the death knell of many construction projects. They are killed by fear. They are killed before they get off the ground. Killed by owners that always expected the worst.

Yet, there are also many owners that are always optimistic – overly optimistic. Everything will go according to plan. The money will be okay. The contractor will deliver what they committed to do. So, frequently projects are started which are risky, where the owner has underestimated the costs, where finance isn't all in place and where proper contracts aren't signed. Some of these projects should never have even been started. Projects are never so easy and eventually these projects and owners end in a mess, usually in financial difficulties.

Every project should be carefully thought through and planned. A proper and realistic budget should be prepared. Control must be kept of every stage of the project. Potential problems must be understood and steps implemented to minimise and solve them before they wreck the project. Following the steps and taking heed of the advice in this book will provide you with a sound basis to a successful project.

Don't let your fear hold you back. Only clearly thought through logical decisions should hold you back if the outcomes aren't expected to be right for you and your family right now. Equally don't let your optimism drive you headlong recklessly into a project which isn't right for you, a project that's ill-conceived, a project that hasn't been carefully planned and budgeted.

Knowledge is power – educate yourself

You should definitely consider attending some training courses before embarking on your building project. For those doing some of the construction work it's helpful to attend carpentry, tiling, bricklaying and other courses.

Any good building course will provide an overview of standard methods and practices, so even if you're using a contractor or subcontractor you'll have some basic knowledge to check that they're following recognised good practices and that the work meets the quality standards.

Understanding building contracts, construction costs and general finances, budgets and cash flow is invaluable.

There are many valuable design courses, including interior design, landscaping, and architecture. Sure, none of these will turn you into an expert, but at least you'll be better equipped to deal with the experts. These courses can be fun, they may save you thousands on your building project and they almost certainly won't be a waste of time.

Always ask questions when in doubt

Never be scared to ask questions from those doing the work, as well as from experts. Before signing the building contract ask a lawyer to look at it. If you have any concerns about what your contractor is doing ask another contractor. Most regions have trade bodies that represent builders and many of the various subcontractor trades such as landscapers, plumbers, pool installers, etc. Many of these bodies can provide helpful advice, or direct you to someone who can help. Sometimes expert opinion costs money, but it could save huge costs if it helps resolve or prevent a problem. It also gives you peace of mind knowing what the right course of action is.

Summary

Knowing the various options that are available to you, and the advantages and disadvantages of the options, should help you decide what help you'll need and who you should contact. It's important that these decisions aren't based only on what you can afford, but they should consider your abilities, time and expertise. Trying to save money by doing everything yourself may end up being much more expensive than engaging the correct professional assistance.

But, if you have the time, ability and knowledge, then there's nothing (well almost nothing – you do need the appropriate licenses to do some work) that you can't do yourself. But, do research, read books to understand the construction details, read Chapters 5 and 6, ask experts for advice, and attend courses to fill in your knowledge and experience gaps. Never think that you know everything – none of us are too smart that we can't learn new and better ways of doing stuff.

Maybe there's somewhere in the middle that's suitable for you and your project – where you do some work and employ professionals for the bigger and more complex portions of the project.

Put together a list of professionals in your area that you think you can work with and who will be suitable for your project. Research and find out more about them. Check their references.

Chapter 3 – Preparing for Construction

Some people rush straight into their renovation or home construction project without proper planning, thought and preparation. This frequently results in additional costs and delays later. It's important to ensure that you have sufficient funds for the project and that you've carefully considered the budget. It's also about ensuring that everything is in place so that the contractor isn't delayed and so that the project can progress smoothly without problems and delays.

Budgets – do I have enough money?

Budgets involve not only what the project will cost, but also when these payments are due. It's important to understand the construction schedule as well as the payment terms of all suppliers and subcontractors. (Read about cash flow in Chapter 10.) Late payment could lead to work stopping, supplies of materials being cut off, and you could incur additional costs, including losing discount provisions and incurring interest payment charges.

The construction and other project costs are paid from money you have in the bank, money from the sale of assets (like another home) and payments from bank loans. It's important to understand when these funds will be received. Funds from the sale of assets can take time to be received and these transactions frequently take longer than envisaged. Of course, there're often pitfalls along the way, for instance sales could fall through even after everything appears settled. Banks seldom pay loan funds out as a lump sum at the start of the project. The release of funds usually depend on the project reaching particular milestones and on the quality and progress of the project being checked by the bank's representative. Banks may also require to see copies of insurances, invoices, permits and contract documents before releasing funds. It's important to understand all the conditions relating to the loan. Inevitably there will be delays in the process and bank holidays can play havoc with your best laid plans.

But equally, it's important to understand what other costs will be incurred. There are the usual costs of managing your monthly household bills, but invariably there'll be unexpected costs, such as illness, cars breaking down, unexpectedly high bills, and certainly your monthly costs will increase with time.

In addition, there'll be additional project costs that weren't allowed. There will be some changes and variations.

It's important to accurately calculate the project costs, including all the items discussed in the next section. These costs should be regularly checked and as the actual costs come in the numbers should be updated. Once the project starts it is good practice to update the budget every week. This involves ensuring that all suppliers and contractors submit their invoices and variations regularly and that you make allowances for those invoices and variations which you haven't received.

EXAMPLE OF A BUDGET

ORIGINAL ESTIMATE

UPDATE THIS COLUMN AS COSTS ARE INCURRED

DESCRIPTION	B ESTIMATED VALUE	C ACTUAL VALUE	D OVER OR UNDER BUDGET (B-C)	
PURCHASE LAND	150,000	145,000	-5,000	
LAND TAX	7,500	7,250	-250	
PROPERTY SURVEY	1,500	1200	-300	
DESIGN FEE	30,000	28,000	-2,000	
DESIGN VARIATION 1 - ALTER LAYOUT 3 TIMES		3,000	3,000	
PERMITS	2,000	1,800	-200	
CONSTRUCTION CONTRACT	250,000	256,000	6000	
CONSTRUCTION VARIATION 1 - FOUNDATIONS		3,000	3000	
CONSTRUCTION VARIATION 2 - LARGER PC'S		1,500	1,500	
CONSTRUCTION VARIATION 3 - EXTRA TILES		1,100	1,100	
LANDSCAPING	8,000	10,000	2,000	
BOUNDARY FENCE	8,000	8,800	800	
UTILITY CONNECTIONS	2,500	2,300	-200	
INSURANCE	1,000	800	-200	
WINDOW TREATMENTS	18,000			NO COST YET
SECURITY INSTALLATION	4,000			NO COST YET
CABLE TV	1,000			NO COST YET
FURNITURE	22,000			NO COST YET
MOVING COSTS	1,500			NO COST YET
ORIGINAL ESTIMATE	507,000			

	B		D
CURRENT OVER (+) UNDER (-) BUDGET			9,250

=TOTAL COLUMN B

	B	
CURRENT NEW ESTIMATE = ORIGINAL ESTIMATE + OVER/UNDER	516,250	

=TOTAL COLUMN C

=507,000+9,250

NOTE IN THIS EXAMPLE: TODATE, WITH SOME UNKNOWN COSTS YOU ARE 9,250 OVER BUDGET. EITHER SAVE MONEY WITH REMAINING ITEMS OR FIND MORE MONEY

Equally important is to continually check your own finances for unexpected household costs. If you have a bank loan, constantly stay in touch with the bank to ensure that the funds will be received as required.

Prepare two spread sheet of all your costs – one for your household expenses and the other for the costs of your project. The first column with the item description – leave place at the bottom to add additional items you uncover as the project progresses. The second column with the estimated costs. The next column with the actual costs (which you complete as the project progresses and invoices come in and the costs are confirmed) and the fourth column with the difference between the actual and the estimate – which could be a negative (saving) or plus (more). The sum of the second column would be the total expected costs, while the sum of the fourth column is the variation of the budget, either a saving on your estimate, or additional costs over your budget. If you are exceeding the expected costs you must cut costs somewhere or find additional funds. You can add another column with the date when you expect to pay the cost. This is essential to estimate your cash flow – see Chapter 10.

In the same way you can prepare a spread sheet for your expected income. List all the income sources in the first column. The dates when you expect to receive the money, the third column with the expected income, the fourth with the actual income received and the last column with the variance in the income, which could either be more or less.

Compare your estimated income with the estimated costs.

Don't start the project if you won't have sufficient money.

Have you allowed for all the costs?

Frequently costs aren't considered or are overlooked which could result in your budget being too low. Costs for your project could include:

➢ Design fees for engineers and architects.

➢ Project management costs if you appoint a project manager to manage the process.

➢ Land purchases, including duties and taxes.

➢ Property rates and taxes. (Including taxes during construction.)

➢ Costs to maintain the property before construction begins, including security, utility bills and keeping the property tidy.

➢ Construction costs.

➢ Protecting existing structures and facilities which could be damaged by the construction work.

➢ Modifications to areas of an existing house which are impacted by the construction work. Often existing floor and wall finishes have to be changed in the existing building to match those that are installed in the new areas.

➢ Upgrading existing buildings which are being added to or changed. This could include requirements to improve the plumbing pipes and electrical wiring and distribution boards to bring them up to code and standard, or to allow capacity for the additional expansion. It may also include installing additional structural supports and beams to the existing structure.

➢ Demolition of existing structures and site clearing.

➢ Clearing existing trees and other vegetation where necessary.

➢ Levelling the site where required.

➢ Constructing ground retaining walls where required.

➢ Specialist foundations if required.

➢ Additional insurances.

➢ When you have to move out of the house while the construction is in progress, then the cost of temporary accommodation during construction.

➢ Interest on finance loans.

➢ Security during construction.

➢ Fencing during construction.

➢ Permanent fences, walls and gates on the property boundary.

➢ Temporary construction sheds and toilets.

➢ The provision of water and electricity for the construction works.

➢ The provision of water, sewer, gas, telephone and electrical connections to the new house. These include connection fees and deposits for the utility provider or the local council. The deposit could be equivalent to one or two months usage. Although this deposit is refundable it's an immediate expense that must be allowed.

➢ The cost of permits, plan approvals and building approvals by the local authorities, and when the property is within a housing estate then the body overseeing the running of the estate.

➢ The cost of arranging road closures if required for cranes or other equipment. These could include for traffic control and signage as well as fees to the authorities.

➢ Providing access to high areas, which could be scaffolding or access equipment. Often the time required for maintaining access is underestimated and costs quickly blowout when it's required for longer.

➢ Testing expenses.

➢ Hire charges for specialist equipment such as large cranes.

➢ Removing rubbish, including general construction waste such as packaging, breakages and offcuts, disposing of excess soil, rock and unsuitable ground, as well as getting rid of rubble from demolitions.

➢ Employing a clerk of works if you require one to oversee the quality of construction.

➢ Land survey, boundary demarcation and setting out the structures.

➢ When required, undertaking soil and geological investigations.

➢ Dealing with hazardous materials, or ground water, which may be encountered on the project site.

➢ The costs of finishes, such as tiles, carpets, bathroom fixtures and tapware, and lights.

➢ Fitting out of cupboards.

➢ Furniture, carpets and window dressings, such as curtains, blinds or shutters.

➢ Security installations.

➢ Inspections and approvals.

➢ Legal costs.

➢ Contingencies.

➢ Costs of moving into the new house

➢ Constructing driveways.

➢ Making good damage to the surrounding roads, pavements and buildings. Often a deposit has to be lodged with the local council which is refundable after the work is complete and the local authorities have checked that the roads, kerbs and sidewalk are in the state they were before construction work started.

➢ Landscaping, including installing irrigation sprinklers if required. This could include importing suitable topsoil.

➢ Taxes, which include GST and import duties.

➢ Fees for specialists, including town planners and quantity surveyors.

➢ Other costs, which could include mailboxes, street numbers, TV antennae and dishes, telephone and data connections, and new appliances.

Knowing your capabilities

It's easy to get carried away and go gung-ho diving straight into your project. But it's imperative to understand what your abilities are, and what your liabilities and weaknesses are.

You must take an honest approach because it could be costly to find out halfway through the project that you were wrong. Knowing your capabilities and liabilities will better inform you how you should construct your house and what help you'll need to complete it successfully.

When to start? Is right now the right time?

You probably can't wait to start building your new home or renovating your current home. But, is this the right time? Decisions which could impact your start date include:

➢ Have you got sufficient finance?

➢ Will you have time to supervise construction or visit showrooms to choose fittings and fixtures? If there's a new baby coming soon, or if you'll be particularly busy at work for a few months, then you may want to delay the start.

> What activities could impact the project? These could include planned holidays away, visitors who will stay over, and even big events, such as weddings or major birthdays. You might not want to be in the middle of renovations when friends and family visit!

> Are builders busy? If there's lots of construction happening in your town then contractors and suppliers may increase their prices.

> When are the holidays? Many contractors close for a couple of weeks over Christmas which means your project will stand for several weeks.

> What will the weather be? You possibly don't want to be starting construction in the middle of the rainy season, or when it could be snowing. Ideally you'll want to get the roof on before the onset of poor weather.

> When can you get time off work? If you're planning to do some of the work yourself you may want these activities to happen when you have time off work.

Planning permissions – is the red tape sorted?

Most construction work requires planning permissions from the local authorities. Usually there's a fee payable to get your building plans assessed. Unfortunately some authorities work slower than you expect. Verbal promises of when you can expect to receive the permissions are often broken. Then, when you finally get feedback it's to say that there's a problem which you have to fix before the permission can be granted. Invariably this delays the start of the project.

Starting the project before permissions are received could result in work being stopped, even work having to be torn down, or fines to pay.

If you're responsible for obtaining all the permissions ensure that these are submitted timeously, in the correct format and with all the required supporting documentation. Employing an expert could speed up the process and prevent mistakes which cause delays. Talk to the authorities and ensure that you thoroughly understand their requirements. Give them exactly what they want – even more. Continually stay in touch with them to see that the process stays on track, and that paperwork hasn't been lost.

Don't give your contractor a start date, only to find that you haven't received permissions by this date. Your contractor may charge you standing time waiting for the permits and permissions.

Insurances – are you covered?

Always ensure that all insurances and bonds are in place before construction starts. See Chapter 9.

Always advise insurers when there're any major changes to the project, such as changes in the completion date, problems encountered or changes in the value.

Property boundaries – not on your neighbour's property

Just because there's a fence doesn't mean that's the actual boundary of your property. More than one owner has found that land they thought belonged to them was actually their neighbour's. If you're planning to build a structure close to the boundary then it's important to employ a surveyor to check and mark the physical boundary of your property. If you don't do this and it's later found that your structure is too close to the boundary, or is actually on your neighbour's property, you could be forced to demolish the part of the structure that's the problem. Alternatively, you may be able to negotiate with your neighbour to purchase some of their land (which may only be a couple of square metres (twenty square feet)) at their price, and you would have to arrange at additional costs to register the revised boundary with the authorities.

Locating and protecting utility lines – don't break that pipe

Before starting excavation you must ensure that all underground services are known and have been clearly marked and pointed out to those doing the excavation. Striking a utility cable or pipe can:

➤   Be dangerous. Cutting a gas pipe could set off an explosion and damaging an electrical cable can electrocute people.

➤   Interrupt service supplies to you, the construction activities, and neighbours. It could lead to costs and claims when the contents of fridges go off, or businesses have to shut.

➤   Be expensive to repair. A severed fibre optic cable could cost thousands to repair.

➤   Delay construction works until the damage is repaired.

➤   Result in water pipes flooding the area causing damage to the works and the surrounding property.

➤   Result in problems later if the damage isn't detected, or if the damaged pipe or cable isn't repaired properly.

Utility lines can be located by:

➤   Checking the available drawings. But always remember that cables and pipes might not be exactly where they're shown on drawings.

➤   Contacting the utility providers to ask them what you should be aware of.

➤   Scouting the surface to locate valves, markers and manholes.

➤   Hiring equipment to locate buried services. If you do this always ensure you know how to operate the equipment and that it's setup correctly.

➤   Hire an expert to bring equipment to detect the service lines.

Unfortunately even when the utility lines have been detected accidents still occur because those excavating are careless and gung-ho and dig without taking due care, or the service lines aren't clearly marked, or the markings have disappeared, or the crew doing the excavation aren't aware what to look for.

But it's not just the existing lines that need protecting. Frequently workers dig up newly installed lines placed during construction. New lines must be clearly marked and protected.

Unfortunately, on occasion cables and pipes are damaged, but the damage isn't reported, or the person doing the excavation isn't aware they damaged the line. This could lead to an undetected fault which only becomes apparent much later. Electrical cables which have their outer casing damaged could fail months later when water enters the cable. Water pipes could leak for months, making for very expensive water bills, only becoming apparent when the ground becomes saturated. Sewer and stormwater pipes could become filled with sand which enters through holes broken in the pipe, blocking the pipe, or causing areas above the pipe to settle. Unfortunately when the problem eventually becomes apparent it's often difficult to locate the exact location, and invariably the area has been paved over, or has a concrete slab above it, or is grassed and landscaped. Fixing the problem can be costly, so it's vital that all existing and new cables and pipes are protected, and that workers exercise extreme care when digging around known lines, immediately reporting any concerns that they might have, or where they may have inadvertently caused damage to the cable or pipe.

But it's not just underground lines we must be careful with. Overhead power cables can be extremely dangerous. Even equipment coming within a couple of metres (yards) of the line could cause the power to arc, or flash, between the cable and the equipment, damaging the equipment and possibly causing injury or death to the operator and bystanders. Be careful when carrying long ladders and objects under low overhead high voltage electrical cables.

Always stay well clear of fallen power lines and notify the utility provider immediately a power pole or overhead cable is damaged.

Cables and pipes installed within the floors, walls and roofs of houses can easily be damaged by workers cutting and drilling. Countless almost completed houses have water pipes and power cables cut when fittings and fixtures are installed. These especially include when installing bathroom mirrors and towel rails. Not only is this dangerous, but it costs money to repair when tiles and walls have to be chopped open to fix the damage. Flooding from damaged water pipes can damage cupboards and floor finishes.

Relocating services (utility lines) – moving pipes and cables

Sometimes it's necessary to arrange with the authorities to move a power pole, electrical meter, services manhole or water valve because it's blocking access to your property. This can take months to achieve, require reams of paperwork and often requires a fee. It could delay access to start construction work unless you can make alternative arrangements in the interim.

Pipes, cables and services on your property usually can be moved elsewhere by a licensed contractor appointed by you. Moving these services should be done ahead of the construction work so it doesn't impede contractors. Although, if this work is included in the contractor's scope of work they can schedule moving the lines at a time convenient to them when it won't hamper construction progress.

Getting connected – water, power and other utilities

Providers of gas, water and electricity usually provide a connection to the house at a specific point on the property boundary. There's normally a connection fee, plus a deposit for one to three months' estimated usage. Some providers require specific boxes, or installations, for their connection. In particular, electrical providers may have very specific specifications for the type of electrical box that they'll connect to. This specification includes the size, colour, locking mechanism, as well as the height of the fixture.

Sometimes utility providers install a temporary 'builder's connection which must be replaced with a permanent connection before the finished house can be connected.

If you're going to be generating power through solar panels investigate options to sell excess power back to the supplier.

The operator of the town sewer system will often want to inspect the sewer pipes (wastewater) on your property to ensure that they're compliant, or they may require inspection certificates from a registered plumbing inspector or plumber to confirm the installed pipes are to code before they'll allow you to connect to the town sewer.

The connection of telephone, data and cable television is often done by the provider or their contractor. However, you usually have to provide the ducts for the cables from a connection point on the sidewalk to your house, and in the floors, walls and roof space to reach the points in your house where you want a connection. There're specific requirements for these ducts, which include their size, materials, radius of bends and the location of draw boxes. In addition these ducts must be clean and they usually should be fitted with draw wires so the installer can easily pull their cables through. Sometimes these ducts have to be positioned away from electrical cables which could interfere with the signals in the cable.

Gas providers will usually only connect to your house at the sidewalk and also often require a specific type and size box. They'll only connect once the pipes and systems in your house have been checked and they have paperwork signed by a registered gas installer.

Water providers usually fit a valve and a meter at the property boundary. Sometimes these are available in different sizes (possibly fifteen, twenty or twenty-five millimetres (half inch, three-quarter or one inch) diameter), with the bigger sizes costing more to install and in some cases even incurring a bigger monthly charge. Larger sizes could mean that you have more water pressure in your house when more than one tap is used at the same time.

Utility providers often require several weeks, even months, warning to arrange installation, so the connections must be booked in advance of when they're required.

It's important to liaise with all utility providers when designing and planning your house or renovations to ensure that you fully understand their requirements and the exact location of their connection point. This should preferably be in writing. Failure to meet their requirements could result in their installers arriving, looking at the setup, then going away without connecting the service. Only once you've fixed the problem can you reschedule the connection. Meeting and greeting the installers, especially with a cup of coffee, may just help smooth over any problems that might arise.

Design - is information available to start construction?

If you're responsible for the design, or you've appointed the designer, then it's best to ensure that the design is complete before construction starts. If the contractor has to wait for information they'll submit a delay variation claim. Of course it's costly when work is completed on a section only to find that the design changes, meaning that the completed work has to be altered.

Equally important, is to check the design to ensure that it meets all your requirements, and of course to check that there aren't any stupid mistakes, like for instance the house being orientated in the wrong direction.

If the contractor has prepared the design check it carefully to ensure that you are happy with it and there aren't any obvious mistakes.

Lead times - why are you waiting for materials?

Some materials take time to manufacture and deliver. Sometimes the manufacturer has to take measurements, design and detail the item, prepare drawings, then manufacture and finally deliver the item. Some items might not be in stock and come from interstate or another country. The lead time for an item is the total duration it takes to order, manufacture and deliver the item to the project.

Using standard and stock items could mean the items are immediately available. But materials which must be imported or manufactured need to be ordered well ahead of time so that they arrive on the project when they're required. Having items with long lead times may cause delays to the construction schedule if they can't be ordered in time.

The shortest reasonable lead time for any item is at least a week from when the contractor receives the drawing or information, to when they can physically start the activity. This allows them time to plan their work, order the items and get started. Some specialist items could take nine weeks to fifteen weeks, so always ensure that the contractor has the information well ahead of time, or keep things simple and standard. Of course sometimes items can be fast-tracked, but this will cost more money - do you really want to pay extra money to airfreight items from overseas, or for manufacturers to work nights and weekends? For more on scheduling see Chapter 6.

Demolitions – what stays and what goes

If you've engaged a contractor to carry out demolitions, which could include removing complete structures, ripping out some walls, cutting new window and door openings in walls, or removing floor and wall tiles and fixtures, then it should be clear in their contract as to:

➢   Who's responsible for marking out areas to be cut and demolished.

➢   Who removes the demolished material.

➢   What items you want protected and salvaged.

➢   Who will protect the surrounding areas from dust, vibration and damages.

➢   Who will provide temporary protection to the existing building when external walls or the roof are removed. This protection is from the weather as well as from criminal activities.

➢   Ensuring that hazardous materials are handled appropriately, separating them from other waste and disposing them in the correct manner.

Unfortunately there are some 'fly by night' contractors that illegally dump waste construction materials on vacant properties and you may be held accountable.

Before demolitions start:

➢   All hazardous materials must be identified.

➢   All demolition permits must be in place.

➢   Electrical, gas and water supplies must be cut-off to the structures and the lines made safe.

➢   All salvageable material should be removed.

➢   Safety steps must be in place to prevent injuries to workers and the public.

➢   Steps must be in place to minimise dust.

Main Contractor (general contractor) or subcontractors

If you've appointed one main contractor (general contractor) they'll manage the project, engaging subcontractors to do the work as and when they're required. You can let them get on with the project. They'll be responsible for any no-shows of their suppliers and subcontractors, and the knock-on impact caused by one of their contractors not completing their tasks on time.

If you've appointed some subcontractors you'll need to coordinate their work with the main contractor to ensure that your contractors are available when they're required and that they work with, and around the main contractor's work, without holding up the main contractor.

If you've elected to appoint all the subcontractors and manage their work it's critical that each has a clear scope of work which doesn't overlap with another contractor, or leave any gaps. It'll be vital to ensure that subcontractors arrive when they're required, that the various subcontractors cooperate with each other, and then to check that the subcontractor completes all their work before the next contractor is ready to start. Subcontractors who arrive only to find that the work area isn't ready for them could charge you standing time and the costs of their aborted trip. Frequently, if a contractor can't do their work they must be rescheduled to return when the previous contractor has completed their work. Often the contractor isn't able to return on your desired day because of other prior work commitments which could push your project out, delaying the following trades even further.

It's therefore imperative if you're managing the construction that you prepare an accurate construction schedule showing all the tasks and who will be doing the work. (See Chapter 6 for notes on preparing a construction schedule.) Understand from each contractor how long they need to complete their work, then lock them in for the required time and day. But it can't just be left there. Contractors should be contacted a few days ahead of time to confirm that they'll be there on the allocated day. Frequently contractors have projects which overrun the time they expected and suddenly your job gets forgotten. Staying on top of your contractors can ensure that they're reminded of when they're needed and if they let you down that you then have some warning to make alternative arrangements, or to reschedule the following contractors. It's always wise to allow extra slack in the construction schedule for when problems occur and contractors don't show up, or they take longer than anticipated.

Once the contractor is on the project they usually need to be managed. Unfortunately, some workers can arrive, then find there's a problem and disappear without you knowing that the job hasn't been done. It's also important to check the quality of workmanship and ensure all items are complete so that the following contractors can continue with their work.

If you've appointed a project manager they may be delegated to manage these contractors on your behalf. However, you may be liable for delay claims should they mismanage the contractors.

Never let cost be the only driver of decisions

While designing your house, selecting the contractor, and during construction you'll be faced with hundreds of decisions. From the choices of floor coverings, tiles, bathroom fixtures, kitchen cabinetry, counter tops, light fittings and much more. It's important to always focus on costs and know what your budget allows. However, it's also important that your focus on costs doesn't drown out other essential factors. Just because something is on sale or much cheaper than another item should never be reason enough to choose the product.

When making your decisions you should consider:

> The quality. You should never be tempted to purchase something that's of an inferior quality, that's unreliable, or which is damaged already. Do you

really want to include a chipped bathroom fixture or cracked tile in your bathroom? Do you really want to install an air-conditioning unit that fell off the back of a truck?

➢ If the product is suitable for the house? Will it match the architectural style and the other materials you purchased? Nobody should be choosing a countertop or tile solely for the reason that it's the cheapest.

➢ Is it what you really want?

➢ Is it practical?

➢ Is it really going to be the cheapest decision after you've factored in all the other costs, such as transport, installation and running costs?

Unfortunately, frequently owners become so focussed on costs that their new home becomes a mishmash of clashing ideas and colours which have been selected purely because they were the cheapest or the products were on sale. The vision of that dream home with your favourite colours could turn into a nightmare containing colours that nobody likes, least of all when they're mixed together. Of course this doesn't mean that you shouldn't purchase items that are on sale, or use second-hand items, rather that these should be appropriate and fit the house's style and décor without compromising quality. Nor should you be so fixated on a brand or particular item that you overlook or ignore products and materials which are cheaper, but which will be just as suitable.

Summary

It's important that before starting construction you:

➢ Review your budget, taking account of when you'll receive money and when payments will be due. This budget should take account of all the costs and allow a contingency. The budget should be regularly updated.

➢ Check that all permits and permissions are in place.

➢ Ensure the design is complete and correct.

➢ Check all insurances are in place.

➢ Make sure the property boundary is clearly marked.

➢ Ensure that all contractors have a clearly defined scope of work and time by when they should complete their work.

➢ Locate and protect existing utility lines, or get them removed as required.

➢ Timeously arrange for power and water connections, understanding what must be done to ensure your installations are compliant and won't delay the installation of the utilities.

➢ Ensure materials will be available when required.

Chapter 4 – Renovating Your House

Renovations range from minor cosmetic touches, like repainting a house, through to bigger changes, such as redoing paving and constructing pergolas and verandas. Then there are more major changes, for example extending the house by adding additional bedrooms, bathrooms and garages. More complex and major changes could include structural changes and even adding an additional upper floor to the house.

Sometimes these renovations are done in stages to match time and budgets, while occasionally they're necessary because of changed circumstances (an extra child arrives, elderly parents move in, or you've got older and are less mobile). Often they're a necessity because items have become worn, structures have weakened, the house has leaks (in the roof, around windows and even through walls) and cables and pipes have become non-compliant. Of course, frequently renovations are done because you've decided you don't like things as they are, you would like an extra bathroom, you want a different colour scheme, or you want to upgrade and modernise your home.

On occasion, investors purchase older houses and carry out renovations to make them smarter, newer, more upmarket, with additional bathrooms and bedrooms, so that they are more appealing to buyers and they can then sell them at a profit.

Sometimes you even decide you want to move to another house or area, maybe upsize or downsize, but in order to make your house more appealing to potential buyers you've decided to make some changes and improvements.

Even minor cosmetic changes can make a huge difference to the value of the house, or to your enjoyment of the property. (See my book 'An Introduction to Building and Renovating Houses: Finding your ideal property and Designing Your Dream Home' where I devote a chapter to simple home improvement ideas.)

Restrictions – what could impact your plans?

There are restrictions which could limit what you can and can't do to an existing house. These include:

- ➤ Physical restrictions which include:
    - The location of sewer pipes which might be in the way of a planned extension. The location (including vertical alignment) could impact where new bathrooms, laundries and kitchens can be added and

even the position of new toilets, bathtubs and sinks.

- The layout of the current house.
- The structural integrity of the existing building. (See later.)
- The design of the existing roof. Modifying an existing roof is often costly and can result in leaks and colour and material differences. Extending an existing house is cheaper and easier if it can be done without altering, or tying into the existing roof.
- The materials incorporated in the existing building.
- The topography of the property. Sloping sites require level areas to be created for the extension, which require ground excavations or filling with earth.
- The foundations under the existing walls. These foundations may prohibit, or make it problematic, to add another floor or storey, or could make it difficult to relocate internal walls.
- The location of the current building on the property. Is there space for the planned extension?
- The current architectural design of the house. The alterations, changes and additions should generally match the existing architectural style of the house, or the existing style (interiors and exteriors) need to be modified so there's a coherent design flow. For instance, adding a modern cutting edge extension to a Victorian existing design in most cases will result in a mismatched poorly coordinated design. So matching a modern extension with an existing vintage house could require extensive modification of the existing fixtures, fittings and finishes (at additional costs) to maintain continuity. Having said this though, clever architects have managed the transitions with sympathy and good effect.

➤ Local or council bylaws and estate rules which could dictate the distance that the new building can be from the property boundary, the location and size of windows overlooking your neighbours, the height of the building and sometimes even the architectural features of the house. (Much of this I discuss in my other book, but needless to say it's important that you familiarise yourself with all these rules, or at least engage a design professional who understands the various rules and requirements.)

➤ Heritage listing – some older houses are heritage listed houses which limits what can be done on the exterior of the house, and in some cases, depending on the type of listing, could even restrict what can be done internally. Heritage listed properties can be very expensive to change.

➤ Neighbours' objections.

➤ Access for construction.

➤ The requirement to continue living in the house. (See later.)

➤ Your budget.

What permits do you need?

Minor changes such as repainting interior walls and modifying the interior of the house usually don't require permissions. However, apartments and houses located in estates may require that the managing body is notified that contractors will be busy on the property.

It should be noted that when renovating apartments particular rules may apply, which could limit the hours of work and the amount of noise. Often apartment complexes have rules which dictate what type of floor coverings can be used, in particular that hard materials like concrete and ceramic tiles cannot be used (this is to prevent the transmission of nose to apartments below) and they also limit internal structural changes and dictate the type and location of plumbing waste pipes. In fact changing the location of many plumbing fittings in an apartment can be difficult as it often requires access from the apartment below.

All exterior changes, and usually internal structural changes will require various permits and permissions, which could include from local authorities, estate managers (where applicable), fire authorities, in some cases in environmental sensitive areas then environmental agency approvals, road authorities when driveways are to be constructed that enter public roads at a new location, and where required heritage authority approval.

The soundness of existing structures

It's pointless renovating the inside of your house if the roof leaks. You could recover the roof, but that might only be a temporary fix if the roof timbers are rotting and need replacing. You could think that patching those cracks and repainting the wall will make the cracks vanish – well they may vanish for a time, but, if the foundations are moving the cracks will probably reappear.

In addition, you need to have the foundations and floor slabs assessed if you're planning on constructing additional walls, or building upwards adding another floor, to ensure that they can take the extra loads. Ceilings needs to be strong enough to support the new ceiling fans or chandeliers you're planning to install.

But, even construction works can damage existing structures. You probably don't want to replace your driveway because delivery trucks were too heavy for it causing it to crack. Workers should take care when working above ceilings and on roofs that they don't damage them or even fall through.

Unfortunately, more than one renovator has had their budgets destroyed because costs escalated when it was found that structures and foundations needed to be replaced or strengthened so that the new renovations could be completed.

Existing mould, dry rot and termite infestations could be hidden problems that are uncovered during renovations and which require rectifying.

Caution should be taken when excavating for new foundations or pools that the existing building isn't undermined resulting in the building settling.

Sufficiency and location of existing plumbing and electrical

Sometimes, what appears to be a minor renovation can become costly if it's found that the existing plumbing, gas or water pipes and electrical cables aren't up to code and specification. For final approvals to be granted the plumbing and electrical networks for the whole house may have to be upgraded. In addition, it's also important to confirm that the existing power and water supply is adequate to supply the additional facilities. If it isn't it could involve installing bigger connections, cables and pipes. Before embarking on a renovation project it may pay to have experts assess the current plumbing, gas and electrical systems to confirm that they meet regulatory requirements and that they can supply the extensions.

In particular, look at hot water systems which might be too small, or might be situated far from where hot water is required, meaning the water cools as it traverses the lengthy pipes supplying the new bathroom. Lagging or insulating the hot water pipes can help reduce the problem.

Often a lack of water pressure is a problem, especially if the existing supply pipes are small, or when the renovation involves building upwards.

Sometimes, pipes and electrical cables are in the way of the extension and have to be relocated at additional cost.

Structural modifications – don't bring the house down

Often the first thing we want to do is chop out internal walls to change the size of rooms and the configuration and layout of the house. Unfortunately, some of these walls may be holding up the roof or the floor above, so removing them can cause the roof or upper floor to sag, or worse even collapse. In some cases it's possible to put in extra permanent supporting structures for the roof or upper floor, but these should be designed by and engineer and installed before demolition work starts.

Even cutting additional doors and windows, or enlarging the existing windows can weaken load bearing walls. Additional beams may have to be installed to transfer the loads over the openings. The remaining portion of the walls must be checked to ensure that they're able to carry the additional loads from above.

All buildings are supported by some form of foundation. The detail of the foundation will depend on the ground on which the structure is built, as well as the load that the foundation must carry. If the building is on rock the foundations may be light, while buildings on weak ground will have more substantial foundations, even including reinforcing steel. It may appear easy to demolish an internal wall and rebuild it a few centimetres (inches) away, but if the new wall isn't constructed on a foundation and only on the existing concrete slab there'll be problems if the concrete slab has insufficient strength to support the new wall. The concrete slab could crack and the wall settle and crack. This is unsightly and can be dangerous.

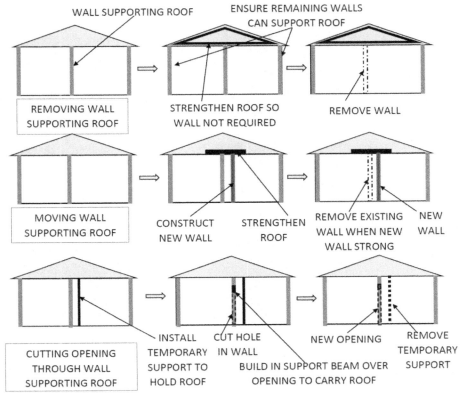

WALL SUPPORTING ROOF

ENSURE REMAINING WALLS CAN SUPPORT ROOF

REMOVING WALL SUPPORTING ROOF

STRENGTHEN ROOF SO WALL NOT REQUIRED

REMOVE WALL

MOVING WALL SUPPORTING ROOF

CONSTRUCT NEW WALL

STRENGTHEN ROOF

REMOVE EXISTING WALL WHEN NEW WALL STRONG

NEW WALL

CUTTING OPENING THROUGH WALL SUPPORTING ROOF

INSTALL TEMPORARY SUPPORT TO HOLD ROOF

CUT HOLE IN WALL

BUILD IN SUPPORT BEAM OVER OPENING TO CARRY ROOF

NEW OPENING

REMOVE TEMPORARY SUPPORT

Sometimes foundations aren't only there to support the structure but they also must hold the house down. For instance, houses made of lightweight materials in an area prone to hurricanes, tornedos and cyclones need be firmly anchored to the ground.

> *Case study: The owners of an apartment building had to replace the existing asbestos roof with a tin roof. Now tin is much lighter than the asbestos roofing materials. The lighter roof meant that it was more susceptible to being ripped off by the wind. An engineer had to design additional roof tie-down rods that were installed two metres (six feet) into the existing brick walls. In addition, all the existing roof structure connections were checked to ensure that they were robust and adequate to withstand the wind forces.*

Chopping out an internal wall – not always straightforward

It seems so simple – cut out an existing wall to make a room larger, or to create open plan living areas. But there're issues you should consider which could add to your costs. These include:

➢ Is the wall load bearing, supporting the structure above? (See the previous section.)

> ➢ Are there pipes or electrical wiring in the wall which have to be accommodated elsewhere? These need to be isolated, made safe and then relocated as necessary.

> ➢ Will the floor levels on the two sides of the wall be the same? If the floors have been constructed separately it's feasible that they aren't perfectly level and even though they are the same level at a connecting doorway they might be different elsewhere. Even a level variance of five millimetres (a fifth of an inch) can be a problem when you try join the floors after the wall is gone.

> ➢ Will the ceilings be at the same height between the adjoining rooms? Ceilings may not be exactly level across the room and you may find that the ceilings don't perfectly line-up. Even a five millimetre difference (fifth of an inch) may result in you having to redo the ceiling in one of the rooms.

> ➢ Will the floor finishes match? Replacing carpets may be simple, but tiles involve more work. Even when the floor tiles match at a connecting door between the rooms they may not match further along when the wall is removed. It's possible that the tile pattern in one room isn't perfectly square, or the joints between tiles are fractionally larger. This may result in tile patterns mismatching further from the door when the wall is removed.

> ➢ Will the walls at right angles to the wall that's removed line-up between the adjoining rooms? Sometimes one wall could be slightly out of square or a few millimetres thicker, which could mean that once the wall is removed the adjoining walls don't join perfectly flat. You can manage this transition by including a small nib where the wall you removed joined the other walls.

> ➢ Usually lights have to be changed so they are controlled by one common switch. Lights mounted in the ceiling may have to be relocated so they are placed evenly and symmetrically across the enlarged room. This may entail minor repairs to the ceiling.

> ➢ Ducted air-conditioning may have to be modified so there is one control for the room. The ducts feeding the two rooms could have to be combined to take account of the new enlarged room.

Dealing with hazardous materials

There're a number of hazardous materials that can be encountered when renovating an old house. The most common of these is asbestos. Asbestos material should be handled and disposed of by a specialist. Not only can it be hazardous to people in the area, but most countries have strict legislation governing the handling and disposal of asbestos. Failure to adhere to the rules could result in fines, as well as the costs of remedial work to correctly dispose of contaminated materials.

Asbestos could be encountered in roofs, ceilings, walls, insulation, electrical equipment, water pipes and floor covering materials. If there's any concerns about asbestos it's recommended that experts are called in to test suspect materials. An expert from your area will be familiar with the type of materials used in buildings of the same age and can usually quickly test suspect materials and prepare a report.

Additional hazards to consider when doing renovation work include:

➤ Mould, which often forms in damp and enclosed conditions and can form in walls and under floorboards. Breathing in mould spores can be hazardous. When removing areas infected with mould always wear suitable breathing masks and dispose of the contaminated materials where it won't contaminate new building materials. Call in experts to ensure that areas of mould are removed or treated. Existing mould will easily spread. Living in a house with mould is dangerous to your health and the mould can destroy furniture and clothing.

➤ Dry rot is a mould that rots timber. It spreads if left untreated and it weakens timber until it becomes weak and collapses. Replace all areas that have dry rot.

➤ Termites eat timber and they can literally eat a whole house. Get experts to exterminate termites and use timber products that have been treated to protect against termite infestations

Damage to existing structures – it could be costly

Partially renovating a house sometimes results in damage to the rest of the house. This damage results in additional costs.

➤ Dust from construction works can penetrate the whole house. Not only does this result in additional cleaning bills, but it could even result in requirements to repaint walls and replace carpets. Dust can damage equipment and appliances. To limit the spread of dust:

▪ Consider hoarding off the areas where renovations are taking place and ensure these hoardings are as airtight as possible.

▪ Cover areas with plastic dust sheets – these could include light fixtures, carpets, furniture and walls.

▪ Remove fixtures and fittings, curtains, blinds and furniture that could get dust on them.

▪ Lightly wet down dust making activities.

▪ Regularly remove building rubble and clean the work areas.

➤ Dirt is brought into areas on shoes and equipment. Limit the spread of dirt by covering and protecting floors and providing alternative access for construction workers so they don't have to go through unaffected areas.

➤ Scuffing, chipping and scratching.

▪ Floors - particularly timber, tiles and carpets can be damaged when workmen move equipment and materials through and over areas not being renovated. Consider covering floors with heavy duty cardboard which should be stuck down so that dust and grit can't get under the cardboard between the floor and the cardboard which will cause scratches. Where walls are being demolished place timber boards to protect the floors from falling debris.

- Doors – consider removing and storing doors from doorways that will have construction traffic passing through. Also protect the door frames by taping heavy duty cardboard or timber to areas which could be scuffed and damaged.

➤ Structural, which includes cracking and even structural failures. This could be caused by:

- Stacking of heavy materials on slabs and paving, or even against walls. Most slabs are not designed to have heavy loads on them.
- Moving heavy equipment on slabs and paving. Use timbers to protect the surface and to distribute the loads. Always check that the structure is suitable to support the weight of the machine.
- Excessive vibrations caused by equipment. Heavy compacting equipment shouldn't be used close to buildings since this can cause cracking. Equipment breaking parts of a structure can transfer the vibrations to other parts. Using smaller equipment and pre-cutting the break lines can reduce the impact of the vibrations.
- Cutting out essential bracing or load bearing elements. Always get an engineer to check the structural integrity before breaking openings and demolishing walls.
- Cutting out bracing walls. Removing some walls may mean that the remaining structure becomes unstable and could easily fall in high winds, or if knocked by a vehicle. Have an engineer assess the structure before demolitions start. Additional permanent, or temporary, supports may be required to support the structure.
- Constructing new walls and floors on existing foundations and floor slabs which weren't designed to receive these.
- Leaving areas open or exposed to the wind which could cause wind damage and even result in the roof being blown off, or walls collapsing.
- Damage to buildings when knocked by heavy construction equipment, including trucks and excavators.
- Undermining of the existing foundations when digging trenches for new pipes and cables, or new foundations and basements. Care must always be taken not to excavate too close and below existing foundations. Some ground can easily collapse, especially if water gets into the excavation. Ask for professional advice and always fill the excavation in as quickly as possible to lessen the risk of flooding.

➤ Water could come from pipes damaged by work, pipes or drains that have become blocked and cause flooding, rain entering the building through openings cut into the existing roof or walls, or from external sources when construction has damaged stormwater drains or where the natural path of the water has been blocked or diverted. It's therefore important to:

- Ensure that water pipes are isolated where they could be damaged by the construction work.
- Check that building material and rubble doesn't enter drains.
- Ensure that all pipes are located, marked and protected before work starts.
- Check that external work, including the stacking and tipping of sand and building materials, doesn't block the natural path of stormwater.
- Cover all openings with suitable tarpaulins or plastic sheeting that can keep the water out. These protections must be secure so they can't be blown open by the wind. In addition water shouldn't pool on these coverings as this can cause them to tear or collapse.

Connecting to the existing building

Adding on new structures to an existing building poses a number of challenges.

➢ Floor levels should preferably match. Where there are steps between the new section and the original building these need to be planned so that the size of the stair treads and risers are a consistent size that match the recommended comfortable and legal stair sizes. See Chapter 12.

➢ It's often difficult to match the existing finishes – particularly face bricks, textured or coloured render work, floor tiles and timber flooring. The problem of matching finishes often results in a permanent mismatch and the new work always appears different from the original building. The alternative is to change the existing finishes and materials to match the new work, which can add significant extra expense which wasn't foreseen when the budget was prepared.

➢ Tying in a roof structure poses many challenges, the most obvious being to ensure that there are no leaks. But even getting the same materials of the same colour can be a problem.

➢ Where floor finishes are carried through from one room to another, such as ceramic tiles or timber, it's difficult to find the same matching materials and colours. In fact, even when the exact colour is found you'll frequently find that the existing material in the house has faded with time and use.

➢ Existing floor levels may dictate the type of materials used on the new floor. Generally we don't want small steps between different rooms in the house. So, if you're chopping up the floor tiles in the bathroom and re-tiling it you're often restricted to use a product of similar thickness, or thinner. Using a thicker tile or product will mean the top surface is probably higher than the finished level in the adjoining room. It's not recommended to reduce the top level of the existing concrete slab to accommodate a thicker tile because this is expensive and it will weaken the slab. Using a thinner tile will necessitate using more glue, or applying a layer of grout under the tile to ensure the top of the new tile is level with the adjoining room. In addition, changing the floor level will impact the doors. If floor levels increase doors may scrape on the floor so they'll need to be cut shorter - not usually a major problem. But if the new floor level is lower, then the doors may have a large gap underneath which could be unsightly and allow noise and light to enter from the adjoining room. You may have to install new doors of the correct length. Sometimes door frames and architraves end at the top of the finished floor. Installing a floor finish which is thinner than the existing floor will mean that the bottom of the frame is now raised above the new floor level. This is unsightly and is a place for dirt to be trapped and it could even be a hazard that cut people's feet.

➢ Sometimes, simply moving a wall, or even a kitchen cupboard may seem simple, but often timber and tile floors have been laid around the existing wall or cupboard. Moving the wall or cupboard exposes a bare piece of floor. Patching the timber or tile often results in colour differences (assuming the product is still available).

Case study: in our house we undertook renovations in the main bedroom. This involved moving a few walls slightly and the timber floor had to be patched in a couple of places. Firstly we had to find the exact same timber for the patches. Then the complete bedroom floor had to be sanded and sealed. But the timber floor continued from the bedroom out the door through the whole upper level floor. The newly sanded and treated floor was always going to have a different colour from the original floor which had aged in the sun and with use. We eventually had to sand and seal all the existing timber floor upstairs to achieve a uniform coloured floor - about one hundred square metres (a thousand square feet) because one square metre (ten square feet) had to be patched!

To live in the house while it's being renovated or not?

You probably don't want to move out of your house unnecessarily. It involves additional costs, which include moving out of the house and back again, as well as the cost of renting another property. It also involves a certain amount of disruption to your family's life.

However living in a house that's been renovated could involve:

➢ Noise.

➢ Dust.

➢ Interruption of water and electricity supply.

- Security issues. See the next section.
- Risk to pets which could escape the house or property through temporary openings in walls and fences, or through doors or gates that workers have inadvertently left open. Also, noise, dust and strangers in the house could frighten the pets, causing them distress, even leading to them running away.
- Danger where you or your family could trip over hazards or fall into unprotected openings.
- Restrictions to the use of portions of the house and garden – which could be inconvenient, especially when it's the kitchen or bathroom.
- Storage and protection of items from rooms impacted by the renovations.
- Continuous coming and going of construction workers which can disturb your family's daily routine and privacy.
- The risk of furniture being damaged by the construction work.
- Parts of the house being open to the weather. Even workmen traipsing through the house will let cold or heat indoors.
- Tramping dirt, mud and water into the house by workers.

In addition, planning to live in the house while it's being renovated can put restrictions on the planned changes and the construction work. This could include:

- The design and changes would be limited so as not to impact areas of the house where you and the family will be living.
- Construction may have to be done in stages to work around requirements to provide living areas at all times.
- Some changes may have to be accelerated to limit their impact on occupants.
- Access for construction workers may be limited to prevent intrusion into your living areas, adding to costs. Even working hours may be reduced.
- There may be additional delays and construction costs caused by staged building methods and requirements to hoard off work areas from your living areas.

For bigger renovations it may be more cost effective to move out of the house while the contractors are busy with construction.

Security during renovations

Security of a building undergoing renovation is often compromised because:

- Security alarms may be turned off due to dust and vibration setting them off, or because of power interruptions, or they're disconnected to facilitate their relocation.
- Perimeter walls or fencing could be cut to allow access for materials and equipment. Yard gates are usually left open to allow construction workers in and out of the property, or they could be accidently left open by careless workers.

➤ Construction workers generally have access to the existing house and they could steal your family's personal effects as well as fittings and fixtures.

➤ When modifications and additions are made to the exterior of the house, holes for new windows, doors, or where the new extensions tie into the existing building are left open for several days while old openings are built closed, or the new doors and windows are installed. Alterations to existing roofs often take several days, leaving parts of the roof open in the interim.

➤ Exterior access scaffolding can provide easy access to unguarded upstairs parts of the house.

➤ External doors are often left open for workers to enter the building, which could allow criminals to also enter the house.

Insurance during renovations

Before starting with major renovations it's important to notify your insurer and inform them when work will start, what it entails and how long it's expected to take. They should be kept informed of any changes. Read the small print of your insurance policy. Even moving out the house for an extended period while renovation occur could void your policy. When the project is complete always update your insurer.

Measure existing structures – they may not match drawings

Never assume that what's shown on drawings is exactly how the existing building was constructed. Sometimes renovations or changes were done to the structure which aren't show on the drawings. But anyway, often doors and windows aren't located in the exact location as shown on the drawings. In particular waterpipes and electrical cables are often not in the precise locations as shown on the drawings.

Summary

All of us do minor work around the house, whether it's some painting, small maintenance, working in the garden, or getting into slightly bigger projects like adding a barbeque or installing a new patio.

But launching into a full renovation project requires more thought and planning. Regrettably some jump right in without knowing what they're in for, how long it'll take, how much it'll cost, or indeed, without knowing what the end result will be. Suddenly they're left with a house with bits knocked out here and there and the family is living in a building site – a building site that could last for several years. Worse still, you could spend all this money and energy and find that what you've done is illegal, or that it hasn't added value to the house.

Before starting your renovations you should:

➤ Have a master plan of what you want done.

➤ Understand what permits are required.

➢ Know what restrictions there are on your property.

➢ Consider how the work will impact you and your family.

➢ Prepare a budget.

➢ Have a timeline for how long the work will take.

➢ Sequence the work so that urgent repairs are attended to first and that work that could be damaged by other trades is done last.

➢ Check that the existing plumbing and electrical is sufficient.

➢ Confirm the soundness of the existing remaining structures.

➢ Take care when carrying out structural modifications to the existing building not to weaken the structure where it could crack or even collapse.

➢ Locate and protect existing services so they aren't damaged by the work.

➢ Identify hazardous materials and ensure these are removed and disposed of by experts.

➢ Understand the problems of living in the house while the renovations are carried out.

➢ Protect the existing structures and finishes from damage caused by the renovation work.

➢ Understand how the new areas will tie into the existing building.

➢ Always physically measure the existing structures to confirm that the existing drawings are an accurate representation of what's there.

➢ Implement suitable security measures and precautions during construction.

➢ Ensure that you aren't wasting money, or that there aren't other better options available.

Renovations will be messy, they will involve noise, dust, dirt and inconvenience and unexpected problems will be encountered. You need to be prepared to be flexible and always have money in reserve for the unknown. But breathing new life into an old house and living in a completed renovation that's been well planned and executed will be rewarding and should provide years of joy and comfort to you and your family.

Chapter 5 – Building Processes – What You Should Know

Right, so you've finally decided what you want and where you want it, you've completed your design and you're deciding who is going to build (or renovate) your home. There are still a few hurdles to clear and some boxes to tick before construction can start.

It's also good to understand some of the construction processes so that you are more aware of what can go wrong, why things are done as they are and what you should be looking out for.

Clearing site– not simply sending a bulldozer in

Clearing the construction site could involve:
- Demolishing existing structures.
- Removing vegetation. It's important to clearly mark trees that shouldn't be removed and fence off vegetation which you don't want damaged. A bulldozer or excavator can do big damage in a few seconds when your back's turned. Vegetation can be chipped and mulched and stockpiled to use as compost and mulch for landscaping at the end of the project.
- Stripping topsoil. In general, topsoil is the top layer of the ground suitable for plants to grow in, which could be between 50mm and 200mm thick (two to eight inches). It isn't suitable under houses and roads and must be removed, and shouldn't be used for filling in trenches. Topsoil is usually a valuable commodity and should be separated from construction debris and other soil. Good topsoil is essential for landscaping and sufficient quantities should be stockpiled on the property (space providing) to be spread in new garden areas when all building work is complete. Importing new topsoil is expensive, plus there's the cost of carting away the material stripped from your property. Stockpiles of topsoil on the property may need to be protected so it isn't washed away by rain, possibly blocking stormwater drains, or being carried onto neighbouring properties or roads where it must be cleaned up. Excess good topsoil could even be sold, or given away free providing people cart it away at no cost to you.

> ➢   Removing any obstructions and impediments to the project work.

Levelling an area for your house

Generally the area under the footprint of the building should be graded and levelled to the required height specified under the building (this height would be the finished floor level shown on drawings, less the thickness of the floor structure). This may require material from high areas to be moved to areas which are too low. Excess material usually has to be taken away, while a shortage of material will require suitable material to be brought from elsewhere, usually at additional costs. Of course the material that's used to fill and level the area under the building footprint must be suitable and it must be compacted to the required engineer's specifications. Clay, silt, topsoil, and material with vegetation or rubble, as well as material that's inconsistent or which has large boulders, is generally unsuitable for fill. Excavated slopes and filled areas mustn't be too steep so that they'll collapse. These slopes usually require protection with vegetation or other methods so the ground isn't eroded away.

Before starting to level the site the area should be cleared of all topsoil, vegetation and unsuitable material.

It's important to note that material that's excavated from the undisturbed ground usually compacts to only about 80% of the original volume (this varies according to the type of ground and the desired amount of compaction). This means, that assuming the material excavated is all suitable for fill, then for every eight cubic metres (eight cubic yards) of fill we have to excavate about ten cubic metres (ten cubic yards). This is also a problem when trenches are excavated for pipes and cables. Often when the trenches are backfilled you may find there's a shortage of material – nobody has stolen the material, it's just been compacted down into a smaller volume and you'll have to find additional material to make up the difference. See later.

If additional fill material has to be brought from elsewhere there's an additional cost for the transport and often the material has to be purchased. It should be noted that a cubic metre (yard) of loose material on a truck usually compacts down to around 65% (again this depends on the type of soil as well as the desired compaction). So for every six and a half cubic metres (six and half cubic yards) of fill required you usually have to purchase about ten cubic metres (ten cubic yards) of loose fill. (Always ask for expert advice, or test a few loads because with some materials you may be fortunate and the loose material compacts down to only 75 or even 80%.) When purchasing material always check that you're purchasing cubic metres (yards) not tons. If you're paying for tons ask the supplier what that equates to per cubic metre or yard.

Unsuitable material and material that's in excess of requirements usually has to be carted from your property at an additional cost.

It should be noted that during the construction process fill material is usually required to backfill around foundations and under floor slabs. Therefore retain sufficient suitable material created while levelling the site for later use.

To limit the amount of material required to be bought for filling it's important that all material excavated on the property, whether to install utilities or for foundations, is sorted, keeping good backfill material separate from unsuitable material. Unfortunately, often this isn't monitored properly and the good material gets contaminated and becomes unsuitable for use.

An engineer can advise on the compaction required under structures and the type and suitability of material on the property.

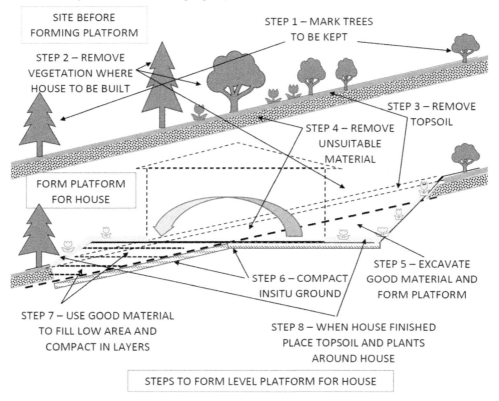

STEPS TO FORM LEVEL PLATFORM FOR HOUSE

Generally, where possible, it pays to design the house and set the floor levels such that the material excavated will all be used for filling, with minimal material to be carted off the property or additional fill to be brought on.

If additional material is required, or you have surplus material, it pays to scout the area and nearby suburbs. Often there're other projects nearby that have surplus material that they need to get rid of, or they may require additional fill material. Of course always check the quality of the material, since nobody wants a load of rubbish material that can't be used and which then has to be removed at additional cost.

It should be noted that it's illegal to dig holes on vacant properties or deposit excess material on them without the owner's permission. But, sometimes even with the owner's permission there may be permits to be gotten, such as environmental.

Where there's some material that's not very suitable, it may be a possibility to use this material for filling lower down, and keep the better material for the uppermost layers – but obviously this is dependent on the engineer's advice. See later.

On bigger properties, if there's an excess of material it may be possible to incorporate some of this into the landscaping, creating low mounds.

Of course below ground swimming pools and basements create additional ground which can either be used to level the property or it has to be carted away.

Retaining walls – holding the soil back

Often level areas must be created on sloping sites. Retaining walls could be constructed to keep the ground back that's been excavated to form the level platform and also to retain the earth that's been tipped to raise portions of the site. Any walls above one metre (three foot) must be designed by an engineer, but it's probably good practice to involve an engineer even on lower walls. Poorly designed walls can easily collapse, resulting in the cost of repairing the damage, sometimes even damage to surrounding buildings, roads, walls and property, and even injury.

Many retaining walls fail due to inadequate drainage. Water is allowed to build-up in the ground behind the wall, which exerts additional pressure on the wall causing it to fail. If there are inadequate drains at the top of the wall and at the foot of the wall, then stormwater will erode away parts of the wall or its foundation, leading to failure.

The top of walls higher than 500mm usually require a fence or protection to prevent people accidently falling off the top of the wall.

Retaining walls must always be designed taking account of the loadings which could be exerted on the ground above the wall, which could include building foundations, boundary fences and vehicles. They must consider the material under the foundations as well as the material that will be placed behind the wall.

Retaining walls usually require a foundation which is generally constructed from reinforced concrete. The size of the foundation will depend on the height of the wall, the ground conditions under the foundations, the type of retaining wall and the loading behind the wall.

Retaining walls can be constructed from a variety of materials which could depend on the required finished aesthetics, the available materials and skills, the height of the wall, your budget, and the available space. Construction materials and methods could include building an in-situ reinforced concrete wall, using block materials (such as clay, cement or stone blocks), using precast concrete elements, using patented precast elements which are packed in such a way that plantings can be introduced between and in the elements which helps soften and disguise the wall, and making use of stone filled 'gabion' baskets.

Block and concrete walls should have adequate water-proofing behind the wall. Walls that have no water-proofing (or poor protection) look unsightly when water penetrates the wall. Not only can this cause staining, but it causes deterioration of the surface, including bubbling and spalling, which results in structural deterioration of the wall, even causing the wall to fail.

Poorly designed retaining walls can be unsightly and even dangerous.

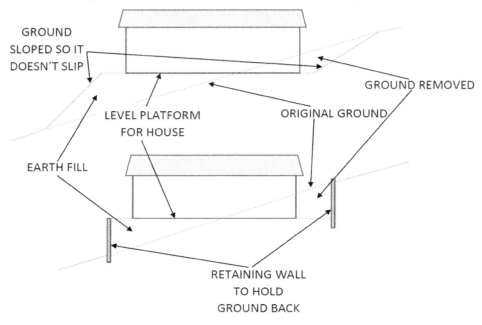

GROUND SLOPED SO IT DOESN'T SLIP

GROUND REMOVED

LEVEL PLATFORM FOR HOUSE

ORIGINAL GROUND

EARTH FILL

RETAINING WALL TO HOLD GROUND BACK

GROUND LEVELLED TO FORM PLATFORM FOR HOUSE. IN FIRST CASE GROUND IS SHAPED TO STEEPEST SLOPE POSSIBLE AND IN THE SECOND CASE THE GROUND IS HELD VERICAL BY RETAINING WALLS

Excavations – not as simple as just digging a hole

Ground has to be excavated to level the site for foundations, for basements, pools and to install services such as water pipes, stormwater pipes, electrical cables and sewer (wastewater) pipes. Sometimes, in the case of basements and sewer and stormwater pipes these excavations are deep.

Remember when you were a child playing on a sandy beach. High up on the beach where the sand was dry if you dug a hole it filled up with sand as quickly as you removed it. The sides of the hole kept falling in. Closer to the sea the sand was wetter so you could dig a hole fairly deep and the sides stood up vertically. But as the sand dried out the sides of the excavation started to fall in. Of course, as soon as you stood near the edge of the excavation the sides collapsed and you fell into the hole. When you tried to dig a hole right at the edge of the sea where the waves were, the excavation filled with water and the sides of the hole fell in immediately they were wet.

Now there's a huge variety of different ground conditions which you could encounter on your building site. These could range from solid rock, rock that is heavily fragmented, ground containing boulders, hard well compacted ground, loose ground, and sand. Excavating in hard solid rock it's possible to have vertical sides to the excavation and the sides won't fall in. Excavating in sand will often have a similar result to what you encountered on the beach and the sides usually won't stay vertical for long, and usually only up to a depth of half a metre (eighteen inches). Harder ground could stand vertically for a couple of metres (six foot), but the sides can collapse if water enters the excavation – water running into the excavation will erode the sides and water sitting in the bottom of the excavation will saturate the ground on the sides eating into the ground, eventually causing it to collapse.

Of course ground that collapses into the excavation results in the excavation becoming larger, and it also requires the ground to be cleaned out of the excavation again, which is time consuming. But if the excavation is more than a metre and a half deep (four-and-a half feet) and somebody is working in the excavation then they could be injured by the falling debris and even buried alive. Unfortunately there are frequent reports of construction workers being killed when the sides of trenches collapsed on them burying them.

Therefore by law (note: check your local safety requirements), and for practical purposes, the sides of all excavations (other than in solid rock) cannot have vertical sides more than one and a half metres (four-and-a half feet). Above that, the ground must be battered back (sloped) to about a thirty or forty-five degree slope, or the sides of the excavation should be in steps or benches. Of course where there's only sand the sides of the excavation can't be vertical and will probably be at a forty-five degree slope from the base of the excavation. What this means is that the excavation at the top surface ends up being much wider than it has to be at the bottom of the hole. Imagine a three metre (nine foot) deep trench that is six hundred millimetres (two foot) wide at the bottom. In sand the excavation could be over six metres (eighteen foot) wide at the top, or in hard ground the excavation could be three metres (nine foot) wide. Not only must this extra material be excavated, but once the pipe is installed, or the wall built, this material must be put back, and compacted properly.

What this means is that excavating a three metre (nine foot) deep basement isn't going to cost 50% more than excavating a two metre (six foot) deep basement, it's probably going to be double the cost. And, excavating a three metre (nine foot) deep trench could cost three or four times the cost of excavating a two metre (six foot) deep trench.

But remember, as discussed when you were on the beach and you stood on the edge of your excavation the sides collapsed, so we have the same on our construction sites where excavations next to roads or below building foundations could easily collapse because of the extra weight on the sides of the excavation from the vehicles and the building.

Of course making excavations wider to accommodate the depth is often not an option, there simply isn't the space. In these cases the sides of the excavations have to

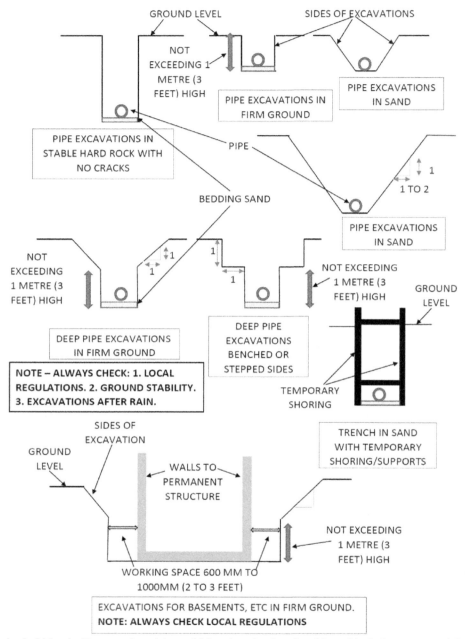

be held back. For trenches this could involve shoring the sides with timbers or special structures, or even sinking caissons (rigid boxes of timber, steal or concrete, strong enough to hold the ground back) into the ground and excavating the ground out between the walls of the caisson. Deep basements, or basements excavated in sand may require walls to be constructed from continuous steel sheet piles or concrete piles which are driven into the ground first. This establishes an enclosed space around the outside of the basement, and the ground can then be excavated from within this enclosed area. When the basement is excavated the basement walls can be constructed against this ring of piles.

Whenever excavating care should be taken to separate the good material which is suitable to use for backfilling from unsuitable material. Invariably the ground varies the deeper we excavate. The upper layer could be topsoil and contain vegetation Below the topsoil could be several layers of ground. Some material could be unsuitable for backfilling and may have to be disposed of. Some material could be okay for filling layers deeper down, while the best material should be kept for filling the uppermost layers of trenches and against walls.

When excavating for foundations or basements. it's often necessary to make the excavation larger than needed so that there's space in which to work and to construct the foundation or wall. The working space required usually varies between six hundred and one thousand millimetres (two to three foot). The area excavated for working space must be filled with ground which is compacted when the wall is complete.

If the concrete is to be cast against the sides of the ground or soil then the excavation should be done as neatly and accurately as possible. If the excavation is larger than it should be then more concrete will be required to fill the space of the extra ground removed. If the excavation is too small then the foundation or wall won't fit and excess ground must be removed to make the excavation the correct size. This will create delays and additional costs.

Usually stormwater and wastewater pipes can't be placed directly on rock or hard ground and require a layer of soft sand 50 to 150millimetres (2 to 6 inches) thick under them. This allows for the pipes to be placed at the correct height and it means that the pipe is supported evenly along its length without lumps and bumps of rock which could damage the pipe.

Ground compaction – making solid foundations

The ground under foundations, ground floor slabs, paving and driveways and in trenches should be compacted. Usually an engineer will prescribe the degree of compaction and the number of layers that should be compacted.

Obviously when compacting trenches care must be taken not to damage the pipes in the trenches as they can often be easily crushed or cracked.

When compacting ground it should be done in layers 100 to 150 millimetres (four to six inches) thick. Thicker layers don't get compacted. Usually ground needs some moisture for compaction, normally referred to as the optimal moisture content. If there's too much water, or too little, you won't achieve the required compaction density no matter how hard it's hit. The amount of compaction also depends on the type of machine and how many times the ground is compacted. Again there's usually an optimum effort and too little will mean the ground isn't compacted properly, while too much won't make any difference to the degree of compaction after a while.

Some soils, such as clean sand, can compact very easily. Topsoil and clay ground is unsuitable for using under structures.

Geotechnical companies provide advice on what materials to use and undertake tests of the ground on the property and of the compacted area to check that the ground has been adequately compacted.

Building on ground which isn't compacted properly will result in settlement of the structure, paving or driveway, which will look unsightly and be costly to repair.

Foundations – essential support to your house

Foundations support the whole house and their failure will inevitably lead to cracking of your house, which could eventually lead to leaks and even structural failure making your home uninhabitable. Repairing poor foundations is costly so it's advisable to get an engineer to design the foundations and then to ensure that the foundations are constructed properly.

Foundations provide a level base for the structure of your house, they support the weight of the house, and in some instances they anchor the house and prevent it from being blown away in a storm. The foundations could be as simple as forming a concrete slab under the house, they could involve concrete beams below the walls, or they could be piles which are concrete, steel or timber columns driven or drilled vertically into the ground. The essential part of the foundation is that it distributes the weight of the house to the ground so that the ground is able to support the load and therefore the house doesn't settle or sink. This may involve excavating through the upper layers of ground to reach soil or rock that can support the weight of the building. Foundations should be rigid to evenly distribute the load and to prevent unequal settlement of the house.

The type of foundations will depend on the ground conditions under the house, the load of the house above (for instance houses with two or more floor levels require more substantial foundations than a single floor house and houses with solid brick walls are heavier than frame houses clad with tin or boards), the weather conditions (houses in cyclone, hurricane and tornedo belts require more robust foundations to keep the house firmly anchored to the ground), and if there's a basement.

Some houses require special foundations. This might be because:

➢ The ground conditions are unsuitable because:

▪ Clay ground often swells or expands when it gets wet. You don't want to live in a house that goes up and down. But invariably it doesn't go up and down evenly, so the house will begin to crack and it could become structurally unsound. In addition, water and sewer pipes crack and break. Either the clay has to be removed and suitable material placed under the house, or the foundations must be designed to accommodate the movement, which often means installing piles. Consulting an engineer is essential.

- Collapsing sands settle under the weight of a house which could cause cracking of the house and pipes connecting to the house. Usually foundations have to be designed for these conditions.
- The house is built on a site which was formerly a rubbish dump.
- The area is prone to the formation of sinkholes. Actually you don't really want to be building in an area prone to sinkhole formation, which are normally areas with dolomite rock. If you really have to then there are steps that engineers can take to design your house foundations, but there may be no guarantee that your house won't be swallowed by a sinkhole.

➤ The house is on the edge of a hill or cliff.

➤ The house is on steeply sloped ground.

➤ The house is on the banks of a river or lake.

➤ The structure of the house is supported on only a few columns or walls which carry the major load of the house. Or, possibly the house has cantilever sections which hang over open space and these cantilevers have to be supported and held back to stop them toppling over.

➤ There's an excavation, such as a below ground pool, that's immediately next to and below the foundations of the house.

Special foundations are usually costly and take additional time to construct. Sometimes these have to be installed by specialist contractors. If large machines are required then access may be a problem if there're overhead restrictions (such as power lines and tree branches) or narrow steep access routes. Always ensure that the design for all structures are complete so that all the foundations are constructed at the same time. Remobilising specialist equipment to construct additional foundations later will add more costs.

Stormwater drainage – don't flood your house

Water could enter your property from a number of sources, which includes rain falling on your roof (which may be collected in gutters and downpipes), runoff from your neighbours' properties, water off the street, natural watercourse flowing through your property, and rainfall falling on driveways, patios and the garden.

Stormwater considerations include:

➤ Water should never be allowed to stand near buildings where it can cause damage to the foundations, including causing settlement, and also cause damp in the walls of the house.

➤ Ensuring water cannot enter the house, even in the heavies downpours.

➤ That stormwater isn't allowed to enter sewer systems where it can cause flooding. It's generally illegal to empty stormwater into town sewer systems.

➢ Ensuring natural watercourses aren't blocked.

➢ Controlling the flow of stormwater. Strong and fast flows of stormwater can cause erosion and scouring which could wash away soil and gardens, undermine foundations and damage driveways.

➢ That water doesn't build up behind retaining walls and property boundary walls where it could cause these walls to collapse under the water pressure.

➢ That you understand the local regulations which cover the disposal of stormwater, the discharge of water into neighbouring properties and public roads, as well as receiving stormwater from your neighbouring properties. In some cases all stormwater landing on your property may have to be channelled back into the ground through soak pits.

➢ You consider catching and storing stormwater (particularly from roofs) to use in dry periods to water your garden.

Stormwater management should be part of the overall design of the house and much of it should be implemented at the start.

Stormwater management includes:

➢ Ensuring that the floor of the house is raised above the surrounding ground.

➢ Landscaping and sloping the property so that water flows away from the house and towards an outlet.

➢ Making the entrance to the property raised above street level so that water from the road doesn't enter the property, even when the street drains become blocked.

➢ Making sure that natural watercourses are kept open and deviated where necessary.

➢ Allowing for water entering from your neighbours' property if you have to accept it.

➢ Installing underground soak pits, storage tanks, major stormwater pipes and culverts early in the building process.

➢ Checking that driveways are planned so that water running off them doesn't flood garages.

➢ Ensuring that stormwater isn't concentrated into one area where it'll form rivers. On steeply sloping ground consider installing features to slow the water down, such as rocks and plants. Smooth concrete lined drains allow water to flow very fast and where these end the water can easily scour and erode the ground away, even causing damage to structures.

➢ Considering driveway surfaces which allow stormwater to soak through into the ground below.

➢ Checking that there are adequate drainage holes in retaining walls and property boundary walls.

➢ Ensuring that stormwater drains and channels are large enough to take the heaviest rainstorms.

Plumbing – pipes and more

Plumbing systems consist of the water pipes which connect from the water supply (usually the town system or utility provider, or from your own source of water such as rainwater tanks or bore) to where it's required at taps and toilets. Pressure forces water along the pipes – either pressure from the town system, pressure created by a pump from your bore or tank, or your own raised tank. Water pipes must be able to withstand the pressure of the supply system. Water pipes are available in different grades to withstand various pressures. They are usually 12 to 25 millimetres (half to one inch) in diameter and made from various materials including copper, galvanised steel and various plastics. Because water is forced along the pipes under pressure water pipes don't have to be installed at a specific level and can go up or down.

The amount of water you get out of a tap or fitting in your house will depend on:

➢ The pressure in the town system. If your property is at the top of a hill you will have a lower water pressure than properties at the bottom of the hill. In addition the water pressure of town systems could vary during the course of the day depending on how many people are using water. So early in the day when everyone is using their bathrooms the water pressure could be lower than at other times.

➢ The size of the pipes feeding the fitting. Long pipes with a small diameter cause extra friction which reduces the flow.

➢ How many other fittings are drawing water in your house at the same time. I'm sure we've all experienced being in the shower and the water has suddenly got warmer when someone flushed the toilet taking the cold water.

➢ The actual fitting. Some fittings are designed to limit the amount of water exiting from the tap. In fact in some water poor regions it's law that you must only fit low flow fittings. This can be really irritating if you're trying to fill a bathtub with water.

➢ The water pressure will be less in the upper floors of a building. This might not be noticeable for a two storey house unless your area experiences very low water pressure.

The water supply pipes must have at least one shutoff valve so that the water can be turned off when repairs are required or there's a leak. But it's good practice to install valves within the house, ensuring they're easily accessible. In more than one instance we've had pipes burst flooding the house, and the sooner you can cut the water supply the less water will flood your house.

The other component of the plumbing system are the wastewater pipes (sewer pipes) which take wastewater to the town system or your septic tank. These are gravity pipes and must always flow downhill. Drainpipes vary from 40 to 100 millimetres (one and half to four inches) in diameter. Each waste outlet should have a trap, which is a U-shaped pipe which permanently holds water, preventing smelly sewer gases from entering the room. Waste pipes need air to allow the wastewater to move otherwise an air-lock will be created. At the higher end of the system a vent pipe connects to the atmosphere. Since this will release smelly air these vents are usually placed above the roof, although a non- return valve can be fitted which only allows air to enter, while preventing air from escaping.

It's always advisable to use good quality plumbing pipes and fittings. There have been several cases of imported tap fittings leaching lead into the water supply. Of course lead is poisonous. Also I've had flexible hoses feeding taps suddenly burst because they were substandard, flooding the house.

Generally there are codes which govern plumbing materials, and plumbing design and installation.

Wastewater pipes – why they can't go just anywhere

Sewer pipes (wastewater pipes) usually have to be connected to the town system. If there's no town system, then depending on the regulations, as well as the geology of your property, you may have to construct a sewer storage tank which has to be regularly pumped into a truck. Alternatively it could flow into a septic tank and French drain system. If your property is located in a clayey area, or on rock, then a septic tank and French drain won't work. Always consult experts if there's no town sewage system to connect to.

Sewer pipes can't flow uphill unless you install a pumping system which is expensive. Sewer pipes feed from the drains in your bathrooms and kitchen to the local town system outside your property. Normally sewer pipes should fall at a constant rate of no less than one in sixty (check your local regulations) which means that for every sixty metres (sixty yards) of pipe the lower end must be at least one metre (three foot) below the higher end. This does depend on the type of pipe and building regulations. When there's insufficient fall the solid material won't flow down the pipe and results in a blockage.

Sewer pipes also need to be a minimum level below the ground level so they can't easily be damaged (they could be squashed or broken by vehicles driving over them, or pierced by gardening tools). Obviously sewer pipes shouldn't be above ground level where they are unsightly, can be damaged and create an obstruction. The location of bathrooms in houses on large properties, or ones where the location of the town sewer is at the higher end of the property could be dictated by their distance from the town system and the depth of the town sewer pipes relative to the floor level of the bathroom. Pipes near the surface will need protection so they aren't broken.

Often sewer pipes are deep and are below the other utility lines, so it's always best to install the sewer lines before the other pipes and cables are installed, and probably at an early stage of construction. Sewer pipes are often installed under floor slabs and are one of the first items to be connected. Always ensure that the open ends of all pipes are adequately protected to prevent sand, concrete and rubbish entering the pipe. See also Chapter 12.

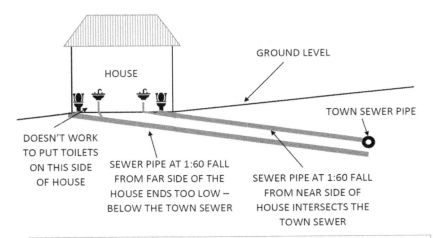

GROUND LEVEL

HOUSE

TOWN SEWER PIPE

DOESN'T WORK
TO PUT TOILETS
ON THIS SIDE
OF HOUSE

SEWER PIPE AT 1:60 FALL
FROM FAR SIDE OF THE
HOUSE ENDS TOO LOW –
BELOW THE TOWN SEWER

SEWER PIPE AT 1:60 FALL
FROM NEAR SIDE OF
HOUSE INTERSECTS THE
TOWN SEWER

EXAMPLE SHOWING POTENTIAL PROBLEM IF THE TOWN SEWER
IS NOT LOW ENOUGH – IN THIS CASE THE BATHROOMS AND
TOILETS CANNOT BE SITUATED ON THE FAR SIDE OF THE HOUSE

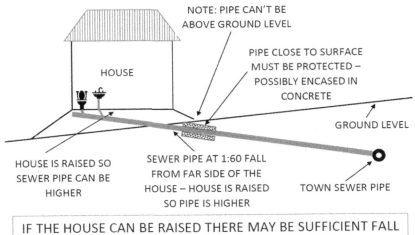

NOTE: PIPE CAN'T BE
ABOVE GROUND LEVEL

PIPE CLOSE TO SURFACE
MUST BE PROTECTED –
POSSIBLY ENCASED IN
CONCRETE

HOUSE

GROUND LEVEL

HOUSE IS RAISED SO
SEWER PIPE CAN BE
HIGHER

SEWER PIPE AT 1:60 FALL
FROM FAR SIDE OF THE
HOUSE – HOUSE IS RAISED
SO PIPE IS HIGHER

TOWN SEWER PIPE

IF THE HOUSE CAN BE RAISED THERE MAY BE SUFFICIENT FALL
FOR THE SEWER PIPE WHERE THE TOWN SEWER IS TOO HIGH

Plumbing and electrical – why it happens in stages

Plumbing and electrical installations have to be coordinated with the other trades and contractors and it usually requires a number of visits from plumbers and electricians. So for instance, these installations could include:

> Before casting the ground floor slab plumbers would have to install pipes under and in the floor slab. Electricians would have to install wires or cable

ducts under and in the floor slab.

➤ Depending on the design of the walls:

- Framed walls would require pipes and wires or cable ducts installed after the frame is erected but before the walls are boarded closed. Taps, plumbing waste pipes, electrical switches and outlets must all be fixed in the correct position.

- Concrete walls and columns would require everything installed before the concrete is poured.

- Block and brick walls which will be rendered may have pipes, wires, ducts and outlets cut into them after the walls are constructed but before the walls are plastered or rendered.

- Block and brick walls which are 'face' (exposed) will not be covered over by a finish such as render, plaster or tiles, so require that pipes, ducts and wires are built into the wall as the wall is constructed.

➤ Upstairs concrete floor slabs will need pipes and electrical ducts and wires that go in the floor to be installed before the concrete is poured.

➤ Once the roof is installed, but before the ceilings are installed, hot water systems and air-conditioning units that go in the roof must be installed. Air-conditioning ducting and plumbing pipes should be installed. In many cases the electrician should install wiring or ducts to the light points.

➤ Before bathrooms are tiled, the toilets and fitted bathtubs should be installed.

➤ When ceilings are installed then lights and air-conditioning grilles can be installed.

➤ When the walls and floors have been tiled in bathrooms and the walls rendered or finished-off in the house then free standing bathtubs can be installed. Toilets, basins and sinks can be connected. Taps can be installed. Electrical switches and sockets can be finished off. Usually it's best that the last two steps aren't completed until the house is lockable since many of these items are expensive and could be stolen.

➤ Before final landscaping, paving and driveways are completed all external pipes and cables should be installed.

It can be seen that plumbers and electricians may have to return to the project four or more times, and air-conditioning contractors usually two or three times. It's important to check that all electrical wires and ducts and all plumbing pipes have been installed correctly, at the right location, with no visible leaks and faults, before:

➤ Concrete is poured.

➤ Framed walls are closed.

➤ Waterproofing is applied in bathrooms.

➤ Brick and block walls are rendered.

➤ Tiles are installed.

➤ Ceilings are installed.

But even these trades must be coordinated between them. Plumbing waste and sewer pipes have to be installed at the exact locations and levels. They usually have little room to change so they should be installed first. Air-conditioning ducting is usually premade in sections, unless it's flexible ducting installed for smaller airflows or at the ends of the main ducts. So non-flexible air-conditioning ducts should be installed next. Water pipes can go up or down and there's some flexibility in location so they're installed next. Electrical wiring has the most flexibility, so can be installed last. However, having said this, it's important to note that pipes and ducts can't obstruct where lights, switches and outlets must go.

Electrical basics

Electrical safety is critical. Electricity kills and it can cause fires. Always ensure that work is done by licensed electricians and that all wiring and fittings comply with best practices and local codes.

Power feeds to the house from the local power supply. The electrical current flows through wires, a bit like water through a pipe. Thinner wire restricts the flow of electricity (much the same as a small hose pipe). There's more friction. Friction causes heat which can lead to fires. It also causes losses so the power you get out at the end of a thin wire is less than that which enters it. This means that the longer the wire the more losses will occur. But thicker wires are more expensive. The size of the wire is measured in gauges or square millimetres. Larger gauge numbers indicate smaller diameter wires.

Electrical wires are normally copper. Sometimes aluminium wiring is used but this is less efficient than copper so needs to be larger diameter for the same equivalent power. The wire is insulated, usually in plastic, to prevent it from transferring the current elsewhere which may happen when it comes into contact with water, metal surfaces or even a person. Wires are often rated according to whether they can be installed in wet areas or dry, and also according to the heat they can withstand. So wires installed in a roof may have to withstand higher temperatures.

All electrical cables have a live wire, neutral and the earth or ground wire. These have different colours which are mandatory in your country. The different wires should never be mixed up or connected incorrectly.

Every item that consumes electricity has a power rating. The power (or watts) is calculated by multiplying the current (measured in Amps or A) by the voltage (V). Power is delivered to your house at a set voltage which is the same throughout your country, normally 120, 200, 220 or 240 Volts. So if you have a heater that's rated at 1kW which is 1000 Watts and your supply is 200V then you require 5A of current. An item that requires 5000W with a 200V supply requires 25A.

Case study: The oven in our house needed to be replaced. When we looked for a replacement all ovens that fitted the space of the old oven required 5500 watts of power. Since we had 240V we required 23Amps, but the circuit breaker was only rated 16A. Investigating further we discovered that the wires supplying current to the oven could not take a bigger current. Installing a smaller oven meant there would be a gap below the oven in the kitchen which required patching. But a smaller oven would also be totally inadequate for the house which is a family home of four bedrooms. Obviously when the wiring was done for the house they gave little thought to installing an adequate supply to the oven. At large expense we had to install a new circuit breaker and new wires to the oven. Installing a larger circuit breaker only would have resulted in too much current going through the wires to the oven, causing them to burn out, possibly even causing a fire.

The power connection from the utility provider could be single phase or three phase power. Single phase connections are usually cheaper and the monthly fees to the provider are less than for three phase power. But some products such as swimming pool motors, larger air-conditioners and even spas require three phase power. In addition three phase power provides more power than single phase. So before deciding whether you want a single phase or three phase connection you should decide what electrical appliances you will install in your house, know what their power requirements are and calculate what the total requirements for the house will be.

Where the power supply enters your property there should be a meter which measures the amount of power that you use every month and a circuit breaker which prevents too much power entering your property. Should the provider experience a problem and there's suddenly a spike in voltage this could damage the wiring and electrical appliances in your house, even causing a fire. The circuit breaker is there to immediately cut the power if there's a power surge and it prevents overloading of your house's electrical system. The meter must be accessible for the authorities to read.

In your house is an electrical distribution board (possibly in the garage, kitchen or storeroom). The power from the street feeds into this and it's then distributed via different circuits (wires). Usually ovens, stoves and air-conditioners should have their own circuits. The lights are normally on one circuit and electrical outlets are on another circuit (or possibly more circuits). The circuits all have a circuit breaker which is usually denoted in Amps and may be 15A, 20A, 25A, etc. These limit the amount of current entering the circuit and they must be matched to the size wires in the circuit. They are designed to 'trip' and cut off power when the current drawn exceeds their capacity. Without this protection the electrical wires could burnout and cause a fire, or at best require the wires to be replaced. It's imperative that a larger breaker isn't used than the circuit is designed for, or that the breaker isn't prevented from 'tripping'. No matter how frustrating it is to have a breaker trip, never be tempted to remove it or stick something in it to prevent it cutting power. You may have a faulty appliance tripping the breaker, or too many items consuming power on that circuit. Simply disconnecting an appliance may mean the breaker doesn't trip.

The circuits should have safety switches, sometimes known as RCD's (residual current device) or GFCI (Ground Fault Circuit Interrupter) that cut the power off in milliseconds should a fault develop. In addition some countries require AFCI's (arc-fault circuit interrupter) which cuts power when the current is causing a spark which could start a fire. Note: please get expert advice for all electrical matters.

Curing and drying – why it takes time

Some items require time to dry, cure and to gain strength. So for instance, when you pour concrete into an elevated beam or slab you can't strip the supporting formwork the next day (see later). The concrete has to gain sufficient strength before all of the supports can be removed. We of course know that concrete could take several hours before it's sufficiently set so that you can walk on it without marking the surface. I'm sure you've seen paving with dog paw marks permanently imprinted in the surface because dogs ran across the concrete when it was still soft. Usually concrete takes at least seven days to gain 60% of its strength and we generally say concrete has only reached its full strength at twenty-eight days. Concrete can still continue gaining strength long after this time, but this gain is only minimal.

The rate at which concrete gains strength is also dependent on the weather, or more accurately the temperature (when it's cold concrete takes longer to set and to gain strength) and it being cured correctly (see the next section).

It's important to allow sufficient time in the construction schedule (programme) for concrete to gain strength before formwork (see later) is removed. Normally the sides of slabs, beams and columns shouldn't be removed until at least 24 hours after casting the concrete, but in cold weather this may have to be increased to 36 or 48 hours. Supports and props under beams and slabs should never be removed until at least seven days has passed, or in cold weather until ten days or more. To be safe test cylinders or cubes should be taken from the fresh concrete and their strength tested after seven days. Usually if the concrete has reached 66% of the design strength the formwork can be stripped. However, care should still be taken when placing loads on this concrete (such as stacking materials on it, or building walls and other structures) so consideration should be given to leaving supports in longer. Always check with your engineer as to when it's safe to remove propping under new concrete. Removing props from under concrete beams and slabs before they've gained sufficient strength to support themselves will lead to the slab or beam sagging – you don't want your upstairs floor to have a bow or dip (which could easily be twenty to fifty millimetres (one to two inches)). Of course, in the worst cases the concrete will crack, even failing completely and collapsing. New concrete is also easily damaged so take care.

It's possible to order concrete that gains strength quicker, or to use concrete with a higher strength than necessary so it achieves the required strength in a shorter time.

As with concrete, other adhesives and products take time to gain strength. Floor tiles shouldn't be walked on for at least 24 hours after they were laid (stuck in place). The mortar used in brickwork takes time to gain strength. Freshly built brick or block walls can easily be blown over by wind if they're partly complete and unsupported. Brick and block walls should generally not be built up in sections more than a metre (three foot) high in a day, because adding more layers adds additional weight which could crush the partly cured mortar below, causing the wall to bow or even fall down. Care should also be taken not to press against, or knock fresh brickwork, otherwise the walls might not be straight anymore.

Generally, before applying carpets, timber, waterproofing or vinyl to concrete floors the concrete should have dried out. It's good practice to read the product guidelines and when moisture could be a problem to conduct moisture tests of the substrate. Using fans, heaters and blowers can accelerate the drying. Obviously buildings in humid and moist conditions will take longer to dry out.

Concrete – why you need to know more

Concrete comes in different grades or strengths. Normally the engineer specifies the design strength of the concrete, which may vary for different parts of the building. Concrete is a mixture of cement, water, sand and stone. The strength of concrete depends on the ratio of cement to water. The more cement the stronger the concrete, while the more water the weaker the concrete. More water usually also means that the concrete shrinks more as it dries, which usually causes shrinkage cracks that are unsightly and which allows moisture to penetrate the finished concrete.

Adding stone reduces the amount of water. But too much stone means that the concrete will be difficult to work with and there will be voids between the stones. It's important to note that the stone should be clean and free of dust and dirt, since the dust and dirt will require more water, which will make for a weaker concrete unless more cement is added. Stone should be generally of a uniform size.

Sand helps create the cement paste that fills the voids between the stones. Sand should be clean and free of contaminants such as roots, sticks, rubbish and impurities. Not all sand is suitable for concrete. The best sand is a river sand which is of even grading (size). Sand which is too fine will require more water to wet it, and as already discussed more water means more cement or weaker concrete. When the sand is very course the concrete may have voids, or be difficult to compact. If the sand is very wet then less water should be added to the mixture. Where possible sand for concrete should be kept dry and covered when there's lots of rain.

Sometimes, depending on the available sands and stone it may be necessary to blend two sands together.

Sand, water, cement and stone must be well mixed so that the cement is evenly spread through the mixture and there are no lumps of material.

The mixture is now known as concrete. Concrete usually begins to set within four hours of being mixed. The time will be shorter when it's very hot. The setting time will be extended when it's cold, or when retarders (certain chemicals) are added. In fact, add sugar and the concrete will never set. So concrete should be placed and compacted as soon as possible. When concreting bigger structures it's important to ensure that the first concrete placed doesn't dry out before the next load of fresh concrete is added next to it. So it's good practice when pouring slabs and beams to start pouring from one side of the structure, first bringing the concrete to the top surface, then steadily advancing with each new load of concrete, ensuring that the fresh concrete knits with the older concrete. If the new concrete is placed against older concrete that has already started to set it won't join properly and there'll be a 'cold joint' (visible joint) which is unsightly and weakens the structure, even meaning that the structure is unsuitable and should be condemned. It's therefore critical to schedule concrete deliveries at the correct frequencies, so that there isn't a long gap between trucks and also so that trucks are not standing, waiting for previous trucks to be offloaded, meaning that the concrete is already starting to set. You must place the concrete at a fast enough rate so that the concrete doesn't start setting before fresh concrete is added.

Concrete is best compacted by mechanical vibrators or compactors to ensure there're no voids in the structure and to bring some of the concrete water to the surface. Concrete shouldn't be over compacted.

The concrete mixture should always be workable, having sufficient water, cement and sand so that it can easily flow into voids, between and around reinforcing steel, and so it can be readily compacted and worked with. However, construction crews should never add additional water to the concrete mix to make it more workable. Remember the golden rule, more water equals weaker concrete! Only the mixing crew should add more water, plus the required additional cement.

As the concrete starts to set the top surface should be finished and smoothed off. The final finish will depend on what will come on top of the concrete. Floors that have a carpet or vinyl floor finish require a smooth ('steel float') finish. Floors covered with tiles may only require a rougher finish. However, in all cases it's important to ensure that the top surface of the concrete is finished to the correct required levels without dips and humps. A smoother finish takes longer, so is more expensive. A very smooth finish could be unsuitable when other layers are added, say when a screed is placed over the concrete.

Concrete shouldn't be allowed to dry out too quickly which will cause shrinkage cracks and slow down the strength gain. Fresh concrete should be cured for seven days so that it retains moisture. This curing should start as soon as it has been worked smooth and set. Curing of concrete is done either by painting the surface of the concrete with a curing compound, or wrapping the concrete in a plastic membrane, wrapping the concrete in hessian or sacking which is then kept wet, continuously wetting the concrete (ensuring it doesn't dry out), or by forming ponds or dams on slabs (building sand walls) and keeping these ponds filled with water.

Extra care needs to be taken when it's very hot or windy as this will accelerate the drying process. The concrete will need to be worked smooth quickly. Cold joints will form more easily so the next load of concrete must be placed sooner.

Formwork – keeping wet concrete in place

Wet concrete is usually retained by formwork (forms or moulds) until the concrete has set and gained sufficient strength to stand by itself. These moulds can be steel, timber or PVC. Concrete is heavy (around two and a half tone a cubic metre (yard)). Unless the sides of the forms are propped and stayed (supported) correctly they'll bend, buckle, bow and even break. Bent and bowed formwork will result in the finished concrete following that profile, which is unsightly and probably means you have concrete where you don't want it, so it has to be chopped back into a straight line. It also usually means that you've used more concrete. If the formwork bursts and breaks the concrete will escape, so the concrete is wasted and the structure has to be cleaned, rebuilt and fresh concrete poured on another day, which creates a delay.

The wet concrete creates the biggest force near the bottom of the structure, so this area usually requires additional support.

Forms can be stayed or supported from the outside, or in the case of walls and the sides of beams which have forms on both sides the two faces of formwork can be tied together, either with removable tie-rods or form-ties (like bolts), or ones which are left permanently in the concrete. There are various propriety ties.

Forms should be sealed to prevent the wet cement paste escaping. If the paste escapes it leaves voids in the concrete which are unsightly, result in weakness and allows water to penetrate the concrete causing deterioration later.

Formwork can be purchased or hired. It should be noted that if you cut, dent or damage hired formwork you'll be charged for it. Usually there's a cleaning fee that the hirer charges if the formwork isn't returned clean.

Formwork should always be cleaned before it's used. Dirty formwork can result in rough imprints in the new concrete and colour disfigurations. It's easiest to clean old concrete from the forms when it's still fresh. The longer it's left on the forms the harder it gets and the more difficult it becomes to clean.

Immediately before pouring concrete it's good practice to blow the forms clean with an industrial blower to remove loose debris.

Coating the forms with a form or shutter oil (kind of like greasing a baking tin) allows the forms to be more easily stripped (removed) since the concrete is less likely to stick to the face of the forms.

Support-work under concrete beams and elevated slabs has to support the weight of the wet concrete, plus reinforcing steel and the workers placing the concrete. The support-work or scaffolding usually consists of timber, steal or aluminium props or poles. These props must be firmly supported on the level below. Where the props are resting on ground it's important that the ground is firm and that there are base plates or pieces of timber under the prop to distribute the load so the props don't sink into the ground. The number and size of the supports will depend on the weight of the concrete (which depends on the thickness of concrete) and the length of the prop. Props must be locked together (braced) so that the support-work can't lean over or collapse sideways. The boards on top of the props must be fixed in position so they can't come loose and fall off, which could allow concrete to escape, or worse a worker to fall.

It's best to have an expert design the support-work for concrete. If you're hiring the formwork then the supplier may prepare the layout of the support-work for you. Always follow their drawings exactly.

When placing the wet concrete in elevated beams and slabs never allow the wet concrete to heap on the formwork in such a way that it's thicker and heavier than the support-work is designed to hold.

Reinforcing steel – why it can't go anywhere

Reinforcing steel comes in bars which are normally tied together to form a cage. The bars come in different grades or strengths and can be smooth or deformed (with small ridges). Sometimes the reinforcing is in a readymade mesh which comes in standard sized sheets or rolls.

Reinforcing gives concrete structures their strength and also prevents shrinkage cracking. Engineers design the reinforcing that goes in the structure. It's important that the reinforcing is placed in the positions indicated on the reinforcing drawings, and that where the reinforcing (or mesh) joins it overlaps with the next bars. It's obvious that the right size bars (or mesh), of the right grade and deformations is used, otherwise the structure could fail.

Reinforcing should not be too close to the bottom, sides or top surface of the concrete. Usually the reinforcing is designed to have a minimum cover (distance from the outside edge of the concrete) which could be 25, 30, 40, 50 millimetres (one to two inches). The cover often depends on the structure and the conditions the concrete will be exposed to. Harsh conditions near water, and especially sea water will require a bigger distance from the edge of the concrete so that the reinforcing is better protected. Reinforcing that's too close to the edge of the concrete could mean that the concrete can't get around and under the steel bars so the bars could be left exposed, which means that the reinforcing will corrode and also that it won't do its job. Water also penetrates the first layers of concrete and steel close to the surface will rust. Rusted reinforcing expands, which then breaks the concrete around the steel. This is unsightly and weakens the structure. Rusting reinforcing also leaves ugly rust marks on exposed concrete.

Unfortunately, sometimes reinforcing isn't adequately supported and when the concrete is poured workers walk on the reinforcing squashing it deeper into the concrete and below where it should be. Reinforcing which isn't where it should be in the concrete can result in a weakened structure and cracking on the surface. Always ensure mesh reinforcing layers are fixed correctly so that they stay in the right position, even after the concrete is poured.

For reinforcing to be effective it should be clean, not contaminated with grease and oils and relatively free of rust so that the concrete sticks to it. When reinforcing is delivered to the site it should never be stacked immediately on the ground, but should rather be raised off the ground on timber poles. Reinforcing should be used as soon as possible after it's delivered, certainly within a few weeks.

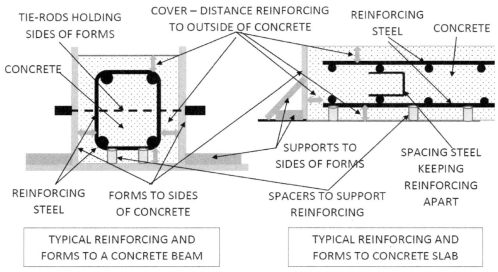

TIE-RODS HOLDING SIDES OF FORMS

COVER – DISTANCE REINFORCING TO OUTSIDE OF CONCRETE

REINFORCING STEEL

CONCRETE

CONCRETE

REINFORCING STEEL

FORMS TO SIDES OF CONCRETE

SUPPORTS TO SIDES OF FORMS

SPACERS TO SUPPORT REINFORCING

SPACING STEEL KEEPING REINFORCING APART

TYPICAL REINFORCING AND FORMS TO A CONCRETE BEAM

TYPICAL REINFORCING AND FORMS TO CONCRETE SLAB

Generally an engineer should inspect structures before concrete is poured to ensure that the correct reinforcing has been used and it's fixed in the correct place.

Sometimes engineers replace steel reinforcing bars with fibres, which could be steel or synthetic. The fibres are mixed into the concrete during the mixing stage.

Construction rubbish – dealing with a problem

Never underestimate the amount of rubbish generated on a construction project. This could be:

➤ Packaging of equipment and materials. This includes paper, cardboard, polystyrene, timber, plastic and strapping.

➤ Debris from structures that had to be demolished so that the new structure could be constructed.

➤ Breakages from cutting and handling. Particularly of bricks, blocks and tiles.

➤ Off-cuts from tiles, bricks, blocks, pipes, timber and boards.

➤ Left over materials, which could include, timber, concrete, mortar, sand, cement, stone, bricks, blocks, tiles, reinforcing steel, pipes, paint and adhesives.

➤ Debris from structures which were broken because they didn't conform to the quality requirements.

➤ Wash water from concrete and mortar equipment and mixers. This often contains large quantities of cement, sand and stone and often sets hard.

➤ Vegetation that had to be removed from the site.

➤ Unsuitable ground and soil.

➤ Excess soil.

Case study: We purchased a new house which had a garden which consisted largely of lawn. We decided to do some more landscaping and laid out gardens for trees and plants. Everywhere we dug up the lawn to form new garden beds we struck building rubble. In all we removed at least six cubic metres (six cubic yards) of broken bricks and tiles, together with bits of concrete, glass, wood and more. We never could remove all the rubble and even several years later we were still finding rubbish in the garden. Then we noticed that a large patch of lawn about nine square metres (ninety square foot) never looked as healthy as the rest of the lawn and in hot weather it started to die. I investigated and removed a patch of this lawn, only to discover that there was what appeared to be solid concrete only centimetres (inches) below the lawn. We had to hire rock breakers to remove this, which we found to be solidified mortar (probably excess material from the bricklayers). It was as hard as rock and probably at least thirty centimetres (one foot) thick, covering an area of ten square metres (one hundred square foot). Nothing was ever going to grow properly in this area until it was removed.

Getting rid of building rubbish is expensive, so many contractors will try:

➤ Dispose of it illegally by dumping it on a vacant lot, or on state land.

➤ Bury rubbish on the property, which is a nuisance, causing you extra work and costs to dispose of it. It'll also restrict the growth of trees and shrubs in your garden. Some rubbish such as glass and asbestos is hazardous.

➤ Throw rubbish in your rubbish bins which the city collects. Usually the local authorities object to the inclusion of building rubbish in the general waste bins and they may refuse to clear the bins.

➤ Throw rubble into the building foundations and under floor slabs where it means that the ground can't be compacted properly, which could cause the ground to settle under the foundations and floor slabs.

Construction waste can be reduced by:

➤ Shredding and chipping vegetation that's been cleared, then storing it to use in the landscaping as compost and mulch.

➤ Planning the ground floor levels of the house and the landscaping so that excess ground isn't created.

➤ Separating recyclable material.

➤ Ordering materials in lengths to avoid excessive off-cuts, and planning cutting to minimise waste.

➤ Handling material carefully to avoid breakages.

➤ Ordering the correct quantity of material.

➢ Ensuring that all work is done right first time, so there's no demolition of faulty and poor quality work.

➢ Ensuring that good excavated material doesn't become contaminated with rubbish. Frequently on construction sites building rubble gets moved around the site. It gets mixed in with the ground until eventually what was only a few cubic metres (yards) of rubbish has become a pile of several cubic metres (yards) because it's been mixed in with usable soil, which now also has to be thrown away because it's contaminated.

➢ Separating hazardous materials, such as asbestos, oils and paints, and ensuring these are disposed of correctly. Adding hazardous material to normal building rubbish contaminates all the material, resulting in the quantity of hazardous material being larger than it should be.

➢ Not letting concrete and cement mortar waste accumulate into large solidified lumps that are difficult to break up and dispose of. Break the concrete into smaller pieces when it's fresh and hasn't become too hard.

➢ Crushing clean building rubble to use for backfilling. Suitable material which is crushed into small particles may be suitable in some locations.

Swimming pools – when should they be built?

Pools are often only constructed after the house construction is nearly complete. However, it may be wise to consider building the pool earlier. Constructing the house before the pool could restrict getting excavating equipment to the area, which may mean the pool must be excavated by hand and the excavated material is removed with difficulty. Pre-formed pools usually have to be put in place using cranes, and if cranes can't get close to the pool location because of the new building then larger cranes will be required, making the pool more expensive.

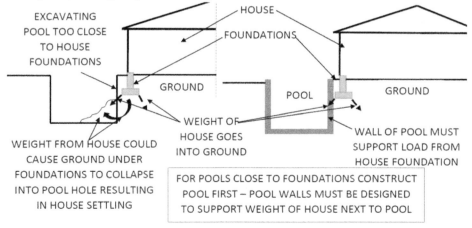

Of course, when the pool is constructed right next to the building foundations, then excavating the pool may cause damage to the foundations, even causing the foundations to be undermined. This's particularly a problem when the foundations are on sand. In these cases it's essential to construct the pool first and ensure that the building foundations are designed taking into account the adjacent pool.

Excavating the pool when the site is being levelled and prepared may allow the excess material to be used to create the level area for the building, or to landscape the garden, saving the cost of carting it away.

Always employ a reputable swimming pool contractor to design and build your pool. When a below ground pool is constructed near the foundations of any building always get an engineer to provide expert advice.

But excavating the pool early may create other problems, such as blocking access to construction of the house and it needs to be protected from damage.

Perimeter fencing – securing your property

Fences and walls can provide security to the building and the contractor's equipment during construction so sometimes it's helpful to construct the permanent fences or walls at the start of construction. They also help ensure that the building work doesn't overflow your property, damaging your neighbours garden or the council verge. In addition they help keep the public out of the construction site where they may become injured. However, boundary fences may become damaged during construction, and they can also impede access for large trucks and equipment. Care should be taken to ensure that the permanent fence or wall isn't constructed before the site has been graded to ground levels which are close to the final finished levels. Walls which are constructed on ground that's too high, or low, may have to be demolished and rebuilt when the ground is eventually graded to the correct levels.

Landscaping – gardens and more

Landscaping, or planning the garden and the area within the property around the house can add immensely to the enjoyment and the use of the property as well as to the value of the house. Well planned plantings can screen the house and property from neighbours, or hide ugly walls or structures. Poor planning of the spaces around the house may impact the amenity and lead to problems and additional costs later. Early thought about the exterior areas of the house is advisable, and consideration should be given to engaging advice from a landscaper or landscape architect.

The wrong choice of trees and plants, or planting them in the wrong place can lead to problems. Some trees have invasive roots which damage water and sewer pipes, they may push up paving, crowd out other plants so that nothing else grows near them, and in the worst cases even damage building foundations.

Trees that grow very large could eventually shade the whole garden, blocking out light and making the interior of the house dark. Trees that are planted too close to the house may eventually become difficult to prune and experts will have to be employed (at great expense) to trim them. Trees planted too close to the neighbours can lead to complaints of overhanging branches, invading roots and fallen leaves blocking pools, gutters and drains. Disputes with neighbours are often caused by trees too close to the dividing boundary.

Deciduous trees are often nice to have because they lose their leaves in winter, allowing more sunlight to reach the house and garden during the cooler months. In summer the tree has leaves which shade the garden and house. However, the falling leaves can be a nuisance, requiring to be cleaned up and disposed, and they also block drains and gutters and dirty swimming pools.

The type of trees, shrubs and plants used and their arrangement should depend on:

➤ The size of the property. Some trees and plants aren't suited to small gardens.

➤ The climate of the area. Tropical plants won't survive in areas that experience colder weather. Some plants are better suited to coastal areas, while extreme heat, cold or winds will damage most plants.

➤ The ground conditions. This includes the acidity or alkalinity of the soil. Some plants grow better in acidic soils while others prefer alkaline soils. Most plants won't grow on rocks or in stony or rocky ground. Clay ground could become waterlogged, while some plants grow best in sandy well-drained ground.

➤ How much sun the plants will get. Some plants only grow in shade while others prefer sunny conditions. Some parts of the garden may be permanently shaded while other could be always in the sun, or get the hot afternoon sun.

➤ The amount of water they'll receive. It's pointless using plants that require lots of water in areas where water is scarce.

➤ The amount of care and maintenance they'll get. Hedges and grass need regular cutting. Some plants require additional care and protection, particularly in harsh climates or when they're young. Fast growing plants need to be regularly cut. If you don't enjoy gardening, or are time poor, you should select plants that require less maintenance and ones that are hardier.

➤ The types of pests and diseases in the area. Some plants are more susceptible to diseases, while diseases may thrive in certain climates and in particular areas.

➤ The desired use of the property, for instance if you have children they probably want grassed areas, or paved areas for ball games, there may be a requirement for additional parking, or you might want to include plants and trees which provide food, such as fruit trees and vegetable gardens.

➤ The plants that are readily available in the area.

➤ The type, size, colour and shape of other plants selected and existing trees.

Watering gardens by hand can be time consuming. The use of automatic sprinkler systems can take away this hassle. These systems should be planned to take account of the type and the size of the plants, and should provide a consistent even watering, or provide additional watering to areas which contain plants that require more water. Watering and reticulation may have to be considered during design and construction to ensure that watering points are provided where they'll be needed and so that sleeves and pipes are installed before external paving is completed. The provision of automatic sprinkler systems can add value to the property as most prospective buyers prefer gardens that require less maintenance. But, even with automatic sprinkler systems remember to allow sufficient outside taps so that paving and cars can be washed and that all areas of the garden can be easily watered with a hosepipe if necessary.

In some cases it's possible, and even advisable, to install bores to tap underground water. However, this can be costly and it depends on obtaining water licenses and the suitability of the underground water.

When planting new plants be careful not to damage the existing utility lines and sprinkler pipes.

When preparing new garden beds, or planting near buildings care must be taken that the soil does not become heaped against the building, or come higher than the installed waterproofing or dampproof membrane in the walls, since this can result in water entering the walls resulting in damp problems.

When selecting new plants always consider how the plants will look in the different seasons as well as their eventual size. Some plants can look spectacular when they're in bloom (which is usually when they are displayed in garden centres) and look quiet ordinary for most of the year. Plants that are a good size now can quickly outgrow the garden and need to be removed after a few years.

A good idea is to prepare a rough plan of the garden (with expert advice) and then slowly plant it up as you get the time, inclination and funds. This also allows you to experiment with which plants are more suited to the garden, which you really like, and gives the chance for individual plants to grow and fill the available space. Invariably there will be some plants that aren't suitable and die, while others flourish. You may find that you don't actually need all of the plants you originally thought you required.

There are many valuable books on gardening and landscaping, but ensure you select books which deal with the plants and gardening in your area.

Before planting make sure that the ground is properly prepared, this includes removing all unsuitable material and building rubble. Prepare the slopes and landscaping to avoid low-lying areas and sudden bumps or uneven areas.

It should be noted that when building in rural areas or in towns which are prone to bushfires that special thought should be given to the location and the types of trees and plants on the property. Generally, on larger properties it's good practice to maintain a firebreak around the property perimeter and to avoid planting too close to the buildings. Some trees and plants are more fire resistant than others and should be used in preference to those that are readily combustible.

Summary

Construction projects involve a number of processes and these need to be scheduled and managed so that you don't incur additional costs and delays. These processes include clearing the building site, levelling the area under buildings as required, demolishing existing structures, excavating, filling excavations and low areas, building retaining walls, constructing foundations, locating and protecting utility lines (those existing, plus new ones), installing stormwater drainage, laying sewer pipes, connecting to water and power, concreting, installing reinforcing, constructing swimming pools (if required), landscaping, securing the construction site and dealing with building rubbish. It's important to understand these processes and what's involved so that they are done right, so sufficient time is allowed for them and so they happen in the correct sequence. Failure to understand them could lead to misunderstandings, additional costs when work has to be redone, and even accidents.

But even when the house is finished construction, there are still a myriad of items to be sorted which often aren't included in the building contractor's scope.

Chapter 6 – Doing the Work Yourself

As discussed in previous chapters you could decide to do most of the construction work yourself. This could depend on the size and complexity of the project, how quickly you want it finished, your knowledge and skills, the time you can allocate to the project and your budget. Alternatively you may do some of the tasks and employ subcontractors to do work you aren't licensed or skilled to do. Anyway, most of us undertake simple home maintenance projects and work in the garden. I'm sure we've all done a bit of painting, woodwork and hanging pictures in our homes.

Don't kill or injure yourself, or anyone else

Construction is an inherently dangerous job. Unfortunately injuries caused by people carrying out do-it-yourself maintenance and renovation tasks at home are one of the leading causes of hospital admissions. An injury to yourself could, in the worst case, lead to death or permanent disability, but at the very least will lead to pain, inconvenience and additional costs. Some people are highly dependent on the full use of parts of their body, so consider how losing a finger or suffering a hand injury could impact a surgeon or a dentist (even if they lose the use of a finger or their hand for only a few days, the lost earnings could far outweigh the savings of doing the work themselves). How dependant is your job on your fingers, limbs or eyes?

Important safety tips include:

➢ Working at heights is a leading cause of injury. Always ensure that when working off ladders these are structurally sound, that they're placed on a firm footing and are held in place so they can't slip or fall over. Where possible another person should anchor the ladder.

➢ When working on an access scaffold always ensure that the scaffold is on a firm footing, where one leg can't suddenly settle into the ground causing the whole scaffold to tilt. Scaffold legs should have base plates and even timbers under them to distribute the load. The planks on scaffolding should be firmly attached so they can't accidently tip, or fall off. Scaffold towers should never be higher than three times their width. If the tower is higher it should be tied to a wall, or have side props to prevent it toppling over. Never overload scaffold platforms. Don't erect scaffold on the edge of excavations.

➢ Wear proper personal protective equipment.

- Your eyes are valuable so it's vital you wear glasses that provide full protection so that dust and other construction debris can't enter your eyes. Also, some solvents and liquids can damage the eye should they splash into your eye.
- Safety shoes are essential. They help prevent trips, slips and falls, they'll protect your feet if something heavy or sharp falls on them, and protect the soles of feet should you stand on a sharp object.
- Gloves provide protection to hands.
- Inhaling dust and fibres from cutting can lead to long term health problems, including lung cancer, so dust masks are necessary when cutting or drilling into materials which generate dust.
- Some products, particularly epoxies, solvents and glues can give off noxious fumes, so wearing a proper breathing mask appropriate to the task is essential, and only mix and use them in ventilated areas.
- Safety harnesses are essential when working at heights where there's a possibility of falling. These need to be anchored to a firm support that will hold and arrest your fall.
- Darkened visors must be used when flame cutting or welding.

➢ Always get an injury treated properly, then take precautions to prevent dirt getting into the wound. Even a minor cut finger can become infected and end with a protracted hospital stay, or even worse an amputation of a finger.

➢ Ensure that live services have been disconnected where there's a possibility you could damage them. Turn off gas and power when you're working near electrical wires and gas pipes. Ensure these can't be turned on accidently by somebody unaware that you're working near them.

➢ Never leave live electrical wires exposed.

➢ Keep all work areas clean and tidy. Rubble and material lying on the site creates trip hazards. Bits of wood with nails and screws sticking out are a leading cause of injury.

➢ Use the right tool for the job. Often injuries are caused when the wrong tool is used, or when a tool is used which is too small for the job.

➢ Check all equipment every time before use to ensure that it hasn't been damaged and that all the safety features are in place. Broken equipment should be fixed by the appropriate repairers. Don't use faulty equipment.

➢ Ensure that all work areas are barricaded. Regrettably serious injuries have been caused when children have been playing on construction sites.

➢ Make sure that materials are stacked properly. Heavy objects leaning against a wall can easily be knocked over falling onto someone.

➢ Check that materials that could be blown loose in a storm are secured at the end of the day or when severe weather is on its way. Stacked materials could be blown over and loose materials such as metal and tin sheets can be blown about, turning into dangerous missiles.

➢   Take care not to damage electrical extension leads. All electrical cables should be checked and equipment with exposed wires, damaged electrical plugs and loose connections should not be used until the item has been properly repaired. Needless to say electrical equipment shouldn't be used in the wet and electrical leads should not lie in water.

➢   Never leave dangerous tools lying around where children could accidently, or intentionally, turn them on causing injury.

➢   Care must be taken when doing any demolition work.

  ▪   No load bearing walls must be demolished (or have pieces cut from them) unless an engineer has inspected the wall and all permanent and temporary supports recommended by the engineer have been installed.

  ▪   Before cutting through any bracings in the walls or roof structures first obtain clearance from an engineer.

  ▪   Care must be taken to ensure that the portions of the structure left standing are stable. Unfortunately, some demolitions are poorly planned so that the demolition work is only partly completed when the rest of the structure becomes unstable and collapses, often causing serious damage and injury.

➢   Always take precautions when working with flammable products.

➢   Read mixing and application instructions carefully.

➢   Never work in totally enclosed spaces, especially when using solvents, glues, chemicals and paints that give off noxious fumes, or when using petrol and diesel equipment, or when using gas.

➢   You shouldn't work alone. If something happens to you, or there's an accident, you could lie undetected for hours without help.

➢   Take care when lifting and moving heavy objects. Keep fingers and toes out of harm's way and ensure that you use proper lifting techniques. Injured and strained backs are a major cause of construction related injuries.

➢   Never attempt work that you aren't licensed to do, such as working on gas pipes and electrical installations.

➢   Always have a properly equipped first-aid kit at hand, a fire-extinguisher, and have a mobile phone handy with the numbers of the emergency services. Accidents happen easily.

➢   Take care when doing any work that generates sparks. Sparks can easily set fire to construction materials and surrounding vegetation. Sparks can also injure you and others in the vicinity. Sparks can damage materials, especially glass and floor and wall tiles – you won't be the first person to have damaged newly installed windows and floor and wall tiles.

➢   Never work in deep excavations with vertical sides that reach above your head. There are numerous cases where the sides of trenches collapsed on workers below, burying them alive – unfortunately in most cases the people never escaped alive.

Accidents happen quickly, and often when you least expect them. Injuries can be devastating and can change your life in an instant. Don't take chances to save a few thousand dollars, the end result could cost lots more. Plan all work carefully, taking account of the possible risks.

Protecting the environment – it makes sense

There's legislation that protects the environment and falling foul of the law could result in monetary fines, the project being stopped, and in some cases building permits being rescinded. In addition, there's often remedial actions required to repair the damage to the environment which can be costly and time consuming. It's therefore important to understand the local environmental laws and restrictions that may form part of the building permit. Anyway, much of the environmental protection is common-sense and involves putting in place simple procedures.

Environmental issues to consider include:

➢ Protecting environmentally sensitive areas. This includes marking trees that shouldn't be damaged and fencing areas that should be protected.

➢ Not discharging oils, chemicals and paints down sewer and stormwater drains.

➢ That equipment doesn't create excessive noise, noxious fumes and excessive exhaust smoke.

➢ Not spilling paints, oils and hazardous chemicals on the ground. Where there are accidental spillages these should be cleaned up immediately and disposed of in specially designated waste facilities.

➢ Ensuring that rubbish is disposed of correctly. Your neighbours don't want paper strewn on sidewalks or blowing down the street. Don't underestimate the amount of rubbish generated on a construction site. Ensure that skip waste bins are placed on the property from the start of the project. Have the bins emptied regularly. If necessary cover the waste bins with netting to prevent paper and plastic blowing out into the road and the neighbours.

➢ Ensure that hazardous materials such as asbestos aren't placed with the general rubbish since it will contaminate the whole bin, adding to the cost of disposing of the material. Hazardous materials must be disposed of correctly.

➢ That waste materials are recycled where possible.

➢ Dust from the site irritates neighbours. Reduce dust by watering work areas that are creating dust. Stop operations causing dust when it's windy. Cover stockpiles of sand to prevent dust, and avoid stripping all vegetation from the site. Vegetation helps reduce dust and retains the ground preventing it washing away when it rains.

➢ Uncontrolled stormwater can wash ground and construction materials into drains blocking them, and onto roads and neighbouring properties where they need to be cleaned.

Following good environmental building practices is beneficial in other ways:

➢ Noisy equipment, or machinery that belches smoke irritate neighbours.

➢ A messy building site is dangerous and upsets neighbours.

➢ Recycling and minimising waste helps reduce the cost of disposing of it.

➢ Excessive clearing of vegetation means that it has to be disposed of at additional costs.

➢ Rubbish and litter can cover stormwater drain inlets and block drainpipes causing blockages and resulting in flooding of the property and even adjacent properties during storms.

➢ Using energy efficient equipment reduces costs.

➢ Utilising local materials which don't have to be transported from far is often cheaper.

➢ Using recycled or second-hand materials is cheaper than purchasing new items.

Poor quality could cost you lots

Poor quality work and materials could be a safety hazard to occupants, be unsightly, mean that doors and windows stick or don't close properly, result in maintenance issues later (such as leaks and cracks), cause the bank (or loan institution) not to grant you a loan, result in the authorities declaring the building as being uninhabitable, make the house unsaleable, or the house or parts of it which don't conform will have to be rebuilt at additional costs.

It's therefore essential that:

➢ Materials with the correct specifications and strengths are used. Materials should always come from reputable suppliers. Remember, products bought online or from another country may not comply with the building codes in your area, and they might not have been manufactured to rigorous safety standards, or incorporate reliable parts.

➢ Sound construction methods are used.

➢ You check that materials are correct before installing them. Just because the supplier delivered the item don't assume it's correct and what you ordered. Items can easily become muddled on the project or in the delivery process.

➢ The design drawings are followed and that all items are installed in the locations specified.

➢ Manufacturers' and suppliers' installation instructions are complied with.

➢ Care is taken to ensure walls, doors and windows are constructed square, plumb and level. That floors are constructed flat and to the correct height.

➢ You take care to ensure you achieve the right quality.

➢   You protect completed work. You don't want to be dropping a heavy object on your new tiles, basin, bathtub or kitchen counter!

Are you licensed (registered)?

Many jurisdictions require that construction work involving building a new house or undertaking major renovations and additions is supervised by a registered builder. It's possible in some areas for owner builders to obtain a temporary building license or an exemption. Alternatively if you don't have a building license you'll have to employ a licensed builder to conduct inspections to verify that the construction work meets the relevant codes and specifications. In any case, this may well be worth the cost to ensure that the building is compliant.

Obviously minor works such as painting, general repairs, replacing joinery, etc doesn't require supervision by a registered builder.

What you aren't licensed to do

There is some work you can't do without a license. This varies between countries, states and local areas so always check. These usually include electrical work, plumbing, gas pipes and connections, flues from gas fireplaces, installing roofs and removing and disposing of hazardous materials.

Failure to have this work done by licensed people will probably mean that the house can't be sold, it may not get the final approval and occupation permit and it will probably result in the work having to be redone. But more important is that the incorrect installation could result in a hazard which could seriously injure or kill you, or a member of your family.

The right skills makes work safer, faster and better

Construction often seems easy when you see the experts doing it on television. However, it often takes months or even years to become a proficient plumber, bricklayer, tiler, carpenter and electrician. Sure, many of us can lay floor tiles, build brick walls and do simple wood working jobs. But can we lay the tiles correctly, ensuring they're level, in straight lines, with constant gaps and that they aren't hollow underneath or won't come loose? Often our amateur attempts at construction are clearly visible to even the untrained eye. Furthermore, our clumsy efforts often take longer than the experts, and sometimes our attempts have to be fixed at additional costs.

However, there are courses that teach you to lay tiles, build walls and do most carpentry jobs. You won't be an expert after these courses because that comes with time, experience and practice, but at least you won't make some of the elementary mistakes that amateurs make.

In addition, having training will help avoid accidents and it'll undoubtedly mean you do the job faster.

Of course employing experts for the bigger jobs, or those that require specialised skills or equipment is probably best.

If you still want to save money you can become their assistant, to do the lifting, carrying and repetitive work. This might save them having to employ an assistant at additional cost, it may speed their work up, but in addition you'll be learning directly from an expert so you'll be better equipped to do similar work later.

Inspections – when and what

It's important to understand what inspections are required. These could include inspections required in terms of the loan facilities you have from the bank, by the local authorities or council, by the local fire authorities, by utility providers, by the design engineer and those done by safety inspectors (usually government) to confirm the project is safe. If it's a heritage listed property then the heritage council may inspect. Projects in environmentally sensitive areas could have environmental inspections.

These inspections are often mandatory and are conducted by a person appointed by the bank, utility provider or local council. Sometimes they accept inspections by a registered agency. Usually inspectors need advance warning to inspect the work, and often work can't proceed and the item can't be covered up until it's been inspected. Safety and environmental inspectors may visit the project unannounced.

Inspections could include the foundations, underground sewer pipes, the roof structure, before structural concrete is poured, when smoke alarms are tested, to check the electrical installation, and to check gas pipes including pressure testing the pipes.

Failure to obtain the necessary inspections could mean that you don't receive the next loan payment, or that the authorities don't grant a certificate of occupancy.

Ordering materials – not as simple as you think

When ordering materials make sure that:

➢   The correct product with the correct specification is ordered. There're pipes and pipes, timber and timber, bricks and bricks and they're not all exactly the same. They come in different grades and strengths. Some can't be used outside, some can't be used in wet areas and some are more hard wearing than others. If in doubt ask experts, or even the supplier what the right product is for where you'll use it.

➢   The correct size is ordered. Timber comes in all lengths, thicknesses and widths. Tiles are different sizes. Understand the difference between imperial and metric sizes because frequently pipes and bolts of the one don't match the other.

➢   The supplier is aware when the materials are required.

➢ You order the correct quantities. Having too much is a waste that costs money to buy and then costs more money to get rid of. Running short of material could delay construction and usually incurs additional delivery charges for the shortfall. But worse, some products might not be available anymore so if you've almost finished laying floor tiles and you find that you're short of a few boxes of tiles (even one tile), you may find that the tiles are no longer available and you'll have to select another floor tile and rip out the first lot and retile the whole floor with the new tiles. When working out the quantities of materials always:

  ▪ Double check the quantities.
  ▪ Allow for cutting and wastage. For instance floor and wall tiles have to be cut around the edges of the room and walls, around pipes and other fittings. Inevitably there'll be wastage, which could be between 5 and 10% - with smaller areas often having a higher wastage factor.
  ▪ Allow for lapping. Reinforcing steel and mesh, roof sheeting, roof tiles, and waterproofing membrane always should be lapped as per the manufacturer's or engineer's detail.

➢ You order the best lengths and widths which fit where the item is required, generating the least offcuts and waste, but also in sizes which you can easily handle. Larger sizes may be less wasteful but you might not be able to lift the product and install it, or it might be too big to get through door openings.

➢ You understand if the supplier will deliver the product. Suppliers must have the correct delivery address, times when the delivery can be made (you don't want deliveries arriving when nobody is around to receive them), and be aware of any special delivery instructions (for instance, if large vehicles can't access the property they need to be aware that they must use a smaller truck).

➢ You understand how the material will be offloaded and who will be responsible for it. You don't want to be offloading a consignment of cement or heavy timbers by hand on your own.

➢ Orders must be clear, with the size, specification, quantity and rates. Understand exactly what you're getting and what you're paying for.

➢ You have ordered everything that you require to fix the item in place, which could include adhesive, grout, bolts, screws, etc.

➢ When ordering an item that must fit exactly in a specific location, that you double check your measurements to ensure there's no mistake. Then understand the supplier's tolerances. If they manufacture or supply the item a couple of millimetres bigger will it still fit? Know how you will move and fit the item into place. Sometimes when the item is an exact fit it's near impossible to move into position.

It should be noted that ordering materials in bulk could be cheaper than ordering materials in small quantities. Small quantities not only incur additional delivery charges, but the supplier may offer discounts for larger quantities. Of course, it may be possible to provide a bulk order, say for all the bricks, sand, or concrete required for your house, but then specify that you want the material delivered as and when you require them. You probably don't want all the bricks for your new home delivered on day one, filling your whole property, but rather you want them delivered as you require them (of course in batches that suit your supplier's delivery vehicles).

Material deliveries – don't mess it up

You probably have limited space to stack and store materials so you need to plan deliveries so items arrive just before they're required.

In many cases you may have to offload the trucks, and this has to be done safely and in a limited time. For instance, trucks delivering concrete come in six cubic metre (six cubic yards) loads (sometimes four, five or eight). Smaller loads get charged at a higher rate. But concrete goes off usually within four hours so the truck needs to be offloaded and the concrete placed in this time. But, concrete suppliers also charge extra if their trucks aren't offloaded within a specified period (often fifteen to thirty minutes) and these charges can quickly mount up. Worse still, some suppliers may refuse to wait long periods while you organise to offload their vehicles or finish other tasks. Of course with concrete trucks you don't want to be waiting for the second truck of concrete while the concrete that's already been placed sets, which could result in a 'cold joint' in the concrete which impacts the structure's integrity. So concrete suppliers must be aware of the gap you want between the trucks. See Chapter 5.

Deliveries have to be carefully planned and timed. You should:

➢ Know where you're going to place the material – this area should be ready.
➢ Know how you're going to offload the items.
➢ Have the correct means to offload the items – which could include cranes and lifting slings.
➢ Be ready to receive the material.
➢ Not be standing waiting for the material.
➢ Know the sizes, quantities and weights of the materials. Having a crane that is too small to lift the materials will mean the items can't be offloaded, or in the worst case even result in an accident.
➢ Preferably place the materials close to where they're required.

Before materials are offloaded the delivery documents should be checked to see that the materials are in fact for your project (you won't be the first project to offload materials which weren't intended for them) and that the materials are correct. You definitely don't want to be placing concrete in a structure that's of a lower strength than what's specified.

Check that the materials are of the right quality. Defective and broken materials should be reported on the delivery document and the supplier should be notified immediately in writing. Preferably the defective and broken materials should be returned to the supplier on the same vehicle.

Materials should be stacked so they're accessible and in a manner that they won't topple over (even in a strong wind) damaging the items and even injuring someone. Materials shouldn't be offloaded where they'll block access to work areas, or block, or restrict, public walkways and roads.

Some materials must be protected from the sun or rain. They should be kept under shelter or covered by tarpaulins. Tarpaulins must be securely tied down after items are removed from the stack. Handle materials carefully so they aren't damaged.

Light items, such as roof sheets and boards should be tied down so unexpected winds don't blow them into the air, which is dangerous and damages the materials and the items they come in contact with.

Expensive items that can easily be stolen should be locked in sheds or chained on the property. Theft of building materials is costly and results in delays.

Hired equipment – why it could be costly

It's pertinent to remember the following:

➢ Hired equipment is paid by the hour or day. The longer you have the item on your project the more it costs. Ensure you only get the item when you require it and that it's returned as soon as you're finished using it. Even experienced contractors forget to return hired equipment when they've finished using it. If the hirer is collecting the item notify them in writing that you've finished using it.

➢ You will be charged if the item is stolen or goes missing, therefore ensure the equipment is insured, either by the hirer or by insurance you arranged. You don't want a bill of thousands of dollars.

➢ You will be charged for damages to the item. It's important to check the equipment when you receive it and notify the hirer of any pre-existing damages so that you aren't charged for these when the item is returned.

➢ Check that the item has arrived with all the attachments and parts on the delivery docket. For example, vehicles usually come with spare tyres, lifting jacks and tools. You will be charged for things that are missing when the item is returned to the supplier if these aren't noted as missing when the item arrived.

➢ Ensure you understand how to operate the machine, and where necessary have the required licenses. Even small electrical tools can cause serious injury and using a machine incorrectly could damage it.

➢ All equipment should be safely stored when not in use to prevent theft or it's unauthorised use.

➢ Get the right item for the job. This includes ensuring that it's correctly sized for the job. Items that are too small are inefficient and may get easily broken. Items that are too large may require additional licenses to operate, they'll use more fuel and they could be more difficult to handle and manoeuvre on the site. Portable electrical tools which are suitable for use around the home are probably unsuitable for a complete home build.

➤ You'll be charged for broken items. So drill bits, blades and moil points that can easily be broken should be bought rather than hired, unless you only need them for minor jobs of a couple of hours. Hiring these items means you pay hire for them until they break, then pay for a new item which doesn't even belong to you, then pay more hire.

➤ Always check if it's cheaper to buy the item than hire it. This is usually the case for portable electrical tools. Of course the advantage with hire is that when the item needs to be repaired (for reasons that aren't caused by you) then the hirer has to fix the item and you can often get a replacement in its place. Frequently people end up hiring an item and their hire charges are far more than if they'd purchased the item new.

➤ Where possible arrange with the hirer that you don't pay for the item when you can't use it, such as when it's raining or there's a holiday.

➤ If you require the item for a long period it may be possible to negotiate a reduced hire rate.

➤ Immediately report breakdowns in writing, or return the broken item. You don't want to be paying hire for an item you couldn't use.

Get the details right

If you have no or little experience of constructing a house then my advice is to ensure that any major renovations or a new house should be designed by a qualified architect. A good designer will show the correct construction details. If in doubt ask professional builders or architects for advice.

Getting the details wrong could result in leaks, structural weaknesses and unsightly workmanship.

Saving money – don't we all want to do this?

There are many ways to save money which includes:

➤ Eliminating waste. This includes:
- Ordering the correct quantity of materials.
- Protecting materials from damage. Breakages often occur because of poor installation methods, or while moving the materials on the site. Always use the correct tools and adhesives to cut and fix the materials in position. Handle breakable materials with care.
- Order materials in the correct lengths and sizes where the off-cuts are minimised, or where the off-cuts can be used elsewhere.

- ▪ Double check measurements. Frequently items are built wrongly or cut the wrong length and have to be replaced.
- ▪ Store items where they won't be damaged.
- ▪ Only mix the quantity that you can easily use before the product sets hard or goes off.
- ➢ Ensure quality is good and elements are installed and built in the correct position. Frequently substandard work has to be demolished, resulting in additional cost to get rid of the rubbish and to rebuild the item.
- ➢ Theft is a problem on construction sites. Ensure that valuable items are locked in secure stores and that the building is lockable before expensive items are installed.
- ➢ Incorporate recycled materials where possible.
- ➢ Make use of standard elements – this applies to windows, doors and cupboard. Purpose built units are more expensive.
- ➢ You can consider purchasing end of the range products (products on sale) such as tiles and appliances. With tiles make sure that you have sufficient stock to cover breakages and cutting as well as stock for future repairs because the end of the range usually means that there's limited stock and you probably won't find more should you run short of materials before the work is complete. Check that suppliers will stock parts for appliances that are being discontinued.
- ➢ Negotiate with suppliers for the best rates. Often suppliers will give discounts for earlier payment or when buying in bulk.
- ➢ Don't employ expensive tradespeople to do manual labourer work.
- ➢ Check all accounts before paying them and keep a record of what's been paid so that bills aren't paid twice.

Don't save money by doing this

Unfortunately some will be tempted to save money the wrong way. Never be tempted to:
- ➢ Use inferior materials.
- ➢ Use materials of a lesser specification or strength.
- ➢ Incorporate damaged materials.
- ➢ Omit items included on the drawing, such as reinforcing steel, waterproofing membranes, brick ties, etc.
- ➢ Not compact concrete and soil adequately.
- ➢ Perform tasks which you aren't licensed to do.
- ➢ Ignore, or cover up, bad quality work.
- ➢ Take short cuts which could endanger your life, like working at heights without proper and safe access, using the incorrect tools, or lifting heavy items by hand. No cost saving is worth risking your life for.

> ➤ Use materials beyond their expiry date.
> ➤ Use mismatched materials.
> ➤ Deviate from the installation guidelines.
> ➤ Purchase sale items which aren't suitable for your house.

Security during construction – more than just the cost

Security is a problem on many construction projects. There's always the risk of the theft of tools, equipment and materials. In some cases even items already fitted in the building are ripped out, creating additional costs to repair damages created by the theft. Even copper wire and pipes are targeted. The theft of tools and equipment can leave workers stranded and stop the job for days while replacements are got.

Project sites are sometimes targeted by vandals who damage walls, ceilings, doors and windows just for fun. There's always the risk that some hoodlum will deliberately set fire to a partly completed building.

In some areas vagrants may move onto the project at night and weekends, causing damage and disturbing the neighbours.

But, there's a bigger danger that someone, especially children, could enter the project site and become injured. Children love to play in sand heaps on construction sites and could easily be run over by equipment, or fall into a hole.

It's therefore important that construction projects are fenced and that gates are locked closed afterhours. Clear signage must warn people to stay out the property. Keys should never be left in construction equipment and all tools should be locked away in sheds or stores. Try and limit material deliveries to only items that are required in the next few weeks. In some areas it will be necessary to employ security guards and take extra security measures to deter theft.

The house should be made lockable as soon as possible, and more expensive fixtures shouldn't be installed before the house can be locked.

Check, check and check again

It's vital to check everything, especially before moving to the next stage. Check:
> ➤ That you've not left anything out that's on drawings. This includes overlooking details, or not looking at all the drawings. Refer to the architectural, engineering, plumbing and electrical drawings. Check the plans, sections, elevations and detail drawings.
> ➤ That you've allowed for all your subcontractors' requirements – this could for instance include water or electrical points. If your subcontractors and suppliers require specific dimensions so they can install their materials, fixtures and equipment make sure that everything is built to these requirements.
> ➤ That you've installed all the electrical wiring (or wiring conduits) and all pipes before moving onto the finishes. Before rendering (plastering) or tiling check that all electrical and plumbing points are where they should be.

Take the drawings and physically tick the points off. Have you allowed for fans, fan and air-conditioning controls, security installations, heated towel rails, underfloor heating, etc. You don't want to be chopping holes in finished tiling and render! Not only is it costly and causes delays, but it often leaves patches which are difficult to disguise.

➢ The quality. Are all window and door openings in the correct location and are they built square and plumb? Are all corners square and walls plumb? Are all dimensions correct? Are floors flat and at the right level? Are there any imperfections which will show through after the final finish is applied? Discovering errors after the finishes have been installed will be costlier to rectify.

➢ That all orders are correct. Do they have the correct quantities, dimensions and specifications? Are they clear and unambiguous?

➢ You have correctly set out the building, walls, foundations and pipes. Even experienced builders make mistakes.

Case study: We were installing the finishes in a small theatre and found that some fixtures didn't fit as expected. On investigation we found that when the building supervisor marked the position of the walls he only marked a line for the inside of the wall. Unfortunately the bricklayers assumed this line was the outside and built the wall accordingly. This meant that the whole room was two hundred millimetres (eight inches) smaller than it should be. Now this error may seem small, yet it even impacted the number of seats that could be installed in the theatre, and a number of the fixtures had to be remade. A costly and embarrassing mistake.

Always ensure that when a surveyor sets out the building you understand whether these lines are for the inside, outside or the centre of the walls. If you've marked something out make sure you clearly indicate what the line is representing so that you and your contractors don't make a mistake.

➢ All dimensions before ordering items and before cutting materials.

➢ All calculations and arithmetic.

➢ Anything you're not sure of. If you're unsure of something on a drawing, or it doesn't look right, ask the designer. Your designer won't be the first to make an error. Never assume anything. Ask for expert advice if necessary – no question is a stupid question.

➢ All invoices, contracts and quotations. Read the fine print.

➢ All materials and items that you're installing and building in. Never assume that the purpose manufactured window or door frames are the correct specification or size, or even that they are square.

Case study: we were finishing a house and the carpets were in and the walls painted when we noticed that one of the doors didn't fit properly in the frame. We tried refitting the door without success. Eventually we found that the purpose manufactured door frame had been supplied out of square. The only way to rectify it was to cut it out the wall and install a new frame. A costly exercise, which meant that the wall had to be patched and repainted, a new carpet installed and a new door fitted. Of course the supplier only paid for the new door frame. It was our fault that we didn't check that the frame was right before installing it!

➢ All suppliers' and subcontractors' shop drawings when these are issued to you for approval. Never assume that the drawings are correct. If you approve the drawing and it's later found that the items supplied are the wrong size because the dimensions on the drawing you approved were incorrect then you may be liable for the costs to rectify the problem.

Insurance – protecting your assets and yourself

It's essential when undertaking major renovations to an existing house that you notify the insurers of the work that you'll be doing.

Before starting construction of a new house ensure that adequate insurance is in place. You wouldn't want your almost complete new house to burn down and then you find that it isn't insured.

Insurance should always have adequate public liability cover. Someone (even a vagrant) could enter your partly completed house and hurt themselves and then sue you for damages.

Check the wording of all insurance policies to see they are adequate and that you are able to comply with their conditions. See Chapter 9 for more.

Construction schedule (programme) – why you need one

The construction schedule is a useful tool to work out:
- ➢ How long the project will take to construct.
- ➢ When particular materials and items are required.
- ➢ When subcontractors are needed.
- ➢ When tasks must be completed so that they're done in the correct sequence, where following activities don't damage them and so work doesn't have to be redone to allow forgotten items to be installed.
- ➢ Your cash flow. It will tell you when you require additional funds.

Most contractors use scheduling or planning software to prepare a construction schedule. But for the average house or home renovation the construction schedule can be prepared on squared or graph paper. Alternatively you could get someone help you set it up using simple scheduling software, such as Microsoft Project.

On the horizontal axis you set out the timeline for the project. This could be divided into individual days or in weeks. At this stage guess how long the project will take, if you think it'll be twelve months then make sure you choose a scale so that twelve months fits in. Note, you may decide to stick two or more pieces of paper together so that you can show the schedule properly. On the vertical axis, starting from the top of the page on the left hand side, write down every activity you can possibly think of. Start in a logical order listing the activities in the sequence that you think they'll occur. Don't worry if you don't get them exactly right. So for instance we could have; prepare design, permits and permissions, deliver the site toilet and shed, erect fencing, check property boundaries, clear the site, level the site, set out foundations, excavate foundations, prepare foundations for concrete, concrete foundations, foundation brickwork, fill around foundations, prepare floor slab for concrete, concrete floor slab, erect walls, erect roof, place roof covering, render walls, etc, through to pave driveway, complete landscaping, house ready to occupy.

(Looking through the drawings you should be able to see all the individual activities that need to be completed. Walking through the inside of a completed house can also help you to list all the activities required in a finished house. Visit construction projects to understand the sequence of tasks and what's involved with each task.)

Then decide how long you require to complete each task and write the number of days next to the task. Always err on the generous side allowing extra time. Ask subcontractors how long they'll need for their tasks.

Then start with the first task and draw a horizontal line from the day the task can start for the length of the duration. So if the design starts today and you expect it to take three weeks then draw a line level with the design activity, starting today and extending three weeks long. Then decide which will be the following activity. Probably applying for permits and permissions. This activity can usually only start once the design is complete. So let's assume that permits and permissions will take four weeks, then start drawing the line for this activity below where the connecting activity (the design) ended and extend the line for four weeks. To show that the start of this activity is connected to the finish of the design activity draw a vertical arrow connecting the end of design to the start of the line for the permits. What comes next? Well once you have the design and the permits and permissions you can start work. So the next activity could be to fence the site, which say takes two days. This will start immediately the permissions are received. In other words seven weeks from today (three weeks for the design plus four weeks for the permits). You should have checked the property boundaries before erecting the fence. This activity could happen at any time from today. Say it takes one day. So you can put a line one day long against this activity anywhere in the next seven weeks, providing it's complete before you erect the fence. After the fence is complete you might want to clear the site. Say this takes one day. You can start the line for this activity immediately the fence is completed. Again link the end of the fence activity to the start of the clearing activity with a vertical arrow. It should be noted that the start of the fence has two activities which must be finished before the fence is erected, namely the checking of the property boundaries and the receipt of the permits. (See an example of a construction schedule on the next page.)

Once you've cleared the site you'll want to level the area for the house. Say this takes five days. The start of this line will be linked to the end of the clearing line.

At some time when this is happening you can schedule the site toilet and shed to arrive. You need them to be on site as early as possible, but probably not before the site is fenced and cleared. Let's have them arrive the first day the site levelling commences. Following this we excavate the foundations, place concrete, etc. Linking all the activities so that there's a preceding and a following activity, all the way through to when you have a completed house.

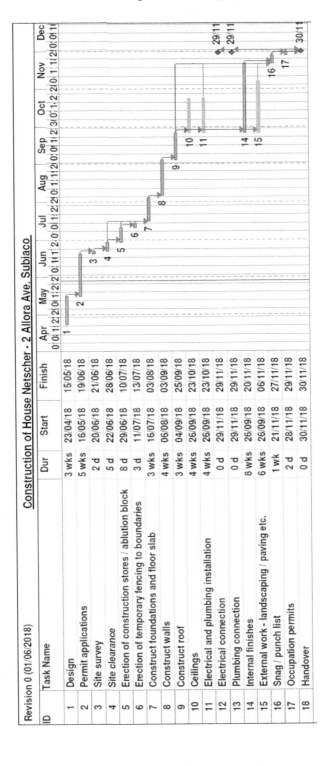

Revision 0 (01/06/2018)

Construction of House Netscher - 2 Allora Ave. Subiaco

ID	Task Name	Dur	Start	Finish
1	Design	3 wks	23/04/18	15/05/18
2	Permit applications	5 wks	16/05/18	19/06/18
3	Site survey	2 d	20/06/18	21/06/18
4	Site clearance	5 d	22/06/18	28/06/18
5	Erection of construction stores / ablution block	8 d	29/06/18	10/07/18
6	Erection of temporary fencing to boundaries	3 d	11/07/18	13/07/18
7	Construct foundations and floor slab	3 wks	16/07/18	03/08/18
8	Construct walls	4 wks	06/08/18	03/09/18
9	Construct roof	3 wks	04/09/18	25/09/18
10	Ceilings	4 wks	26/09/18	23/10/18
11	Electrical and plumbing installation	4 wks	26/09/18	29/11/18
12	Electrical connection	0 d	29/11/18	29/11/18
13	Plumbing connection	0 d	29/11/18	29/11/18
14	Internal finishes	8 wks	26/09/18	20/11/18
15	External work - landscaping / paving etc.	6 wks	26/09/18	06/11/18
16	Snag / punch list	1 wk	21/11/18	27/11/18
17	Occupation permits	2 d	28/11/18	29/11/18
18	Handover	0 d	30/11/18	30/11/18

You may be able to shorten the overall duration by shortening some of the activities and seeing if you can overlap some activities with others, or have more than one activity happening at the same time. If you only have a small team you'll probably only have resources to work on one item at a time. If you have subcontractors they may be able to work on some activities while you're doing something else.

So there should be a logical progression of one activity following another, from the foundations, through the walls to the roof. Many of the internal activities of the house can't start until the house is weathertight. Then we have some activities that could be damaged by other activities, so for instance carpets are usually installed near the end so they aren't dirtied and damaged by the other activities. The last coat of paint is often also applied near the end, while the paint undercoat could be done when carpenters and tilers are busy in the house.

Remember to take account of poor weather which might cause work to slow down or stop. Also factor in holidays and times when you or your contractors won't be working.

The construction schedule can be broken down into more detail, so for instance the foundations could be split into excavation, preparing the foundation, fixing reinforcing steel, concrete and backfilling. This detail is not always necessary and depends on if there are subcontractors that need to know exactly when they must be on site. So for instance a reinforcing subcontractor would need to know when the foundations will be ready for them to fix reinforcing in place, which isn't the day when the foundation activity begins, rather only once the excavation is complete.

This simple construction schedule, or programme, should provide an indication of how long the project will take. Ask someone with building knowledge to review your construction schedule to see that it's reasonable.

Of course, it's not just good enough to plan the project, but you also need to monitor your progress against the schedule at regular intervals, say weekly or fortnightly. By monitoring progress you can take action when work falls behind. This may entail delaying the delivery of materials, rescheduling subcontractors to arrive later, or calling in additional help to speed up the work. If your house is going to take longer to construct than you anticipated you may have to make alternative arrangements to accommodate your family.

It may be pertinent to add additional activities for items that require time to be manufactured and get to site. For lead times refer to Chapter 3.

Keeping track of the costs – don't run out of money

Costs can quickly spiral out of control if you aren't careful, causing you to run out of money before you're finished construction. It's easy to make decisions without considering the cost implications, to walk into a store and make a purchase.

It's important to prepare a spread sheet which you should update at least weekly, but preferably daily, or as soon as the purchase is paid or the order is placed. It's easy to lose invoices, forget costs, or pay a cost for the project as part of another household bill. See chapter 3 on budgets.

The spread sheet of costs could include columns for the date, what the item was, the supplier and when the invoice was paid. All orders and invoices should be kept in a file, no matter how small the amounts are. A few dollars here and few more there, can quickly add to the hundreds, and the hundreds to thousands. Make copies of invoices and mark them off as paid when you pay them so they aren't accidently paid again. Always check the invoices (see Chapter 10) against the order values to ensure that they're correct.

Continually check the total spent against your budget. If it appears you are going to overrun the budget take action sooner than later. This might include arranging additional finance, or possibly cutting back expenses.

Summary

It's possible to plan and do all the work associated with renovating or building your home yourself. But for the novice builder, those who aren't good with their hands and those that are time poor it can lead to an expensive mistake.

The essentials of doing the work yourself include:

> Ensuring you have the right skills. Attending training courses is essential.
> Plan the process from start to finish. Know what the end goal is and try not to deviate from it.
> Talk to experts. Visit suppliers. Look at other houses.
> Make sure you will have time to do the work.
> Engage a professional to prepare detailed drawings.
> Enlist help – especially when muscle and extra hands are required.
> Make sure your family is behind you and will help out when required.
> Prepare a realistic budget. Obtain prices from suppliers. You don't want to run out of money before the project is finished. Always add a large contingency – things will go wrong, there will be extras and changes, and items will be more expensive than estimated.
> Use the right tools and equipment. It's tempting to use the tools you have, or do things by hand, but this is slow and often leads to accidents. Most equipment can be hired. Allow in the budget for excavators, cranes and a good set of power tools.
> Safety is a priority with any construction project. It's pointless saving thousands on your project doing it yourself and ending with a permanent back injury, losing a finger, damaging your eye, or worse. Your health and the health of others must always be the number one priority.
> Understand what hazards you could encounter on the project.
> Don't bury problems.
> Make sure that you don't undertake work which you aren't licensed to do.

➢   Ensure you produce good quality workmanship.

➢   Have the required inspections done as work proceeds.

➢   Ensure that all insurances are in place and that you don't void your current insurance policies with the work you undertake.

➢   Get the details right. Even a small error, or what seems an insignificant change to you, could lead to costly problems later.

➢   Order the correct materials in the right quantities and sizes.

➢   Know how you will offload materials and place them in position.

➢   Store materials correctly where they won't become damaged, fall over, be stolen, clutter the workplace and where they won't overload existing structures.

➢   Avoid wasting materials.

➢   Don't try and save money by using inferior materials, omitting items, working unsafely or taking short cuts.

➢   Take care when hiring equipment to use the item correctly so it's not damaged. Read the hire contract carefully. Always check that it's cheaper to hire the item than purchase it.

➢   Make sure that you get the sequencing of activities right so that tasks are done in the correct order, where completed work won't be damaged by the following tasks, or have to be redone to allow access to do tasks that should have been done earlier.

➢   Keep track of all the costs.

➢   Prepare a realistic schedule or programme.

➢   Never be too proud to ask for advice or help.

Always execute all work professionally, delivering a quality house that will be structurally sound, aesthetically pleasing, satisfying all the codes and specifications, a house that will be safe for you and your family to live in, and a house that you'll be proud of. Never take short cuts which could impact the integrity and value of the house. If you lack some skills and knowledge then engage an expert, attend course or ask for advice.

Chapter 7 – Finding Contractors

Frequently construction projects go wrong because the wrong contractor was employed. They didn't have the skills for the work, they ran out of money, their work was substandard, there were safety incidents, the project didn't look like you envisaged, it was finished late (sometimes not at all), the contractor went bankrupt before the work was finished, or there were problems (such as leaks) after the project was finished. Indeed, the project was a nightmare which cost you more than you budgeted and left you with a building you weren't happy with. Unfortunately there are many contractors that give the industry a bad name. Fortunately there are also many reliable and reputable contractors who can deliver the house you were expecting with minimal fuss. The important thing is to select the right contractor, provide them with all the necessary information to accurately price your project, carefully check the price comparing it to other contractors' prices, and then ensure they're appointed using a sound contract document. The process of finding and selecting a contractor should never be driven by price alone. Regrettably, the cheapest contractor often ends up being more expensive than some of the other prices you may receive.

Display homes, standard designs and kit homes – the pitfalls

Many contractors have display homes which you can visit. The contractor offers to build the same home wherever you want it at an advertised price. Many contractors also offer standard home designs which you can select and have them build at their advertised price. While others offer a kit home, which you can purchase and erect on your property. This all sounds like a great idea, you know what you are getting and the price! But is that the case?

As with any contractor it's important to understand the contractor's reputation and their reliability. In many cases owners fall in love with a particular design which is within their budget. It seems an easy process then to sign a contract and get your new home underway. Little thought has been given as to who the contractor is, and whether you'll be getting the advertised product, at the price you envisaged and within the timeframe required. It's important to choose your contractor wisely (see later in this chapter on selecting the contractor and questions to ask your contractor) and not become solely focussed on a particular product.

When selecting a display home or standard plan you must consider the following:
- ➤ Will the house meet the local and estate rules and permit conditions?

> Is the price really the final price? What provisional sums and prime cost allowances are in the price (see later)? The display home may have more expensive finishes and fittings than the contractor's advertised price allows. To get the same quality fittings and finishes could add considerably to the final price. Items to consider include:
>   - The type of light fixtures.
>   - Bathroom fixtures, including bathtubs, basins, toilets, towel rails, toilet roll dispensers, shelving and tap fittings.
>   - Counter tops in kitchens.
>   - Kitchen cabinetry, including how many, doors, handles and finishes.
>   - Windows, including if insect screens, double glazing, tinting, etc, are included.
>   - Appliances, including the make and size.
>   - Air-conditioning, including the size, make and efficiency. For ducted air-conditioning consider the type and location of air grilles.
>   - Wardrobe, including the material, the number of shelves and drawers and whether cupboards have doors (if required).
>   - Doors, including the kind of locks and handles, the type and quality of door and the frame. Some front doors can cost several thousand dollars so don't automatically assume that the door you see on the display home is the one that you'll get installed in your house.
>   - Garages, including the internal finishes and the type of door, it's material and whether it's automated.
>   - The extent of wall tiles in bathrooms and kitchens.
>   - The type of vanity slab in the bathroom.
>   - Bathroom cabinetry.
>   - The number of electrical outlets.
>   - The type of floor finishes, including the quality of carpets.
>   - The type of skirtings.
>   - The type of cornices.
>   - Patio, including floor finish and roof covering.
>   - The type of shower door and enclosure.
>   - The type of tiles.
> What's included and excluded in the price (see later)? There could be additional costs for site clearing and levelling, connecting utilities, approval by the authorities, landscaping and even for the foundations.
> Will the house plan actually fit onto your property? Indeed is it actually suitable for your block considering the property slope, shape, size, orientation, access and the neighbours?
> Is the house design and materials suitable for your climate?

Subcontractors – contractors doing portions of the project

As discussed in previous chapters you could elect to appoint a number of specialist contractors, each to do a portion of the works. These could include a plumber, electrician, concreter, bricklayer, tiler, carpenter, cabinet maker, roofer, etc. Each would have to quote on their specific section of work. You have to ensure that there're no gaps or overlaps in their work. So for instance, for the air-conditioning, you would have to check who will install the electrical connection for the air-conditioner, and who will install the base to support the air-conditioning unit.

You need to be clear what work each contractor is expected to accomplish, as well as the anticipated timing of when they're required to execute their work. Some subcontractors may have to return to the project several times. So for instance, the plumber may have to install their drainpipes in the ground before the floor is installed. They could then have to return to install pipes into the upper storey floor slab. They would return to install pipes in the walls, possibly again to install pipes in the roof, again to fit baths and toilets, then finally to install tap fittings. Every time they visit is a cost to them, which is really your cost. Where possible the number of visits should be limited to keep costs down. Should the number of visits be more than they could reasonably have expected you will incur additional costs. Of course, if the contractor isn't available when they're needed it could result in delays to other contractors who could claim from you, and invariably the project will be delayed.

Main contractor – one contractor for everything (or almost)

Appointing a contractor to complete all the work is the simplest since you're dealing with only one contractor who's then responsible for finding their subcontractors and for managing and coordinating them. Make sure the contractor understands what's included in their scope and what's excluded from their scope.

The role of the project manager

Depending on the terms of the contract with your project manager (if you have one) they could be tasked with the preparation of the pricing documentation for your project, finding suitable contractors to price the project, evaluating the prices received, then recommending to you which contractor to appoint. They would then appoint the chosen contractor using an appropriate contract document which you then sign.

The tender or quotation – what's the price?

It's best to obtain between three and six quotations to ensure that you receive a competitive price. Frequently you'll receive at least one price that's much more than the others, which is often indicative that the company isn't really interested in the project (it could be too small for them, or they could be too busy on other projects).

You don't want to ask too many contractors to price since it's not fair on them as they each spend money on preparing their price, and it requires extra work from you.

Steps to finding and appointing the contractor

If you are going to find the contractor and appoint them then:

➤ Ensure that you're clear about what you want them to construct. If you already have drawings then these will form the basis of the contractor's price.

➤ Make a list of all your requirements, as well as any restrictions which could hinder or limit the contractor's work.

➤ Preferably, know what form of contract you want to use (see Chapter 9) and what contract terms and conditions you will consider.

➤ Find suitable contractors – see later in this chapter.

➤ Investigate these contractors to see that they are a match for you and your project, that they have the capabilities to execute the project and that they want to do the work.

➤ Provide them written instructions of what they should price and the restrictions on the project.

➤ Provide them as much information as possible. This could include drawings of the new work, drawing of existing structures, estate rules, contact details, specific concerns, and preferably the contract document to be used.

➤ Walk the contractor around the project site so that they're familiar with the working conditions.

➤ Give all contractors the same information so that you're able to easily compare their prices.

➤ When the prices are received carefully adjudicate the prices – see later.

➤ If there's anything unclear with the price, or the price doesn't include items it should, then send questions in writing to the contractor. Carefully evaluate the answers and adjust the price (or your additional costs) if necessary.

➤ Once you've chosen the contractor issue them with a contract document for them to sign. You and the contractor should each keep a copy.

➤ Once you've appointed the contractor it's good practice to notify the other contractors that they weren't successful.

Finding the contractor – not just anyone

A contractor must be selected that can do the type of work expected, that has the capabilities and who operates in that region. There are often thousands of contractors operating in a country, but even so it can be hard to find one willing and capable to do your project.

➤ The best solution is to approach contractors you've previously successfully worked with on other projects. However, it will still be necessary to check that they're interested in doing the work and that they have the required resources available. Since you last worked with the contractor circumstances may have changed and they could for instance have new managers who aren't as focussed as the ones in place when they last worked for you. They may also now be committed to other projects and have limited resources, or only the 'B team' is available for your project.

➤ A simple solution is to search for contractors on the web. By typing in the trade and the area it's possible to obtain a selection of contractors. Visiting their websites usually provides more useful information including their contact details. Often websites provide details of previous projects. Sometimes though, not all possible contractors come up in a simple search since some may not have websites and others might not be shown as operating in your location even if they are. There's also often little indication of the size of project the contractor can undertake, nor of their resources. Websites also only give examples of their satisfied customers.

For example: I required a retaining wall to be replaced, but a number of contractors I approached weren't willing to price the project. For some the project was too big, while for others the project was too small. This wasted lots of my time.

➤ Looking through local newspapers, or even the relevant trade publications will sometimes produce advertisements of contractors working in the area. Again it's difficult to gauge their reliability or their capabilities.

➤ There're often forums and associations in many regions, such as 'Master Builders' or specific trade organisations and groups. These associations should have a list of contractors operating in the area who would be capable of undertaking the project. The fact that the contractor belongs to such an organisation provides some level of comfort, although often there's no restriction or qualifications required to belong to the forum or association (other than paying a fee), and few of these organisations can punish members that don't perform, unless they're serial offenders.

➤ Driving through the area you'll often see sign boards, vehicles or equipment with the names of contractors working in the area. Stop at these work sites and talk to the project owner, perhaps even view the contractor's work to see their quality and professionalism.

➤ Often acquaintances, colleagues, businesses and neighbours may have contacts for contractors that have worked for them in the past.

➤ In some areas, local tradespeople and building companies can register with a central tendering or quotation company. The central company can be contacted and the project's requirements and location specified. Usually a number of suitable companies will respond and provide a price for the work. Sometimes these systems have a well-established website and it's possible to review what past clients said about the work of each of the contractors. This is usually only useful for smaller projects.

➢ Designers, architects, quantity surveyors, project managers and engineers working on the project will always have an extensive list of suitable contractors that they, or their colleagues, have worked with in the past.

Choosing the contractor – they will be your partner

Contractors are hugely varied and range from the one-man business where the owner does almost everything themselves, through to multinational construction companies that construct projects valued at hundreds of millions of dollars. Some contractors are specialist, only doing electrical, plumbing, carpentry or bricklaying work, while others provide a full construction package. Those that do the complete construction may have all the resources and trades in-house for the project, while others employ subcontractors to do many of the specialist trades. In fact, some construction companies are more like project managers employing subcontractors for all of the work, and they merely manage them. Some contractors specialise in particular projects, for instance some do home renovations, others only build new houses (some contractors specialise in luxury houses, others in typical middle income houses, some construct low cost housing, others use particular materials or methods), or civil structures, apartment buildings or office buildings. Larger companies may have different divisions that specialise in different types of construction. Most contractors work in specific towns, regions or countries, with only the larger companies having the ability to work across a wider geographic area and across states.

Many projects go badly because the wrong contractor is selected, often the contractor that submitted the lowest price.

When selecting a contractor it's important to consider the following:

➢ Does the contractor have the required experience to deliver the services required? Have they worked on similar projects? There's a difference between contractors that build low-cost houses to those that build luxury houses. A heritage restoration requires particular skills.

➢ What services they offer? If you want the contractor to design the building then check that they have good designers who will interpret what you want and deliver a design that works. Do they offer planning services and can they help with the interior design, fixture selection and finishes (such as bathroom, kitchen, tiles, materials and colours)?

➢ Do they have the applicable registrations for the work? Usually there's a requirement for builders to be registered in the country or state. Check with the registration body that the registration is current, that it's in the correct trading name of the contractor and that it's for the trade that you're looking for. Companies also usually have to be registered for tax purposes.

➢ Can they produce acceptable quality? Have they produced good quality work on their previous projects? Do they have the required skills available to produce good quality work?

➤ Do they have the resources to carry out the work? This includes; equipment, management and the tradespeople. If they don't have the resources, can they get the resources and will they be able to manage them?

➤ Do they have the financial means to carry out your project? Are they financially secure. If the contractor is suffering losses on other projects this could cause them financial stress which could mean that they can't pay for people and materials. In extreme cases the contractor could become bankrupt partway through your project, leaving you facing delays and additional costs while you find another contractor to finish the project. You'll probably also lose deposits and advances that you've paid them.

➤ What other work are they currently doing? If they're involved with other large projects they may not have the resources or the finances to successfully undertake your work.

➤ What's their safety record? A poor safety record is often indicative of poor management. Contractors with a poor safety record shouldn't be used. Accidents delay projects and they could get the project stopped by the authorities until the contractor rectifies safety breaches. See Chapter 8.

➤ Do they have a good reputation?

➤ Have they got a previous record of being claims orientated and having legal disputes with owners? You don't want your budget blown by extra costs!

➤ Are they reliable and complete their projects on time?

➤ Do they use good subcontractors? Who will their main subcontractors be?

➤ Has there recently been a change in management?

➤ What insurances do they have? See chapter 9.

Past performance however isn't always indicative of how a contractor will perform on a project and I've on occasion had good contractors perform poorly because they were overcommitted on other projects, which meant they had insufficient and poor quality resources for my project.

Questions to ask your contractor

➤ Will you prepare the plans (if this is a requirement)?

➤ Will you arrange council and other required approvals?

➤ Do you have insurance – including worker's compensation insurance?

➤ Is your company registered? (Check the registration provided.)

➤ Do you have the required building licenses to work in this state? (Check that the license is valid and current.)

➤ Can I have references of previous clients?

➤ Will there be a full time project manager? If not how often will they be on site?

> ➤   Will I be welcome to visit the project at any time?

Questions to ask the contractor's references

Ask the references provided by the contractor the following questions:
- ➤ What was the scope and size of the project that the contractor completed and when was it finished?
- ➤ Were you satisfied with the work?
- ➤ Was the quality good?
- ➤ Did they finish it when they said they would?
- ➤ Did they communicate regularly with you?
- ➤ Was management frequently on the project?
- ➤ Were there problems? What were they and how did the contractor handle them? Were the problems sorted promptly?
- ➤ How easy were they to contact?
- ➤ Did they work safely?
- ➤ Did they keep the project site tidy?
- ➤ Were there extra costs? Why? Did they advise you ahead of time that you would incur these additional costs? Were they fair and reasonable?
- ➤ Was the contractor helpful? Did they provide good advice?
- ➤ What advice would you give me if I was to hire this contractor?

Adjudicating (checking) the price – looking for tricks

All quotations (prices) must be in writing. Once the tenders, or quotations, have been received they must be carefully adjudicated (checked) ensuring that 'apples are being compared with apples', like with like. It's important not to just look at the total price, but rather consider the whole price submission.

Not all tenders are equal, so it pays to check:
- ➤ That the contractor has priced all items they were asked to price, and that they haven't excluded anything.
- ➤ Their start and completion dates are acceptable. It's important to note that longer durations could result in additional costs for you if you're renting alternative accommodation for the project duration. However, shorter durations could strain your cash flow abilities.
- ➤ They meet the requirements discussed previously in this chapter for selecting a contractor.
- ➤ That the specifications of the products they propose using are acceptable.
- ➤ The resources they propose to commit to the project are acceptable and sufficient. It's useful if the contractor has provided résumés of the senior staff that will manage the project so you can assess their qualifications and experience. You don't want a contractor whose project staff are all new.

➢ Their proposed construction methodology, in particular how this will impact your family if you continue living in the house while it's being renovated. If the construction method involves using preformed panels and elements it could be difficult to alter the house in the future.

Case study: A few years back we had our main bedroom and bathroom renovated as well as a portion of the upstairs living area. We continued to live in the rest of the house while the work was carried out. The builders constructed a temporary timber hoarding (partition) from floor to ceiling to separate their work area from the rest of the house. They accessed the work areas from outside, causing us little disturbance and allowing them to carry out the work without hindrance from us. The hoarding also limited the noise and kept most of the construction dust from the rest of the house.

➢ That their payment terms and conditions are acceptable. Some contractors may want earlier, or more frequent payments, upfront payments or they may have added money to items they'll be undertaking first, which could impact your cash flow.

➢ That the contractor has evaluated all the applicable drawings (sometimes the contractor provides a list of drawings used for their price and these should be checked to ensure that none issued to them have been omitted).

➢ They've included for preparing designs and drawings where necessary.

➢ The contractor hasn't included additional requirements which you must supply, such as, cranes, scaffolding, toilets, accommodation or offices. If they have then the additional costs must be factored into your comparison.

➢ They've included all taxes.

➢ The contractor understands the project requirements.

➢ They've allowed for all testing and quality requirements.

➢ They haven't got any contract conditions or exclusions which are unacceptable, or that will make their price more expensive than the other bidders.

➢ They've complied with the site-specific conditions, which may include items such as working hours, types of hoardings and fences.

➢ They've adequate insurance in place. See Chapter 9.

➢ That their warranty periods are acceptable.

➢ That the equipment to be incorporated into the project comes with suitable warranties and that spare parts and servicing will be available locally. For instance, you don't want an air-conditioning system where the servicing is difficult and parts not readily available.

➢ The contractor has included for receiving and handling materials supplied by you.

➢ Their provisional sums and prime cost items and compare these to other contractors. See later.

➢ Whether the price is fixed or subject to change. See Chapter 10.

Something that's often not done is to ensure that the price is fair and achievable. Sometimes contractors make a mistake with their price, or the contractor is inexperienced and doesn't understand the project fully, so they submit a price which is too cheap. Be wary of prices that are much cheaper than other prices. You shouldn't become focussed on a 'bargain price' and award the project to a contractor who then loses money. A contractor that's losing money will try and save costs, possibly using inferior quality materials and putting too few resources on the project. In addition, they'll probably do anything to try and recoup their costs, which could include lodging additional variation claims, some of which may be spurious, which will waste your time to argue them, even incurring you additional costs to engage experts to fight the claims through the legal system. Contractors that lose money may become bankrupt or insolvent part way through the project, leaving you with an unfinished house. But, just because a price appears cheap shouldn't be reason to discard it, rather be cautious and understand why the price is low – for instance, the contractor may propose using innovative construction solutions which will give you the product you're looking for at a cheaper price.

The adjudication of tenders must be seen to be done in a fair manner. Keep a record of the adjudication process and the reasons why particular contractors weren't selected. However, it's usually not necessary to inform a contractor why they weren't selected.

What's included in the price (or excluded)

It's important to check what each contractor has included or excluded in their price. A contractor may be cheaper than another's price because they haven't priced all items included in the other price. Check whether these items are included:

➢ Clearing and levelling the project site and removing vegetation and excess material from the property.
➢ Construction of driveways.
➢ Landscaping.
➢ Property boundary fencing.
➢ Garden irrigation.
➢ Appliances in the house, such as ovens and cooking tops.
➢ Air-conditioning.
➢ Preparation of drawings.
➢ Obtaining permits and permissions from the local authorities.
➢ Connection of the utilities of the new house to the street utilities.
➢ Security systems.
➢ Cupboards and cabinetry. The extent, internal layout and their materials.

But even the type and quality of floor tiles, carpets, windows, light fixtures, tapware, bathroom fixtures, doors, door handles and locks, cabinetry and cupboards and counter tops can vary hugely, impacting the price.

Some contractors can include unreasonable provisional sums and prime cost items (see below) which are far too low, meaning that their price will inevitably increase before the project is complete.

Prime cost items (PC items) – unpleasant surprises

A prime cost is a monetary amount the contractor puts against an item that could ultimately have a different price depending on the final product you choose. So for instance, contractors frequently put in a prime cost item for, tiles, bathroom fixtures, tapware, light fittings, door locks and handles, etc.

> *For example: If the contractor has a prime cost for tiles of $50 per square meter and you select a tile that costs $55 then you'll pay an additional $5 per square meter, plus mark-up (see next section). So if the house has 100 square meters of floor tiles and the contractor's mark-up is 20% then you'll pay an additional $500 plus mark-up of $100. If the house price was $150,000 it will now be $150,600. Obviously if you selected tiles that cost $48 then your house will cost $220 less ($2 + 20% by 100 square metres).*

Unfortunately some builders deliberately specify low prime cost values to make their price cheaper and more attractive. Of course this doesn't mean that you won't find a product for the specified price, but your choices of colours and quality will be limited and the products may not suit your style of home.

To protect yourself from unexpected surprises on the final price of your project you should:

➤ Before signing the contract, check the products available within the specified prime costs to ensure the amounts are satisfactory.

➤ You could ask the contractor to revise the prime cost amounts upwards. It's easier to negotiate with the contractor before signing the contract, and some may even increase the prime cost amounts at no extra charge if they think this is a deal breaker.

➤ During construction try and ensure that the chosen products fit within the stipulated allowances.

Provisional sums (allowances) – why the price isn't the price

Don't think that the contract price is the final price that you'll pay the contractor. Inevitably there will be some changes and variations (see Chapter 9). In addition, most contractors include provisional sums and prime cost items in their price. (Provisional sums are an estimate of the final cost while prime cost is an allowance.)

The provisional sums cover the cost of items which the contractor can't price fully now. Unfortunately, some contractors also use provisional sums as a means to make their price appear low and attractive, then after the contract is signed they hit clients with additional costs (sometimes with excessively high mark-ups). Sometimes contractors are simply too lazy or too rushed to price some items so they insert a guestimate provisional sum.

Contractors may have provisional sums for some of the following; clearing the project site, foundations for the house (foundations often vary depending on the actual ground conditions encountered), levelling the house site, excavating rock, preparing drawings, landscaping, kitchen cabinetry, built in cupboards, air-conditioning and items that haven't been designed yet.

A provisional sum is basically a guestimate of what the item will cost. The final cost is only known when the contractor submits a price for that item – usually after the work is complete.

> *For example: if the contract price for building a new house is $150,000 and this includes a provisional sum of $2,000 for clearing the site and then the actual price for clearing is $3,000, then you'll pay the contractor $150,000 plus $1,000 (being the difference between $3,000 and $2,000) meaning the house will now cost $151,000. Of course if the cost of clearing the site is only $1,5000, then your house will cost $500 less (the difference between $1,500 and $2,000) in other words $149,500.*

The problems with provisional sums are that:

➢ It's difficult to determine an accurate budget for your new home since the final price will vary depending on the final cost of the provisional sums.

➢ As mentioned, some contractors could have deliberately included provisional sums which are too low, thus making their prices appear cheap.

➢ It's difficult to check the price is reasonable when the contractor eventually submits the price for the provisional sum item after the work is complete.

➢ If the contractor's price for the provisional sum is determined using their actual costs incurred for the item (see Chapter 10 on cost plus) there's no guarantee that the contractor has utilised materials, people and equipment efficiently, giving you the best price possible.

You can protect yourself by:

➢ Having the contractor accurately price the provisional sums before you sign the contract. This usually means you have to make decisions and choices about the items now.

➢ Check what the price for the provisional sum will actually give you. So for instance if the provisional sum is for kitchen cabinetry – how many cupboards and drawers, what are the shelf layouts, what materials, doorhandles and doors? Will you be happy with these options?

➢ Comparing the provisional sums with those used by the other contractors to see that they're reasonable.

➢ Ensuring there's agreement in the contract how the final price will be determined. If this is on a cost plus basis then the contractor should include a selection of rates for people and equipment that may be used for this work, as well as the expected mark-up they'll apply to their costs.

➢ When work begins on these items it's advisable that you monitor the work, recording types of equipment and people and the hours each expended on the work. Regularly taking photographs helps. If the contractor is aware that you're keeping records they'll be less inclined to cheat you.

➢ Asking an expert to review the contractor's price, in particular the provisional sum amounts.

➢ Ensuring you have contingency in your budget should the provisional sum amounts increase.

Profit (mark-up or margin) – not too much

Contractors add profit to their work, including on materials, labour, equipment, overheads and the subcontractors they employ. Their profit is included in their total price and it's usually impossible to figure out how much they've added. It could vary between 5% and 40% depending on how desperate they are for the job. Usually contractors add about 10 to 20% profit.

In addition contractors add profit to all variations and changes on the project. So in the example above, if you choose a tile that's $5 more than the prime cost and the contractor's profit is 20% then they'll charge you an extra $6 ($5 plus $1 profit) per square metre of tiles.

If you don't know what the contractor's profit margin is they could add any profit to their variations. It's therefore important that the contractor specifies what their profit or mark-up will be for changes and variations and this amount should be specified in the contract. You should not accept any amount over 20% and should argue that 10 to 15% is fairer. Beware of contractors with cheap prices and excessively high profit or mark-up for their variations.

Also check that this mark-up includes overheads (see Chapter 10).

The contract – the book of rules

Once you've agreed the price with the selected contractor it's important that there's a proper, legally binding contract between you and the contractor that covers the full scope of works which the contractor must undertake. See Chapter 11.

Oh no, you're over budget – what now?

Sometimes the prices received from contractors exceed your budget. When this happens there're a number of options you could consider:

➢ Ask the contractors for a discount – but usually this will only be a couple of percent at best.

➢ Revise some terms and conditions in the contract and ask the contractors to update their price in accordance with these amendments. This may include asking the contractor for discounts for removing some of the project risks from the contractor (including say inclement weather), supplying storage or office place (especially for home renovations where the contractor could use your garage for storage), or earlier payments or more frequent payments.

➢ Ask other contractors to price the project. Asking for new quotations will delay the project and add further costs which could outweigh the possible advantages.

➢ Seek other avenues to finance the project.

➢ Talk to the lowest bidders, seeking ways to optimise the project and reduce costs where possible. This might mean selecting cheaper fixtures and finishes – always taking care that the overall project isn't compromised.

➢ Consider that you supply some of the materials and equipment.

➢ Possibly, build the project in phases to enable finance to be raised for later phases.

➢ Attempt to do some, or all of the work yourself.

➢ Request the designers to redesign the project. This may entail reducing the size of the house, using less expensive materials, equipment and finishes, or simplifying the design. Of course this adds additional design costs and will delay the project, which adds further costs, possibly outweighing the cost savings.

➢ Cancel the project.

Many of the options above will delay the project and add to the project costs. It's therefore important that an accurate budget is prepared for the project before requesting contractors price the work. This will help ensure that the building as designed is affordable.

If there's doubt about the budget before contractors are requested to price the project then the pricing documentation issued to the contractors could have options which might include requesting contractors price the project as two or more phases, and then for all the phases together, or to price a 'slimmed down' or basic project with additional prices for extra packages. Depending on the prices received it's then possible to select the best option that fits your budget.

> *Case study: When we renovated our main bedroom and bathroom and upstairs living area we also wanted to enlarge the window in our bedroom. We weren't sure how much it would all cost, so we asked the contractor to price the work including the window and then excluding the window. We received two prices and decided we could afford to change the window. But, if we had decided that changing the window was too expensive we would have accepted the lower price excluding the window.*

In some cases it could be prudent to delay the project if there's a possibility that construction prices will fall (say for instance, when construction work is scarce then suppliers, subcontractors and contractors often reduce their profit margins), or where there's a possibility that extra money will become available, maybe personal circumstances change and you're able to obtain a bigger loan. Of course, things may go the other way and construction costs could increase, or lending institutions could introduce restrictions reducing the size and availability of loans.

It's therefore important to have realistic expectations and budgets and to not get carried away planning a project which you can't afford. Not only are there wasted costs but inevitably there'll be disappointment and recriminations.

Bid shopping – telling contractors what's the lowest price

Bid shopping is when a contractor with a high price is told what the lowest bidder's (contractor's) price is. The contractor with the higher price is given an opportunity to drop their price below this, and if they comply they're awarded the project. This practice isn't ethical and should be avoided. In some jurisdictions it's also illegal. The higher priced contractor can be requested to drop their price (in which case all contractors should be given the opportunity to review their price), but they shouldn't be given the other contractor's price and told to beat it.

Contractors spend considerable time and effort pricing projects and they expect to be dealt with fairly.

Summary

The success of your project will depend on selecting a suitable contractor.

If you've appointed a project manager the task of finding a contractor could be allocated to them, in which case they must find suitable contractors to price the work, prepare pricing documentation, have the contractors price the work, then adjudicate the contractors' prices, recommending which contractor you should appoint to carry out the work. Of course you're free to select another contractor if you're not happy with their recommendation – although you should have good reason for doing so.

You may consider selecting a display home, standard design or kit home. In this case it's important to not only focus on the house design, but also to check that the house is suitable for your property and meets all the regulations. Also check the contractor's reputation and capabilities. Ensure that the contractor can deliver the house in the time you require it. Thoroughly understand what's included in the price and what extra costs you could incur.

If you don't have a project manager then:

➤ Decide how you'll break the project down into sections and trades and then what each contractor must price.

➤ Preferably contractors should be given a written scope of work and contract conditions with drawings to price.

➤ Find suitable contractors who are willing to undertake the work and who have the required resources and capabilities.

➤ Obtain at least three prices for larger items.

- ➢ Once you've received the prices they should be checked and compared against others you've received. Understand what the price includes and excludes, what the payment conditions are and what warranties you'll receive. Factor in additional costs you may incur when selecting each contractor.
- ➢ Check provisional sums (allowances) and prime cost items to ensure that the amounts are realistic and that you won't be caught out of pocket. If possible eliminate as many of these items by deciding exactly what you want now and have the contractor firm up their price before awarding the contract to them.
- ➢ Check that the contractor can do the work. Check references of their previous projects.
- ➢ If the prices are within your budget then appoint the contractor using a suitable contract document. This document should have been included in the pricing documentation.
- ➢ If the prices are over budget you could take steps to lower the prices or to increase the amount of money available for the project.

It's important that you select the right contractor for your project. One that's reliable, who can deliver a quality project with minimal fuss and delays, that has constructed similar projects, and importantly, a contractor that you're comfortable working with. Never be swayed by price alone, or select a contractor only based on a house design you like. Always diligently research your contractor, then carefully check their price to ensure there won't be unexpected hidden extra costs or unpleasant surprises. Check that the contractor's price, including all other costs and extras, will be within your budget.

Chapter 8 – Managing Your Contractors

Frequently clients think that they can appoint a contractor and then let them get on with the job and they'll see them at the end of the project to collect the keys to their new house. Regrettably it doesn't always work out like this and contractors usually need some management. Appointing a project manager, or delegating the responsibility of managing the contractor to the designer can relieve some of the responsibility from you of overseeing and managing the project. Of course, if you've selected a reputable contractor that can be trusted, that has good supervision, skilled workers and reliable subcontractors, then your input may be minimal.

In this chapter we consider some of the project management tasks that you need to be aware of, and the steps that you should be taking to manage your contractor so that you receive your desired project with minimal fuss and within your budget.

Questions to ask before construction starts

Before construction starts, ask these important questions:
- Is there a signed contract between you and the contractor?
- Are adequate insurance policies in place? If the work entails renovating an existing building has your insurer been advised that construction will be occurring. The contractor should have suitable employees' insurance in place to cover medical costs in case of accidents involving their workers.
- Have you received the contractor's surety or insurance bond to cover for their non-performance? (See Chapter 9.)
- Have the necessary approvals, permits and permissions been received from the various authorities?
- Are all your finances in place to pay for the work?
- Do you own the land?
- Are the site boundaries clearly demarcated?
- Have you reviewed and approved the latest construction drawings?
- If you or your designers are providing construction drawings to the contractor have these been issued to the contractor.
- Is everything ready for the contractor? Will they have the required access to the work site?
- Have you removed, or arranged suitable protection for items that mustn't be damaged during construction?

➢ Have you procured materials that you must supply and will they be delivered before the contractor requires them?

➢ Does everyone know where the existing utility lines are and are these clearly marked?

➢ Will the required utility connections be available for construction?

Checking drawings – your responsibility

Depending on the contract, either the contractor will prepare construction drawings or your architect/engineer will prepare drawings. It's imperative that you check these drawings to ensure they comply with your design brief. Once you've agreed that the drawings are correct then changes that you make during construction will be for your cost, unless these changes are rectifying drawing errors or supplying missing details and information.

It should be noted that if you make changes to the drawings which the contractor, engineer or architect could argue result in changes to your brief to them, then the cost of changing these drawings could be to your account, and it may also delay the project. It's easy to become carried away at this stage, making changes and adding extra items, causing project costs to quickly escalate and go over budget. However, making these changes at drawing approval stage will always be cheaper than making changes during construction.

It's important to ensure that construction doesn't begin until the drawings have been approval by the required regulatory bodies.

Kick-off meeting – setting the ground rules

It's good practice to have a meeting with the contractor and their supervisory staff before they start work on the project. This meeting is useful to:

➢ Know who the responsible people for the project are.

➢ Exchange contact details.

➢ Discuss the planned construction methods and what the first tasks will be.

➢ Understand if there're any problems or potential problems.

➢ Set up communication channels and protocols.

➢ Ensure that the required access will be provided on time.

➢ Check that the contractor has sufficient information to start the project.

➢ Ensure that all permits and permissions have been received.

➢ Ensure that everyone knows what has to be done.

➢ Understand the contractor's requirements for laydown areas (place for materials and equipment).

➢ Ensure that everything is in place from all parties so that work can proceed unhindered.

➢ Check that the contractor is aware of any hazards.

> Confirm that the contractor is aware of project specific rules.
> Check that the contractor has a safety plan and has procedures in place in case of an accident.
> Check that the contractor will provide toilets for their workers and that the project site will be suitably barricaded.
> Confirm the process for instituting changes and submitting variations and invoices.

Contractor facilities – what they need for construction

Contractors normally require:
> Toilets for their workmen.
> Power and water points for their work.
> Areas to store their tools and materials. Some of this space should be secure to prevent theft. They could provide their own shed or store, or use and existing building or garage on the project site.
> Preferably an office to work from and store their plans.
> An area for rubbish – which could be a location for a waste bin.

The contract document should have spelled out whose responsibility it is to supply these items, and even their location.

Communicating with neighbours – why it's good practice

It's good practice to inform your neighbours of what construction work will be taking place, when it will start, the expected duration and how it will impact them. This can be done in a letter drop or by visiting them. Try and allay any concerns they may have. Be honest – don't tell them there won't be noise when there always is with construction. It's useful to provide them with your contact details so they can talk to you if they have any concerns during the construction process.

Always notify neighbours ahead of time when access to their properties may be disrupted. Neighbours forewarned are often more understanding.

Always try and resolve conflicts involving the construction work with your neighbours as soon as possible. Never let problems escalate where people could start digging their heals in because they feel their concerns and grievances aren't being heard. Unfortunately minor annoyances can turn into major problems.

Make sure that your contractors consider your neighbours. This includes that:
> They only work within normal hours as permitted by the local authorities.
> They don't make unnecessary noise, especially when people could still be in bed.
> Their workers don't swear or shout.
> They don't damage neighbour's property.
> They are considerate where they park, which includes not blocking

neighbour's driveways and garage entrances, not parking on the neighbour's sidewalk and not blocking roadways.

➢ They don't litter in the street.

➢ They keep the construction site tidy, regularly removing rubbish.

➢ They take steps to reduce dust from the work.

➢ They provide notice ahead of when roads may be blocked by delivery vehicles or cranes.

Is your contractor working safely – why you should care

Construction is a dangerous business and safety should be a major concern on all construction projects. There's no excuse for poor safety and it is possible to complete construction projects without accidents, or additional costs for working safely.

In some countries it's the owner's responsibility to ensure a safe project. But, even when it's the contractor's responsibility it's still important that you ensure that the contractor works safely. Poor safety could:

➢ Result in accidents. I think it would be terrible living in a house knowing that a worker was seriously injured or killed while building your house.

➢ Cause the project to be shut down by the authorities for an extended period while the contractor remedies safety transgressions.

➢ Result in one of the contractor's key people, even the owner of the company, becoming injured which could delay the project.

➢ Result in accidents or injury to your neighbours or others. It would be tragic if the neighbouring children entered the construction area and one of them fell into a hole, or off an unprotected first floor level, seriously injuring or even killing themselves. This could even lead to sizable and costly lawsuits against both you and the contractor.

So how can you, as an inexperienced construction person, ensure that the contractor is working safely? There are a few checks to ensure your contractor works safely.

➢ Only employ reputable contractors.

➢ Before awarding the project ask for the contractor's latest safety statistics. A contractor that works safely will be proud of these statistics and won't hesitate to supply the information.

➢ All workers on the project should wear the appropriate safety gear, which usually includes suitable footwear, safety hats and glasses. If you see workers without this safety gear ask management why they aren't using it.

➢ Safety is often common sense. If a task looks unsafe then ask the contractor.

➢ Ask to see the contractor's safety documentation at the start of the project. This shows that you're interested in the contractor's safety and then they're often more likely to work safely on your project. This documentation should include a safety plan, emergency contact details and safety registers for equipment.

➢   The contractor should display appropriate safety signage and ensure that work areas are barricaded.

➢   The contractor's equipment should be in good condition.

Of course equally important is that you comply with all the safety requirements when you enter the work areas. This would include wearing the appropriate footwear and other required safety gear, and only entering areas after obtaining permission from the contractor. Preferably they should escort you around the project site.

When the work includes renovations to your home while you and your family are living in the house it's important that:

➢   There's always safe access to your living areas for you and your family. This includes providing sufficient lighting at night.

➢   All electrical and gas connections you're using are safe.

➢   Work areas are clearly demarcated and where necessary barricaded so the interface between workers and your living areas is limited.

➢   Heavy objects can't be dropped on anyone below.

➢   When work is done in living areas that these are always cleaned at the end of the day and made safe again.

➢   The contractor's personnel always communicates with everyone when work is done which could impact safety.

Protecting the environment

Protecting the environment is important since environmental damage could result in construction work being stopped, monetary fines, bad publicity and unhappy neighbours. For steps that contractors should take to limit environmental damage see Chapter 6.

Damage to surrounding properties – it can be expensive

Damage to surrounding property can be costly and negatively impact relations with your neighbours. Damage could be caused by:

➢   Contractor's vehicles driving on the neighbours verge or sidewalk damaging their garden, irrigation pipes and sprinklers and driveway.

➢   Materials being stacked against the boundary walls and fences causing them to fall over.

➢   Dust from the construction activities covering neighbours' laundry and entering houses.

➢   Damage to property when building materials are dropped onto them, even from concrete or paint splashes and spillages.

➢   Sparks from welding or grinding leaving burn marks on windows or cars.

> ➤ Spray from spray painting activities drifting onto other properties.
> ➤ Blocked stormwater drains causing properties to flood.
> ➤ Litter from your construction work blowing into neighbouring properties.

Contractors must take care not to damage neighbouring property. Contractors need to be notified of damage they've caused to the neighbour's property and this should be repaired as soon as possible.

Clearing rubbish – the perennial construction problem

Contractors must regularly remove all rubbish generated from their work, such as packaging and breakages of building materials. Contractors shouldn't use your general rubbish bins for their rubbish. They mustn't pour paints and other detritus down your drains, or the drains in the roads and sidewalks.

Wash water from their concrete equipment and mixing trucks should be contained where it cannot run onto public roads and into drains. The sediment from the wash water must be removed once the water has evaporated or drained away.

All oil, paint and solvent spills on the ground should be contained and cleaned and disposed correctly.

Where possible emphasis should be placed on separating and recycling waste materials.

Storage of construction materials and equipment

Contractors will require place to store their materials and equipment. For renovations of an existing home you'll probably have to allocate suitable space which may inconvenience you or cause damage to areas of the garden. They may be able to negotiate to use sidewalks and verges – see below. A lack of space for the storage of materials and equipment could drive up the costs and cause delays. Providing storage in a garage, or part of an existing building could help save costs, especially if this is negotiated before the contract is signed.

Generally contractors require flat areas which are easily accessible to the road (point where deliveries will be received) as well as the work areas.

Sidewalks and verges – they don't belong to you

On small, or congested, properties contractors may have to use the sidewalk (verge) for their materials and equipment. These areas are generally public property. When the sidewalk or verge is used then:

> ➤ In most cases permission must be obtained from the local authorities to use the area. This could entail paying a 'rental' fee as well as a deposit for repairing damages caused by the contractor.
> ➤ Materials and equipment should not spill onto the roadways.
> ➤ There should be a safe alternative route for pedestrians.

> ➤ The public should not be endangered in anyway. Preferably the area should be fenced to keep people away. Trip hazards and dangerous areas should be clearly demarcated.

> ➤ Like the rest of the work site, rubbish and litter shouldn't be allowed to accumulate.

> ➤ Generally use of the sidewalk should not prevent or restrict the access of public workers such as postmen and utility meter readers.

> ➤ The sidewalk should be returned to its original condition when work is complete. This would include repairing all damages to kerbs, paving and gardens. This could be costly so contractors must take due care.

Access for contractors – when and what's required

Access to the work areas should be on the date in the contract document and during normal working hours (or at times specified in the contract document). Preventing the contractor from accessing work areas will be reason for them to claim a delay, with the associated costs.

Access means in a fit state for them to work. So work which may be in your scope, such as clearing of your belongings, or work that your other contractors had to execute (as specified in the contract) such as levelling and clearing the site must be complete. This means ensuring that the work completed by you or your contractors is to the correct specifications and tolerances. So for example, if your contractor had to level the site, then the area levelled should be to the correct dimensions, in the correct location and to the right level (height), within reasonable tolerances. The levelled area usually has to be compacted to specifications nominated by the engineer. If the following contractor finds that the levelled area isn't to the correct height they could claim the additional costs they incurred because of this, which could include, for example, the additional costs for concrete to make up surfaces which were too low, or for the time and costs to remove excess material when the area is too high. Alternatively, they could request that you rectify the area before they start, then claim standing time and an extension of time until you provide them access as required.

Sometimes access to the project could be restricted because of conditions beyond your control. This could be due to flooding, damaged roads and bridges, or other contractors blocking or digging up roads leading to the project site. This may give the contractor reason to claim Force Majeure, see Chapter 9.

Access to your living areas

When renovating an existing house you may have to grant access to contractors to areas where your family is living. This can be intrusive, noisy, cause dirt to be tracked through your home and be a security risk. When access is required to living areas:

> ➤ If possible the area should be locked or hoarded off to keep the construction work separate from your living areas.

➢ Valuables should be locked away.

➢ Pets should be kept elsewhere, or put in boarding kennels.

➢ Items that could be damaged should be removed or covered.

➢ Furniture should be removed from areas that workers have to get to.

➢ Floors could be covered to protect them from damage.

➢ Your family should be aware that workers will be in the house.

➢ Access should be agreed ahead of time.

➢ When the power or water has to be turned off your family should be aware of when it will happen and only the contractor should turn it back on when they've completed their work and it's safe to do so.

Preventing the contractor from accessing the work areas as required could result in delays to the project and standing time claims.

Working hours – don't annoy your neighbours

Neither you nor your neighbours want to be disturbed by contractors. However, you cannot be overly restrictive with the hours of work because this could be reason for the contractor to lodge a variation claim for a delay as well as possible standing time. If you want to restrict the contractor to working within limited hours then this should have been included in the original terms in the contract document so that the contractor could factor these hours into their price.

However, most local authorities have rules governing the hours of work and these are probably limited to weekdays between 7am and 5pm and possibly also on a Saturday. Breaching these hours could result in fines and the work being stopped. It will also irritate neighbours.

Remember you'll have to live with your neighbours for a long time, so good neighbourly relations is important. In addition, once a neighbour is upset they'll invariably find other issues to complain about.

Good communication is vital to the success of projects

Frequently problems occur on construction projects because of misunderstandings and poor communication. It's vital that:

➢ All communication of a contractual nature is in writing. That's communication which may add additional costs, cause delays to the project, or which causes a deviation to a drawing (even moving the position of a light switch by a few centimetres (inches)) should be in writing.

➢ Communication is clear and that the party receiving the communication understands the expected outcomes.

➢ That communication is directed to the contractor's responsible person. The contractor often has a number of employees and subcontractors working on the project, but all communication should be addressed to the contractor's designated representative, unless there's an urgent safety problem.

> ➤ Communication should be conducted in a civil manner. It's easy to get caught in the heat of the moment and say inappropriate things. Construction is a team effort and you'll be working with the contractor for several months so it's important to keep things on a professional level.

> ➤ The contractor should know who they can take instructions from. If various members of your family comment or change items then it will create confusion, probably adding additional costs when instructions are followed from a person not authorised to give the instruction.

Keep track of all conversations and meetings in your diary. The date, who attended and who said what. Always ask questions when you're unsure.

Correspondence – keeping it professional

All communication of a contractual nature, or which raises concerns about quality, progress, safety or other issues should be in writing. People are very quick to forget what was said when, who said what and who agreed to what.

Ensure all correspondence:

> ➤ Has a date.

> ➤ Is addressed to the correct person. Usually the designated representative of the contractor.

> ➤ Goes to the correct address.

> ➤ Is concise and in simple language.

> ➤ Doesn't use emotive language.

> ➤ Uses consistent text. Resist the urge to write in bold, capital text or colours.

> ➤ Doesn't include additional and unnecessary exclamation and question marks.

> ➤ Can be clearly understood by the reader.

> ➤ Where an action is required from the reader, that this is clear.

Poorly written or emotive letters can lead to misunderstandings and disputes. Always stick to the facts. Letters from all parties should be kept because they can form valuable backup should a dispute later arise.

Project photographs are invaluable

Taking photographs (preferably with the date recorded) can be used to record the condition and status of the area before work starts. Particularly for renovations, record the condition of all rooms and the exterior of the house which shouldn't be impacted by the construction work. You almost can't take too many photographs. You want to record the condition of doors, walls and floors, fences and gardens. Frequently damages occur when suppliers deliver building materials or workmen move materials to where they're needed.

Also record the condition of roads and sidewalks since the local authorities could claim for damage to their assets. Even photograph the neighbouring fences and walls that could be accidently damaged or dirtied by construction work on your property. Neighbours and the local authorities will be quick to complain if they believe that their property has been damaged by your construction work. Unfortunately, some of these damages may have been pre-existing, so it's important that they're recorded.

Taking photographs regularly through the construction process records progress. Importantly taking detailed photographs of plumbing and electrical services before they are closed serve as a record of their quality as well as of their size and location.

Quality – What you should be checking and why?

Poor quality work can be costly to you because:
- There's often the inconvenience and cost of having the contractor stay on past the project completion date to fix poor quality work.
- A repair of faulty work often results in a weakness which creates maintenance problems later.
- Defects and poor quality work which has to be fixed after moving into your house results in inconvenience to you and your family.
- There are follow up letters, calls and inspections to ensure that poor quality work is repaired to a satisfactory standard – sometimes even lawyers and construction experts are involved.
- Sometimes you may even give up in frustration and accept a substandard item.
- A fault could be covered up and go undetected until you discover you have a leak in the house, or cracks start appearing.
- Poor quality work has in severe cases caused structures to collapse, or them having to be vacated because they're dangerous and need to be repaired.

Quality is about delivering a house that meets and exceeds the standards and specifications in the contract, meeting the local bylaws and codes and meeting the code and specification requirements of the state or country. These requirements extend to the house's functionality, durability and the finished aesthetics.

It's important to monitor quality during construction. While these aren't necessarily formal checks, and you may not consider yourself an expert, it pays to pick up potential problems early in the construction process. Contractors do make mistakes, or on occasion deliberately take a chance. Being there early to pick up the problem is important. Always notify the contractor in writing of quality concerns you see so there's a record of your concerns. Remember to be consistent. Don't accept an item as being okay one day, then complain about it the next. Don't wait until the end of the project to raise quality issues, by then it's often difficult to fix some problems, and in fixing them other items may be damaged. If the contractor is aware that you're scrutinising the quality of their work as construction progresses they're more likely to take additional care to ensure that they produce good quality work.

Familiarise yourself with the drawings, especially the details. Even take the drawings with you when you walk around the project so that you can check when things don't appear to be in the right place. If you have little construction experience then ask somebody who is more familiar with house construction to join you. Better still, employ a clerk of works to regularly visit the project to check the quality on your behalf. If you've employed a clerk of works you must introduce them to your contractor so that your contractor knows who they are.

It may seem silly, but it's imperative to check that your house is being constructed on the correct property, that it's within the property boundaries (including allowing for setbacks and building lines) and that it's orientated the correct way.

> *Case study: A few years ago a house in Perth Western Australia was completed by the builder, only to find that the house had been constructed on the wrong property, one that didn't belong to the owner. Not only is this embarrassing but it's very costly since the house you've paid for doesn't actually belong to you, it belongs to the owner of the land it was built on.*

Every time you visit the project site check:

➤ That the site is generally clean, tidy and safe.

➤ That the quality appears acceptable. This could include checking the plumbness and squareness of door frames, window frames and walls. Regularly line up door and window openings by eye to see if they all align. Arm yourself with a tape measure, square and spirit level (not a tiny one, rather what builders use) so you can check dimensions, squareness and plumbness.

➤ That the correct materials are being installed.

➤ That there aren't any obvious problems. For instance that doors, windows and electrical points are in the correct position, and that the correct tiles are being used and the right quality and colour of paint.

➤ That the workers are using the latest drawings. Often drawings are revised, or you issue an instruction, but the team executing the work aren't aware of the instruction, changes, or that there's a revised drawing.

➤ That the ground under floor slabs and foundations is compacted.

➤ That before concrete is poured into foundations and slabs that they are clean of dirt and standing water and that the reinforcing isn't touching the sides or bottom.

➤ That all open ends of pipes are temporarily closed so that dirt and concrete doesn't get into the open pipe.

➤ That there aren't obvious holes or damages to pipes, wires and cables, or joints that appear not properly sealed.

➤ That all pipes appear to have been joined correctly. PVC pipes have various fittings and adaptors. It should never be necessary to heat pipes to bend them, or to cut them to slot them together. Pipes of differing diameters should be connected using the correct adaptor fittings and should fit tightly without paper or silicone being jammed into gaps between the pipes.

➤ That pipes and cables in trenches don't have rocks and building rubble thrown on top of them which could cut or crush the pipes and cables. Normally there should be a bedding layer of sand to protect pipes and cables in trenches.

➤ That waterproofing is installed in the correct place with no holes or imperfections. See Chapter 12.

➤ That the contractor is protecting their completed work so it isn't damaged or dirtied.

➤ That insulation is installed in walls, ceilings and under the roof as required.

➤ That brick and block walls are constructed correctly so that corners are vertical, and that one brick course laps over the other so that the vertical joints don't line up with the joints of the row immediately below.

➤ That walls and rooms are square. If in doubt measure the distance between diagonal corners in the room. These distances should be equal.

➤ That adjoining walls are tied together.

➤ Where there's cracking in walls and floors that there isn't a hollow patch behind the surface which could later delaminate completely coming loose.

➤ That the roof is securely tied to the walls below.

➤ That door and window frames are firmly fixed in position so they can't come loose when slammed.

➤ That constructed stairs appear even and are easy to walk up and down.

➤ That where you have supplied materials, the contractor is taking due care to handle them carefully and they aren't wasting the materials.

➤ That aesthetically things look right. Often if something doesn't look right it's because there is a problem. Of course, sometimes the problem may be because there's a problem with the design, so care should be taken to confirm that what's built is in accordance with the design. But if things look wonky or wavy, or there's a colour variation, or if workmanship looks suspect, then ask the contractor questions, or get an expert to check.

See Chapter 12 for insights into some common construction problems so that you know what to look for.

Take lots of photographs, especially to record items that you think might be a quality issue.

Care should be taken that you don't ask for something additional to the specifications, or make changes to the design without considering the additional costs and time which could impact your budget and delay the job.

When entering the project site you should notify the contractor and get their permission (you may have to sign a visitors' register), wear appropriate safety clothing as required by the contractor (in any case never visit the project wearing sandals or shoes which aren't fully enclosed), obey all safety instructions and stay away from work areas, preferably be accompanied by the contractor's representative, and not interfere with operations or give the contractor's personnel or subcontractors instructions (unless there's an immediate safety risk) or yell at anyone (no matter how unhappy you may be with the quality or progress).

It's good practice to arrange a site walk around once a week with the contractor.

It should be noted that the contractor should never restrict you from visiting the project.

Inspections

See Chapter 6.

It's important to ensure that the contractor arranges for the inspections and tests that they're responsible to organise.

Where you, or agents appointed by you, need to check items, then these inspections need to be coordinated with the contractor to ensure that there's sufficient warning that the work will be available for inspection and that there's opportunity for the inspections and the tests to be completed. The contractor should be reasonable with providing prior warning that work will be ready for inspection. This should be a minimum 24 hours, but where you aren't always available, or aren't near the site, then a longer notification may be required, which preferably should be in the contract.

Samples and mock-ups – why they're useful

Providing samples and mock-ups allows the contractor to produce a sample of a material, or a piece of completed work, so that you can approve an accept it. It can also be an opportunity to sort out details, resolve colour choices and agree the final quality. It's important to check that what you're presented with doesn't come with additional charges or delays. Any changes requested by you to these samples and mock-ups must also be within the original contract price.

Agreeing products and the quality of work before work begins means there shouldn't be surprises later, or arguments on the quality required.

Samples and mock-ups should be approved in writing and safely kept until the project is completed.

It's common practice to request samples of bricks, tiles, floor coverings and roof coverings. Often these samples only consist of a couple of tiles or small piece of the finished article. If the sample is too small to enable an informed decision to be made ask for a bigger sample. Even if you have to pay an additional cost it may be worth the expense so that you are able to make the right decision.

Mock-ups could include sample brick walls and paving of a square metre (ten square foot) or so. Sometimes the contractor has samples or mock-ups in a showroom at their office, or at a show or display home. Always take numerous photographs of these from different angles if you're expecting the contractor to replicate them in your house. Showroom displays can be changed and display homes could be sold and be inaccessible when your house is complete and you need to check something.

Preferably the requirement for samples and mock-ups should be included in the contract document so there's no argument about additional costs for providing them.

You should be reasonable about the size of the sample and be specific about what your requirements are. Changes to samples and mock-ups could incur additional charges where these changes are a result of you changing your mind. Obviously there shouldn't be additional costs where the item didn't meet the project requirements or were substandard quality.

If you accept an item or quality standard but later don't like the finished work which matches the approved sample, then the contractor is entitled to their additional costs incurred to meet your revised requirements.

Materials supplied by you – not always straightforward

Depending on the terms of the contract you may have to supply some building materials. To avoid delaying the contractor these materials must arrive on time and in the correct quantities. The contractor should supply the dates when the materials are required.

Know upfront who will receive and offload the materials. You could find that in your efforts to save money you suddenly have a truckload of heavy materials to offload, or you could receive an invoice from the contractor for offloading the items. The contractor might also expect you to store the items until they require them. Ideally you want the contractor to offload the items, store them and be responsible for them from when they arrive on the project. This should be clear in the contract.

If the contractor has to offload the material they must be forewarned of when the delivery is expected so they can arrange to have people and equipment available to offload the items and also so that there's space ready to place the materials.

The contractor should sign receipt for the materials so that if any go missing, or are broken, then they're responsible for the losses.

It must also be clear as to who is supplying the fixings, which could include glue, grout, bolts, washers, screws, etc.

See Chapter 6 for more on ordering materials and Chapter 3 for lead times.

Deliveries of construction materials and equipment

The contractor should take delivery and arrange for their materials to be offloaded. These deliveries should be within normal working hours so neighbours aren't disturbed. Materials shouldn't block public roads and walkways or your neighbour's driveways. If the materials arrive and the contractor isn't on site contact the contractor to let them know there's a delivery for them.

The contractor should plan their deliveries so that the whole site isn't choked with materials.

Coordination of your subcontractors

If you've appointed a main contractor (general contractor) then usually they'll manage and coordinate all their subcontractors. However, if you've elected to appoint some specific subcontractors, or appointed a number of different contractors, then you're responsible to manage the contractors and ensure that they arrive when they're required in terms of the construction schedule and that they complete their tasks within the timeframe allocated in the schedule. Failure of one of your contractors to deliver their portion of work could lead to project delays. Other contractors could be entitled to claim for the impact of these delays on them, as well as standing time for their resources who couldn't work in the interim.

It's important to have an accurate construction schedule so that all contractors are aware of when they're required on site and the time available to complete their work.

It should be noted that if the main contractor is ahead of the agreed construction schedule they can request that your contractor comes earlier to complete their work. However, they cannot claim that your contractor has delayed them if the contractor only arrives on the allotted day according to the approved construction schedule and completes their work in the time allocated.

Construction schedule – why it's important

It's good practice for the contractor to submit a construction schedule. The schedule lists all the construction activities, their duration and the sequence in which they'll be completed. The schedule is usually shown as a series of bars representing the duration for each activity measured against the calendar days of the project. Most construction tasks are sequential with one having to be finished before the next can start. So for instance, the foundations usually have to be completed before the walls can start, and the roof can only begin when the external and supporting walls are completed. The internal ceilings, fixtures and finishes can probably only start when the roof is complete. Sometimes an activity may be able to start before the preceding activity is complete, and sometimes two or more activities can happen at the same time. The duration of each activity will depend on the complexity of the activity as well as on how many resources are available and can be fitted into the area. See Chapter 6 for more on preparing a construction schedule.

In theory construction schedules can be compressed by working around the clock seven days a week. But this is usually more expense than the result warrants, anyway the neighbours may object to late-night noise and there could be regulations which limit working hours. More resources could be put on the project, but inevitably there will be inefficiencies and the costs will be more than the end result is worth.

All construction schedules should allow for the normal weather that can be expected at that location at that time of year as well as other known restrictions which the contractor should have been aware of. See also delay claims Chapter 9.

It's important to check the construction schedule to ensure that:

➢ The completion date agrees with the date in the contract. If the date is earlier you should check to confirm that your budget and cash flow can accommodate the faster expenditure.

➢ The contractor doesn't expect to receive information earlier than your designers have committed to issue it.

➢ The start date matches what's in the contract and you'll have all permits and permissions in place to match the contractor's start date.

➢ The time allocated for your subcontractors' work is sufficient.

➢ You'll be able to supply materials and equipment that are your responsibility in time, so as not to delay the contractor.

➢ The schedule is an accurate portrayal of the contractor's methods of construction.

➢ There's sufficient detail to monitor the contractor's progress.

➢ It's clear when you or your agent must be available to conduct tests and inspections.

Monitoring progress – will you move in on time?

Progress against the construction schedule should be monitored on a weekly or fortnightly basis. Slippage against the schedule should be raised with the contractor to understand why there's slippage and how they intend to get the project back on track. Delays to your project could have ramifications for you which could include:

➢ You getting access to your house late, which means you may have to arrange alternative accommodation.

➢ Loan payments from your bank which are only paid when specific milestones are reached could be delayed.

➢ You may have to delay the follow-on contractors that you've arranged.

➢ You may have other ongoing costs to pay, which could include the costs of project manager if you've employed one, the cost of additional rates and service charges and additional insurance expenses. It's not always possible to claim these costs back from your contractor.

It's essential that the contractor completes the items which are on the critical path. These are items whose delay will delay the completion of the project. Some items have float and could be done at any time without impacting the final completion date provided they are complete before the last items. Catching up lost time on the critical path is often difficult.

Variations – avoiding cost increases

The contractor is entitled to claim for delays and additional costs for extra items that weren't included in the contract scope and which they couldn't have reasonably foreseen when they priced the project. Unfortunately projects are frequently finished late and incur additional costs which weren't expected. From time to time these costs mean that the project budget is exceeded which could result in you getting into financial difficulties. Sometimes projects can't be finished for lack of funds due to variations, or you might have to accept a lesser standard of finishes to reduce the project costs to fit your budget.

It's therefore important to limit variations by ensuring that:

➢ There's a contract which includes a full scope of work, your obligations, the contractor's obligations, and the payment terms and conditions.

➢ Changes are limited once the contract is agreed.

➢ The contractor isn't delayed by any of your actions (or lack of actions), including where applicable:

- That permits and permissions organised by you or your team are in place ahead of time.

- Materials supplied by you are available when required.

- Information provided by you or your designer is available when required by the contractor.

- Approvals (including drawing approvals) required from you aren't unreasonably withheld.

- Access to work areas is available when needed.

- Utilities provided by you are available.

➢ There's an agreed construction schedule or programme, or at least agreed milestone completion dates.

➢ There are open communication channels between all parties.

➢ You understand the impacts of your decisions (or lack of decisions) and actions on the cost and schedule of the project.

➢ Designers and project managers appointed by you inform you of all changes they request which may have a time or cost impact.

➢ You resist the urge to make changes to the project as work proceeds. It's easy to make small changes, then eventually these all add up to a significant sum. Also, what you sometimes perceive as a minor alteration could have knock-on impacts and significant costs.

➢ The contractor is furnished with all the relevant information when they price the project and the contract scope is clear and complete.

All decisions must be carefully weighed-up to ensure that they are the correct decisions and that you understand their cost and time impacts.

All instructions which could have a time or cost impact must be issued in writing.

The contractor must be encouraged to submit notice of a variation (or potential variation) as soon as they become aware of it. This may give you an opportunity to retract the drawing or instruction, or to come up with an alternative solution to limit the impact. Being aware of variations as they occur also means that you can update your budget to take account of the increased cost. Never think that the contractor will do you a favour and not charge you for a change – they seldom do work for free.

Daily diary – recording what happened

It's good practice that you complete a daily diary every day for the project. You can easily draw up a standard diary form where you record:

> ➢ The date.
> ➢ The weather conditions, which should include a record of the rain and the temperature.
> ➢ Who was on the project. This would list the subcontractors, numbers of workers and supervisors.
> ➢ Interruptions to the work, which could be due to the weather, lack of access, waiting for information, or the contractor's own fault.
> ➢ Major tasks completed.
> ➢ Major materials and items of equipment delivered.
> ➢ Records of meetings with the contractor.
> ➢ Other relevant information.

It should be noted that the contractor may bring you their daily diary to sign and agree. You should carefully check what's written to ensure it is correct before signing, then keep a copy for your records.

These diaries could be important should a dispute arise, so they must be an accurate representation of the facts. Carelessly signing the contractor's diary without checking it properly could mean that you've agreed to something that wasn't factually correct.

Control the costs – don't let them get out of control

It's imperative that you have a spreadsheet detailing all the costs. This should be updated every time there's a new invoice and whenever there's a variation. Always insist that your contractor prices variations and changes as they occur. Don't hope that they'll forget or will be nice and simply waive the additional costs they've incurred – it's not going to happen, contractors will never not claim an extra if they have the opportunity. Leaving variations until the end of the project could mean you receive a nasty surprise when a large bill arrives at the end, a bill which you might not have the finances to pay! See Budgets in Chapter 3 and keeping track of costs Chapter 6.

Record keeping – records are vital

Good record keeping is essential. All project records must be filed in a filing system where documents can easily be found. Electronic records should be regularly backed-up since computers can crash or be stolen. Good records are essential for future maintenance, to enable accounts to be paid (also ensuring accounts aren't paid twice), for arguing or checking variation claims, for satisfying the authorities (they may need to see test results and certificates), when the property is sold, and for recovering deposits and fees.

These records could include:
- ➢ All documentation issued to and received from the contractor during the bidding and pricing process.
- ➢ The contract documents.
- ➢ Orders issued to suppliers.
- ➢ All correspondence.
- ➢ Project instructions.
- ➢ Maintenance instructions and product brochures and manuals.
- ➢ Sureties.
- ➢ Warranties.
- ➢ Insurances.
- ➢ Payments and receipts.
- ➢ Delivery dockets.
- ➢ Loan applications and agreements.
- ➢ Test results.
- ➢ Permits and permit applications.
- ➢ Receipts for deposits paid.
- ➢ Compliance certificates.
- ➢ Photographs.
- ➢ Diaries.

When things start going wrong – take action

Regrettably, sometimes despite all your planning and careful selection of the contractor things go wrong. Obviously the sooner you detect that things are going off the rails the smaller the damage and the easier it is to take corrective actions. Signs of trouble include:
- ➢ Quality issues and failure of the contractor to deal with quality problems.
- ➢ The contractor is frequently short of materials.
- ➢ The contractor's subcontractors or employees complain they haven't been paid.
- ➢ Continuing safety issues.
- ➢ Progress is falling behind the construction schedule.
- ➢ Key staff from the contractor leave the project.
- ➢ The contractor has insufficient resources on the project.
- ➢ The contractor's equipment is broken and hasn't been repaired.
- ➢ The contractor appears to be disorganised.
- ➢ You see in the media that the contractor is in trouble on other projects.

Early intervention when you notice things going wrong may prevent the problem getting worse. This could include:
- ➢ Calling the contractor's senior management to a meeting to discuss your concerns.

➤   Ensuring that the contractor hasn't been overpaid and that they've completed all their obligations for work that they claim they've completed.

➤   Ensuring all sureties are valid.

➤   Issuing a letter to the contractor setting-out your concerns and items where they are in default of the contract. Provide ultimatums by when they should have resolved the issues.

➤   Holding regular meetings with the contractor's senior management. Senior management hate attending regular project meetings and to escape these meetings they'll do anything to avoid further inconvenience and hopefully this will include ensuring your house gets back on schedule.

➤   Ensure the contractor concentrates on all the essential work.

➤   Get advice from experts.

However, at no time can you withhold payment of legitimate invoices from the contractor because this could put you in breach of the contract allowing the contractor to terminate the contract, But, of course make sure that you thoroughly check all invoices presented by the contractor and notify them of any errors.

Always be nice to contractors – why it's important

Contractors are human, so learn to treat them well and you'll often find that your project goes lots smoother. Even though those workers may be dirty, sweaty and even of foreign nationality don't look down on them, or consider that they're your 'slaves' to only do what you want them to do. Many of those workers have a skill to carry out tasks which you can't do, or don't want to do. Greet workers on the project, offer them a cooldrink or tea and coffee (never alcoholic beverages unless there's a special milestone celebration and then it should be only after work hours). Say thank you, please, and show appreciation for a job well done. It's amazing what being nice to people will achieve. Simple problems get solved. Productivity improves and a little extra care is taken.

Sure mistakes will be made, and you may be unhappy with some workers. But your place is not to berate the contractor's workers, rather call their managers and report the issue, even request problem workers be removed from the project.

Deplorably there are many cases where construction workers have deliberately sabotaged a project when they've been offended by the owner, or they weren't paid by the contractor. This has included deliberately depositing sand, rubbish and drink cans and bottles in sewer pipes which then cause blockages. Often these blockages are only detected after you've moved into the house. Clearing these blockages costs money and could even result in newly laid tiles being hacked up and walls and floors being chopped open. Sabotage could also include not connecting pipes correctly, or not installing all the fastenings and fixings.

Of course be sure that you don't idly chat to workers distracting them from the job at hand, possibly even adding to the hours they bill you.

Your family's role in the construction process

It's important that your family understand that their decisions and actions can delay the project or cause additional costs. Actions could include barring the contractor from accessing the work areas, failing to provide access to work areas on time, as well as making changes to the design and layout of the house. It might seem simple to ask the contractor to stop work for half an hour so it isn't noisy while on a telephone call, but this could result in a claim from the contractor. It's simple to ask the contractor to move a light switch, but what is the cost? Arriving half an hour late to let a contractor into the house will delay the contractor and they might even not wait around but go to another job, meaning your project stands. Asking a contractor to do extra maintenance work around the house may result in additional charges and construction progress could be impacted. Even chatting to workers may distract them from their work and delay them, perhaps causing an accident, and possibly even meaning you get a bigger bill if they're charging you by the hour.

Instructions to the contractor from different people in the family could lead to confusion and work having to be redone.

Keep everyone in the family informed about construction progress and how it could impact them. Everyone should be aware of hazards and where they need to cooperate with the contractor's team. Inform your partner of design changes, problems and delays. By the same token, everyone in the family should be able to discuss problems they see with the contractor or the quality of work with you.

Everyone in the family must remain civil with the construction crew, no matter how frustrated they may be with the construction process.

Summary

➢ Before contractors start on the project there are a number of items that should be checked to ensure that everything is ready.

➢ Contractors should always work safely.

➢ The environment shouldn't be damaged during construction.

➢ The contractor should have facilities for their use during construction, which includes toilets, stores, etc. Depending on the contract these could be supplied by you or by the contractor.

➢ It's good practice to have a kick-off or pre-works meeting with the contractor's team to set the project ground rules.

➢ You should check all construction drawings carefully to ensure that they are an accurate representation of what you require.

➢ It's good practice to keep your neighbours informed of the construction work and how it may impact them.

➢ Contractors shouldn't block sidewalks and verges unless they have permission from the local authorities.

➤ The site should be kept tidy and rubbish must not cause a nuisance and it must be removed regularly.

➤ Care must be taken that surrounding properties aren't damaged.

➤ You need to ensure that the contractor is provided access to the work areas according to the construction schedules and that these work areas are in the state as stipulated in the contract document.

➤ Contractors should not work outside of the working hours prescribed by the local authorities, but in any case should not create undue noise and inconvenience to the neighbours.

➤ Good communication with the contractor is essential.

➤ All instructions of a contractual nature must be in writing. Any concerns must be addressed to the contractor in writing.

➤ Photographs are an invaluable record of construction progress and concerns.

➤ Asking the contractor to provide samples or to construct mock-ups is useful.

➤ It's important that the contractor's work meets the contract specifications, the local building regulations and that it's aesthetically pleasing.

➤ There are often regulatory inspections which need to be carried out to satisfy the authorities, or the bank loan's officer. The contractor must provide adequate notification that work will be ready for inspection.

➤ You should regularly check the work. Inform the contractor of concerns.

➤ Materials supplied by you must arrive in time so the contractor isn't delayed.

➤ If you have a number of subcontractors employed by you they need to be managed so that they don't delay other contractors and they must work according to the agreed construction schedule.

➤ A construction schedule is a vital construction management tool and you should continually monitor the contractor's progress against the agreed construction schedule.

➤ You must limit variations, changes and delays because these will cost additional money – money which may not be allowed in your budget.

➤ It's good practice to maintain an accurate daily diary which records the contractor's resources, progress and problems. If the contractor requests you to sign their diary this should be diligently checked to ensure it is correct.

➤ Good record keeping is essential for all construction projects.

➤ From time to time things go wrong on construction projects. It's important to notice problems when they arise and immediately take steps to solve the problem, or limit damage caused by the problem.

Always take care not to get in the way, or unnecessarily hold-up progress.

Chapter 9 – Contractual Issues – legal matters

Frequently projects go wrong and the contractor and the owner engage each other in lengthy and costly legal battles. These may arise because:

➢ There's a poor contract in place which doesn't adequately describe the scope of the work and the contractor's and owner's (your) obligations. Or, the contract is flawed with loop-holes and contradictory clauses.

➢ You don't understand the contract fully, including your rights and obligations in terms of the contract.

➢ The contractor doesn't understand the contract.

➢ One, or both parties doesn't act in good faith, or in terms of the contract.

➢ There's a lack of communication between the parties.

➢ One of the parties is obstinate, or doesn't want to admit they're wrong.

It's essential that:

➢ You understand that changes, delays and instructions caused by you, or those acting on your behalf, can have a profound impact on the project giving rise to delays and variations. Even the simplest change could have a knock-on impact on other activities which you haven't considered or aren't aware of.

➢ Your expectations should be clear, consistent and achievable from the start of the project.

➢ You know that failure to understand the contract, or assumptions made incorrectly, is no excuse for non-compliance of the obligations and terms of the contract.

➢ You understand that the contract is the law on the project, and all actions are judged using this document. It's not about who will be nice, who will forgive, rather it's about complying with the terms of the contract. The fact that the contractor has a legitimate variation claim should be no reason to argue that they're being unfair, or to assume that they're crooks only out to steal money from you.

➢ All parties continually communicate with each other, immediately notifying the other party of concerns, changes and possible impacts on the project.

➢ You understand that even if the contractor hasn't said that there will be an extra cost, that this doesn't mean there won't be a claim from them later.

> ➤ When in doubt you ask for expert advice.

The Contract agreement – all the rules for the project

The contract agreement is a legally binding contract which binds the parties of the agreement together, setting out their obligations and rights. Unfortunately, some agreements are one-sided which offer little protection to one of the parties or places undue risk on them. Contract agreements should be fair, assigning risks to the party that best controls them, while offering protection to both parties should the other party not fulfil their obligations. If this document is poorly worded, inconsistent, or incomplete, you may find that you have little protection should the contractor fail to deliver the project or not meet all their contractual obligations, possibly causing you additional expenses and leading to protracted legal arguments.

The contract must be appropriate for the type of work. Construction projects vary, from ones that only have one trade and are worth a few hundred dollars, to contracts to construct the complete house, which could be worth several hundred thousand dollars. Clearly the project worth a few hundred dollars shouldn't warrant a contract document more than a few paragraphs. While the contract for the house is usually a more complex document.

The contract can take many forms and it may be a simple one page document, or a weighty, lengthy legal document. However, care should be taken with lengthy documents that there aren't conflicting clauses, and that the document doesn't contain so many specifics that by implication what's not mentioned becomes an exclusion. The contract document normally doesn't have to be hugely lengthy – less than a dozen pages should suffice. It's also not necessary to be using extravagant legal language. Simple everyday language is normally sufficient. Terminologies and abbreviations used in the contract documents must be used with consistency and explained in the contract document so there're no misunderstandings. Contracts must avoid confusing and ambiguous language and there should be no contradictory clauses.

The contract agreement should include some, or all of the following:
> ➤ Signatures of the authorised representatives of both parties (you and the contractor). The contract could be null and void if the contractor's secretary or supervisor has signed the contract and they don't have the authority to sign on the contractor's behalf.
> ➤ Drawings.
> ➤ The project schedule, or milestone dates when the project must be completed.
> ➤ The scope of work (what the contractor must do).
> ➤ General terms and conditions – including payment terms.
> ➤ The contract price – what the contractor will be paid for the work.
> ➤ Names and addresses of the contracting parties (you and the contractor).

➤ Project specific conditions. These could include complying with specific estate rules and requirements, or explicit requirements that you may have, such as protecting certain trees and vegetation, or limiting working hours. Remember that any additional items which you've forgotten and add after the contract is signed could give the contractor the right to claim a variation.

➤ The location of the project (physical address).

➤ The date when the contract comes into effect (starts).

➤ Defects and warranty periods. See Chapter 11.

➤ Definitions of terminology used.

➤ The obligations and responsibilities of the parties.

➤ Specifications applicable to the project.

➤ Penalties, or liquidated damages, for late completion – although few contractors will agree to this item.

➤ Exclusions and work to be done by others.

➤ Any other specific conditions which you think are pertinent.

Preferably it should also include a termination clause and a dispute resolution procedure.

It's advisable to get an expert to check the contract before signing it. It's important to check that the contents of the contract cover all the work the contractor was asked to price and that there aren't additional clauses which weren't included in the original pricing documents.

When does a contract exist?

For a contract to exist there must be a formal offer which must be accepted in an unequivocal way.

> *For example: If a painter submits a quote to paint a house and you tell the painter you like the price, it doesn't mean that you've accepted the painter's price and appointed them to do the work. For a contract to exist you would have to say something to the effect that you accept the quote and would like the painter to undertake the work.*

The contract can be verbal which can be as legally binding as a written agreement, though a verbal agreement is often problematic since it's difficult to prove what was said and agreed.

An offer can be withdrawn before it's accepted providing the withdrawal is explicit and preferably in writing.

> *Example: To use the same example above, it won't be good enough if the painter submits the quotation and in later discussion with you says he's not sure if their price is correct, rather, the painter needs to formally state they've submitted the wrong price and are withdrawing their quotation.*

In certain cases a contract may not exist, for example if:

➤ The contract is fundamentally flawed.

> ➤ One of the parties is a minor, mentally impaired, bankrupt, a prisoner, or under duress or unfair influence.
> ➤ The agreement includes false statements.
> ➤ One of the parties knowingly causes the other party to commit an illegal act.
> ➤ There's a condition precedent (for example if the contract states that you need to obtain finance for the work and you're unable to do so).
> ➤ An act of God makes it impossible to carry out the terms of the contract (for example a builder is contracted to renovate a house but before they start the house burns down).

Nevertheless, it's important to be familiar with the laws governing the contract as these differ between countries, impacting on whether the contract is legally binding.

Types of contract

Contracts can be standard industry documents, contractor drafted contracts, or even your own form of contract.

For most building projects contractors prefer using their form of contract. This is particularly the case with suppliers, installers and home-builders. However, it's possible to use an industry standard form of contract, or you may prepare your own contract. It should be noted that many contractors will be loath to sign contract documents that owners have prepared. If you want to use a specific form of contract this should be given (or specified) when the contractor is requested to price the work. Asking the contractor to sign a contract document which they didn't have when they priced the project may give them an opportunity to submit a variation claim. If the terms of the contract you propose using are too onerous then contractors could decline to price your project.

The motto of any contract should be to keep it simple and always seek expert advice.

Standard forms of contract – keeping it simple

There are many standard forms of contract which are used internationally, within certain countries, or are promoted by some industry bodies. So for instance there is often a contract for home builders.

The advantage of using a standard form of contract is that they've been tailored to specific needs of that industry, they have been drafted by experts within the industry, have been tested legally in the country, they are usually complete and fair to both parties and they're usually readily understood by contractors.

Unfortunately some contractors are tempted to tinker with the contract, deleting some clauses and adding others. This could make the contract one-sided, even unworkable with contradictions and loopholes.

Some of these contracts are licensed and there's a small fee to be paid to the originators of the document. Failing to pay this fee could make the document null and void. Many of these documents can only be used on condition that the main clauses aren't altered. Usually these documents provide blank spaces to insert the names and addresses of the contracting parties, the contract price, start and completion dates, and project specific conditions. All pages to the contract should be signed by you and the designated representative of the contractor (usually the owner or a person appointed by the owner).

It should be noted that even when using a standard form of contract this will in most cases refer to the special conditions and the specifications pertaining to your project. But again, you should take care that the special conditions included in the contract document don't conflict with the general conditions causing ambiguity.

Contractor drafted contracts

Often contractors draft the contract documents. Many of these documents are flawed since they could offer you little protection, they are often one-sided giving the contractor rights to literally do as they please, they could contain contradictory clauses, or they're incomplete and don't include some important points.

If you're prepared to accept such a contract you need to carefully check the terms to ensure that they're agreeable to you and that you will be protected should a dispute arise. It's always worth having a legal expert scrutinise the contract. Check the contract to ensure that all the items that you want included in the contract have been included.

Memorandum of understanding

A memorandum of understanding is sometimes used as a first stage in establishing a contracting relationship between the parties. A MOU can be legally binding provided it's signed by both parties, it clearly identifies the subject matter and it identifies the intention.

The MOU would normally point the way forward to establishing a formal contract.

A MOU can be used when negotiating resolution of disputes since it serves to summarise progress made at a meeting, confirming points of agreement and often a way forward to resolve the dispute.

Your (owner's) obligations – what you must do

You have certain obligations which include:
- ➢ Ensuring that you have all the finance in place to make payments to the contractor in terms of the contract.
- ➢ That you own the property where the work is to be executed, or have permission in writing from the registered rightful owner.
- ➢ Paying the contractors for all legitimate invoices in terms of the contract.

- Promptly assessing and resolving variation claims.
- Ensuring project issues and queries are promptly dealt with.
- Demarcating property boundaries – unless this is designated to others.
- Putting all building approvals in place – unless this is delegated to the contractor or project manager.
- Checking drawings supplied by the designer or contractor to ensure that they comply with your requirements.
- Dealing with all parties in a fair and reasonable way.
- Adjudicating all quotes and prices honestly and fairly, without sharing prices of other contractors with your preferred contractor who is then asked to beat the price.
- Checking that the contractor and designers have the required skills and resources to deliver the house you are looking for and that they're reputable. Never focus only on price alone when selecting your contractor.
- Checking that the contractor delivers the correct quality through the course of the project. When you don't have the relevant experience to check the quality then appoint an experienced clerk of works or project manager to regularly check quality.
- Not engaging in any unethical practices, such as encouraging contractors and designers to perform tasks contrary to codes, or to pay bribes.
- Not unnecessarily withholding approvals of drawings, samples or of completed work.
- Not occupying the facility until all occupation permissions, approvals and permits have been received.
- Not condoning any unsafe practices or work. In some jurisdictions the owner could be held liable for poor safety practices of their builder.
- Ensuring that there's adequate insurance in place.
- Where you delegate authority to a project manager, ensuring that person has the authority, power and experience to carry out these duties and that they understand the levels of authority you've given to them.
- Ensuring that you have the appropriate expectations for the project and that the designers and contractor understand these expectations and are capable of meeting them.
- Immediately notifying the contractor of any concerns regarding progress, quality, budget and safety.
- Only communicating with the contractor's designated responsible person unless there's an emergency.
- Wearing the correct personal protective equipment (as requested by the contractor) when visiting the construction work. Always obey safety signage on the project and stay away from dangerous activities.
- Not obstructing the work in anyway, other than for safety reasons, or reasons outlined in the contract document.

> Not removing portions of the work from the contractor for undue reason, especially not to give it to a cheaper contractor.
> Fulfilling your obligations in terms of the contract.
> Ensuring that materials and equipment supplied by you and your suppliers are available when required.
> Where required, providing services and utilities to the contractor.
> Understanding the contract documentation.

Project manager's obligations

If you have appointed a project manager then their responsibilities should be stated in their contract document and could include:

> Managing and coordinating the various contractors.
> Ensuring the project is delivered on time.
> Managing and coordinating the designers, ensuring that they provide construction information as required by the contractor and that this information is complete and sufficient for the contractor.
> Checking that the work meets the applicable specifications and quality requirements.
> Ensuring that all contractors work safely.
> Ensuring that the contractor has access to the work areas.
> Immediately notifying you of problems, delays and additional costs.
> Acting within their limits of authority and the mandate you give them.
> Acting in a fair and impartial manner.
> Not engaging in any illegal practices, nor condoning or overlooking illegal actions by other parties, or encouraging other parties to act in an illegal manner.
> Maintaining accurate project records.
> Regularly communicating with you, including providing project progress and budget updates.
> Checking all invoices and variation claims.
> Promptly dealing with all queries and problems.
> Ensuring that the project is delivered according to your requirements.
> Arranging all permits and permissions.
> Preparing contract documentation for contractors, if this is a requirement.

Designer's obligations

The designer's obligations include:

> Ensuring that their design complies with local, state and national design codes and requirements.
> Making sure that their designs are accurate, workable and practical.

➤ Supplying drawings which are complete, with all setting out information, no discrepancies and which have all the information the contractor requires to construct the project.

➤ Taking into account the work and requirements of other designers on the project, such as electrical, plumbing, architecture and air-conditioning.

➤ Taking responsibility for the integrity of the design.

➤ Ensuring that the design takes account of your requirements and scope of work.

➤ Responding promptly to queries from the contractor.

➤ That their design takes account of known project conditions as well as conditions that they should have been aware of.

➤ That their design is a cost effective solution, taking account of your requirements and directions.

➤ Obtaining your approvals of the design.

➤ Informing you when your requests and requirements aren't reasonable, will add unnecessary costs, or are contrary to best practices. That they provide impartial advice. That they inform you timeously when your expectations are unreasonable or can't be met.

➤ Acting in a fair and impartial manner.

➤ Not engaging in illegal practices, and not eliciting bribes or specifying products where they will gain other advantages.

➤ Obtaining all statutory permissions for the design, unless these are the responsibility of another party.

Contractor's obligations

The contractor's responsibilities include:

➤ Managing and supervising their portion of works so that the project is completed on time, without safety or environmental incidents, that it attains the required quality standards, complies with the contract specifications and requirements and with minimal fuss to you.

➤ That they don't subcontract large portions of the work without your permission, or sublet the complete project to another contractor.

➤ When responsible for the design, ensuring that the design meets all the applicable codes and regulations, it's fit for purpose, and it satisfies your requirements and expectations.

➤ Ensuring they have adequate resources with the required skills for the job.

➤ That they don't engage in illegal practices.

➤ That they regularly communicate with you.

➤ That they don't unreasonably withhold permission for you to visit the work site.

➤ Paying all their employees, subcontractors and suppliers on time.

> ➤ That they ensure that all their workers, subcontractors and suppliers conduct themselves in a manner that won't be offensive to you, your family or the general public. This includes refraining from unruly behaviour, unnecessary noise and offensive language.
> ➤ Protecting existing service and utility lines and taking due care to locate them.
> ➤ Protecting existing structures.
> ➤ Not starting work before checking that all permits and permissions are in place.
> ➤ Complying with all state, local council and estate rules and requirements.
> ➤ Making themselves aware of the project site conditions before pricing the work.
> ➤ Ensuring they've priced all of the known project conditions and that their price is complete without errors.
> ➤ Ensuring that they have sufficient finance to carry out the work in terms of the contract payment terms.
> ➤ Invoicing for completed work in accordance with the contract conditions. These invoices should have the relevant supporting documentation so that they can be checked, as well as any other documentation as required in the contract document, which could include test and inspection certificates.
> ➤ Ensuring that their employees, subcontractors and suppliers understand the project conditions and rules, that they work safely and deliver the required quality.
> ➤ Having a duty to enquire (this would include querying discrepancies in information and informing you immediately of any concerns they have with the design).
> ➤ Reviewing drawings to ensure that they have sufficient information to construct the work.
> ➤ Setting out the work.
> ➤ Taking delivery and off-loading all materials they're responsible for.
> ➤ That they ensure all work is inspected and passed as required by legislation, good construction practices and the contract requirements.
> ➤ Notifying you or the project manager immediately a delay or variation becomes known to them.
> ➤ Following instructions from you or the project manager, providing these instructions are lawful and in terms of the contract.
> ➤ Ensuring that there's a delegated responsible representative from them for the project and that you and the project manager have their contact details (including emergency contact details for after-hours problems).
> ➤ Taking every action to avoid disputes.
> ➤ Understanding the terms and conditions of the contract.
> ➤ Rectifying defective work.

> Maintaining accurate project records.
> Not stopping work for any reason that's not outlined in the contract document, unless it's on safety grounds, or due to adverse weather.

Insurances – your protection

It's important that all insurances are in place before work begins. This includes checking that existing policies won't be adversely affected by the work. For instance, work in existing buildings may impact the security of the facility, or expose the property to the risk of damage from the weather or from flooding. You should discuss the work with insurance providers to ensure that the policy is not made void. Additional cover may have to be purchased to cover any shortfalls. Alternatively, the insurer may require mitigating measures to be installed, such as extra security, more firefighting equipment and so on.

Depending on the contractual terms and conditions some insurances will be the responsibility of you and some the responsibility of the contractor. Most insurances are renewed annually so it's good practice to have a schedule of all insurances so that action can be taken timeously before they fall due. In addition, when project conditions change, the contract value changes, or the project time-line is extended it will be necessary to advise the insurer, and in some cases additional insurance may have to be taken out. Failure to notify the insurer of changes could negate the policy.

Insurance that needs to be considered includes:
> Insurance of the project to cover for damage and theft on the project.
> Worker's compensation insurance purchased by the contractor to cover injury of their workers on the project. You don't want to be paying their medical bills or have no hospital willing to treat an injured person on your project because they have no medical insurance.
> Construction equipment insurance.
> Third party liability insurance, which protects you from claims or lawsuits from third parties for damages caused by the construction work. For instance, damage to a neighbouring property or injury to a member of the public.
> Design indemnity insurance which should be provided by designers and contractors who have a design component in their contract. This protects you from additional costs incurred as a result of a design fault.

Insurances provided by the contractor must be checked to ensure that they're valid, that they're of sufficient value and there aren't clauses or conditions which are unacceptable or can't be fulfilled.

It should be noted that insurance claims may be voided if:
> You were found to be negligent – such as failing to take suitable safety or security precautions.
> Construction equipment was operated by an individual who didn't have the

required license, someone who was intoxicated, or a person who wasn't trained to use the item.

➤ Equipment was used which was obviously faulty.

➤ The insurance provider wasn't provided all the details of the project, or the value or methods changed from what they were provided.

➤ The policy has lapsed or premiums haven't been paid.

Like all insurance policies it pays to read the terms and conditions to ensure that the policy is suitable, that it will cover all the expected risks and it won't be rendered null and void. When unsure, expert advice should be got from the insurance broker and other experts. Always get all questions answered in writing. In some instances certain events may require additional insurance, such as for flood or storm damage.

Insurance claims – make sure your claim isn't rejected

Some events are claimable under either your insurance, or the contractor's insurance. These include losses due to accidents, theft, or from weather events. Most policies cover for the cost of removing debris and repairing the work and replacing damaged items. They usually don't compensate the contractor or you for the lost time on the project.

It's always necessary to notify your insurance broker immediately loss or damage occurs on your project, even if you believe it's the contractor's fault, or that their insurance will cover the loss (no matter that the contractor has admitted the fault and told you that they've notified their insurer). Always take date stamped photographs of the damage and the incident. Normally rectification work shouldn't begin until the insurance assessor has inspected the damage, although all areas must be made safe as soon as possible.

Bond (surety) – insurance if the contractor doesn't perform

The contractor usually has to provide a surety bond (performance bond) which is insurance in case they're unable to fulfil their obligations of the project. The bond must be made out in the name of the contracting party and must be valid for the duration of the project and should be for the value of the contract.

The bond should be issued by a reputable institution (bank or insurer). The wording on the surety should be checked, since some wording can make it difficult to claim should the contractor default on the contract, or fail to perform in accordance with the contract terms. If in doubt, get an expert to look at it and provide advice.

The tender and contract documents should specify the guarantees, sureties and insurances required for the project. These must be received before work begins.

Sureties and bonds may have to be amended and reissued if the contract value increases, or if the contract period is extended.

Sureties, guarantees and warranties should be kept in a safe place. Sureties should be returned to the contractor once they've completed all their obligations on the project.

Should the contractor fail to complete the project because they went bankrupt, or they abandoned the project, you can claim against the surety or bond from the institution that issued the surety. You can claim all reasonable costs you incurred to complete the project, providing these don't exceed the value of the surety.

Variation claims – they're going to cost you money

Contractors can claim for any changes to the scope of work included in the contract document, or for impacts caused by events they could not have reasonable foreseen and allowed for. These include:

> Changes to drawings or specifications which cause delays or create additional costs. A change in specification could result in an item becoming more expensive. Changes in drawings after the contractor has completed the work means they must redo the completed work. It should be noted that changes to drawings prepared by the contractor or their designers, where these changes weren't caused by you or someone in your team or family, are not claimable from you.

> Additional scope (more work).

> Errors on drawings which cause them delays or additional work, where the drawings weren't supplied by the contractor or a party contracted by them.

> Delays – see below.

> Changes to the contract or commercial terms.

> Changes in legislation (for example an increase in sales tax, or an additional paid public holiday – however, it should be noted that increases in company or personal taxes don't apply).

> Instructions changing the work, or causing the contractor to redo completed work where the finished work was completed correctly.

> Damage to the completed work caused by you, or your other contractors, which the contractor must repair.

> Site conditions which were different to what an experienced contractor could have been expected to foresee. This could include dealing with rock, hazardous materials, hidden services, etc. These conditions could result in a delay (see next section) as well as additional costs to deal with the condition.

It should be noted that:

> There must be a proven additional cost to the contractor.

> The contractor must provide a breakdown of these costs. This breakdown should relate to similar items in the contract document, or should be proven reasonable costs incurred for the item.

> The contractor should notify you immediately they become aware that there will be additional costs, and where possible, allow you to take corrective actions to limit these costs, such as selecting cheaper alternatives.

> ➤ Some variations can be negative where work has been removed or specifications have been reduced when the contractor hasn't already incurred costs in relation to the original scope or specifications. It should be noted that you can't unilaterally remove scope from a contractor and give it to another contractor without agreement from the first contractor. It should also be noted that the contractor may be entitled to retain the profit difference on the cost between the original item and the revised scope.

When a variation has been agreed the contract sum should be amended to include the value of the variation.

It's good practice to list all the variations (even possible variations) with their amounts and whether they've been agreed or not. Referring to this list you can check off when the work has been completed – sometimes in the rush to complete the project the contractor could overlook completing an item. In addition your budget can be updated whenever a new variation is added and when the value of the variation is agreed.

Delay claims – why your project won't be finished on time

Contractors may submit delay claims. These claims usually request an extension of time as well as additional costs for the contractor to remain on the project longer. Delay claims could arise for a number of reasons:

> ➤ Delays in granting the contractor access to site or to a portion of work.
> ➤ Late construction information supplied to them by you or your designers.
> ➤ Unexpected ground or site conditions which an experienced contractor couldn't have foreseen. This could include the presence of unexpected utility lines, hidden rock, poor founding conditions, etc.
> ➤ Instructions issued by you or your representative which changes the scope of the contractor's work, or requests the contractor to stop work for reasons not attributable to any fault of the contractor.
> ➤ Late permits and permissions caused by you or your project manager.
> ➤ You or your designer changing drawings or specifications.
> ➤ Your actions delay the work, for example, your appointed subcontractor is late, materials supplied by you are late, or work areas aren't ready for the contractor.
> ➤ Late approvals of drawings supplied by the contractor.
> ➤ Drawing errors on drawings supplied by you or your designer.
> ➤ Changes in legislation which were unexpected.
> ➤ Extreme weather events that directly impact the construction work.

It should be noted that contractors aren't entitled to claim an extension of time for:

> ➤ Delays caused by the contractor, their suppliers or subcontractors, or for items that they're responsible for, or when their equipment breaks.

➤   Delays in receiving information from designers appointed by the contractor.

➤   Normal weather events, unless the contract agreement says they can claim for these events. So if the project receives fifty millimetres of rain (two inches) in the month and this prevents the contractor working for two days, they can't claim a delay if the average rain for the area in that month is fifty or more millimetres. However, if the average rain for the month was twenty-five millimetres (one inch) they could probably claim a delay for half the time they lost, since the project received double the average rainfall – in other words they could claim for one of the two days lost due to rain.

➤   Delays caused by late permissions from the authorities where the contractor was responsible for arranging these permissions.

➤   An obstacle or event that was obvious when they priced the project. So for instance, if rock was visible on the property before work started, there were known obstructions or restrictions on the site, or they had access to drawings showing utility lines, then they should have allowed for these in their price and construction schedule.

➤   Their or their subcontractor's poor work, or work that doesn't comply with the specifications or building regulations which has to be redone.

➤   The contractor's work being stopped because of noncompliance with safety, permits, permissions or specifications.

➤   Disruptions to the utility supply, unless this is a direct fault of you, for example, because of unpaid utility bills or damage to the supply caused by your actions.

➤   Drawing errors on drawings supplied by the contractor or their designer.

➤   Weather events which have no impact on the construction work. So for instance, even though it's raining if the work is all inside or under cover then the rain should not impact progress.

➤   Delays that don't directly impact the current progress. So for instance, the contractor usually doesn't require paint colours until a few days before they plan to paint. So they can't claim a delay because you only provided the paint colours two weeks before they were planning to paint

➤   The contractor complying with current legislation or existing good practices.

➤   Where you were unaware of the obligation that the contractor is claiming you haven't fulfilled. So for instance, if the contractor requires details of the kitchen cabinetry eight weeks ahead of when it's installed then at the start of the project they must make you aware of when they require these details so that you have the opportunity to provide them timeously.

➤   A consequential delay. For example, usually a contractor can claim for the time lost during an unexpected rainstorm, but not for cleaning up the mess left by the storm, or for drying flooded work areas.

➤   Delays to them when they're ahead of schedule. The delay must cause the project to slip when measured against the agreed construction schedule.

Therefore, if the contractor is two weeks ahead of the agreed schedule and they are delayed for two weeks because you haven't provided access or information for them to continue, they can't claim a delay if you provided the information on the dates required in the agreed schedule. If you provide the information one week later than the date on the schedule, but the contractor was delayed three weeks, they can only claim the one week delay as measured against the agreed schedule.

Concurrent delays – don't let your contractor double dip

Sometimes, two or more delay events happen at the same time. The contractor can only claim for the overall effect of the combined delays and not for the sum of the individual delays. For example, if the contractor can't start work because the information provided by you was ten days later, and also couldn't start because the materials supplied by you were five days late, then they can't claim five days for the late materials plus ten days for the late information, since these delays occurred at the same time and the overall delay was only ten days.

Sometimes the contractor causes one of the delays, so for example, if the contractor's employees were on strike (work stoppage) for ten days, and during this time materials provided by you arrived five days late, then you could successfully argue that the fact that your materials arrived late had no impact on the project progress since the contractor's employees were on strike for this period and would not have used the materials supplied by you even if they had arrived on time.

Standing time claims – contractors must prove their costs

When contractors have resources on the project which they can't use because you stopped the work for reasons unrelated to the contractor's actions, or because the contractor couldn't access the site, or couldn't do their work because your other contractors hadn't completed their work, then the contractor may claim the costs of their resources (labour and equipment) which are now unable to work. It should be noted that:

➢ The costs must be provable and justifiable.

➢ The contractor should immediately notify you that the resources are standing so that you can verify the numbers, so you have an opportunity to rectify the situation quickly thus enabling the resources to start work again, or that where possible you can give the contractor other work for their resources.

➢ The contractor can't claim standing time for their resources where this was caused by their actions such as their materials being unavailable, unsafe acts by their team, or permits which they had to organise not being available. Nor can they claim standing time for a weather related event.

➢ Where the delay is going to be for an extended period you could elect to instruct the contractor to demobilise the resources and remobilise them again when needed. The demobilisation and remobilisation costs will be for your account, but once the instruction is given the standing time claims should cease by the end of that day.

➤ The contractor should not claim for resources off the site, even if they can't use these resources elsewhere. So, if the resources were due on the project tomorrow or next week, and you informed the contractor that they wouldn't be able to access the work area then they can't claim standing time for these resources because they weren't on the project yet.

Force majeure – when it's out of everyone's control

Force majeure is the term given to events that neither you nor the contractor have control over, such as extreme weather events (for example, rainfall above the norm for that time of year in the area), earthquakes and national strikes which impact the construction. Normally the contractor is entitled to an extension of time for the time lost due to these events, but isn't entitled to additional costs associated with this lost time.

Avoiding disputes – often only lawyers benefit

Submitting a variation claim isn't a dispute. A dispute arises when you and the contractor can't agree that a variation claim is legitimate, or on the quantum of the claim. Other reasons for disputes could be when one of the parties has not fulfilled their contractual obligations despite being repeatedly requested to do so. Disputes can be costly as they invariably involve legal costs. They are also time consuming and they can disrupt the project. Where possible disputes should be avoided by:

➤ Ensuring there's a legally enforceable contract in place which is clear and unambiguous without contradictory clauses.

➤ Ensuring all communications of a contractual nature are in writing.

➤ Understanding the terms and conditions of the contract and complying with your contractual obligations.

➤ Asking the contractor to price variations before giving them the go-ahead to proceed with the work. Once the work is done it's more difficult to argue the cost with the contractor and you certainly can't ask them to undo the work if you're unhappy with the price.

➤ Asking for expert help when necessary.

➤ Keeping personalities and emotions out of negotiations.

➤ Always being willing to talk and negotiate.

➤ Being willing to concede when you're wrong.

➤ Employing reputable contractors who don't have a record of regularly entering into disputes with their clients.

> ➤   Administering the contract in a spirit of honesty and cooperation.

> ➤   Understanding when your actions have caused additional costs for the contractor.

> ➤   Not withholding payment for undue reasons, or reasons which aren't allowed in the contract.

> ➤   Understanding the consequences of escalating the matter so that lawyers are involved.

> ➤   When a dispute has arisen between you and an employee of the contractor, then discuss the matter with their manager to see if they can resolve the issue. Often problems arise because of personalities or misinterpretation by individuals.

> ➤   Always being open to holding a meeting to discuss the problem instead of firing off letters and emails. Many issues are a result of misunderstandings which can sometimes be more easily resolved over a cup of coffee. Needless to say agreements of a contractual or financial nature made at these meetings should be confirmed later in writing.

Terminating the contract – it's not so easy

Terminating a contract is fraught with hazards and must be done with caution, carefully following the procedures laid out in the contract document. Indeed wrongful termination could provide the contractor reason to terminate the contract with just cause, meaning they could claim for their costs incurred because of the termination.

So, even if the contractor is not performing, they are late, or their quality is poor, it doesn't give you the right to terminate the contract. You also definitely can't terminate a contract because you've found a cheaper contractor.

Termination for convenience can be sufficient reason for termination and might be due to you not receiving finance for the project. However, you will have to prove that you've actively sort finance that you had a reasonable chance of receiving. In this case the contractor is entitled to the full costs they've incurred to date plus the costs to demobilise their people, sheds and equipment. The contractor should agree to this termination, which they normally would do as they wouldn't want to do work that they're unlikely to get paid for.

Termination for frustration may happen when due to no fault of either party the work cannot proceed. So for instance, if the contractor was engaged to modify an existing house which was then destroyed by a fire or flood the work would become impossible and unnecessary, so the contract could be terminated. The contract could also be terminated if unforeseen site conditions were uncovered which made the project far more expensive to build, or which would radically change the originally envisaged construction methods. Again the contractor is entitled to all their costs that they've incurred plus their demobilisation costs.

Repudiation is termination because the contractor has refused to carry out reasonable work, has abandoned the project, or employed another contractor (without permission) to carry out the work. In this case you would be entitled to claim from the contractor the costs you've incurred due to their actions.

Before terminating a contract it's important that a process is followed. So for instance, if the contractor is not performing they need to be notified in writing as to what the problem is, how they should rectify the problem and by when the problem must be rectified (this should be a reasonable time frame). This notification must be delivered to the correct address as specified in the contract document. Should the problem not be fixed then a follow-up notification should be delivered setting out the steps that will be taken to terminate the contract if the problem isn't rectified. Only once the time periods have expired can a formal termination notice be issued to the contractor.

It's important to note that once a contract is terminated you have no rights in terms of the contract and can't claim penalties for delays or for defective workmanship (although costs for repairing defective work can be deducted from outstanding monies due the contractor), and the warranties will often become null and void. Contracts also can't be terminated for breaches which could be considered as minor (say that the quality of tiling was poor) or which only impact part of the work.

Contracts should not be terminated without employing expert assistance.

Liquidated damages (penalties) – when the contractor pays

Damages can be imposed on the contractor when they don't meet the contractual milestone dates. These damages should only be applied when you have physically been unable to occupy the house because of a fundamental flaw which means that the home can't be safely used, or when said occupation would create excessive inconvenience to you and your family, or when an occupation permit can't be issued. Minor defects should not prevent you from occupying your home.

The amount of damages should be a justifiable amount which reflects the actual costs of being unable to occupy the house on the milestone date. These costs could include additional rental costs and payments for cancelled removal costs. However, the costs often can't include for inconvenience and disruption to you and your family.

Liens – when your house doesn't belong to you

Some contracts allow the contractor to impose a lien on the project if there's a dispute, or for non-payment. Essentially a lien gives the right to the contractor to take possession of the site and effectively lock you, the owner, out. This could be quite devastating, so it's important to ensure payments are timeously made to the contractor and that disputes are resolved when they arise.

Unfortunately the contractor's subcontractors may have the right to take out a lien on your project, which may then prevent the contractor from handing the project to you. It's therefore important to ensure that the contractor pays their subcontractors on time and resolves disputes with them as soon as possible so that they don't impact your project. In this case you could claim damages from the contractor, but this will be of little consolation to you for the frustration caused.

In some cases it may be possible (indeed preferable) to delete lien clauses in a contract document to prevent the contractor exercising a lien over your new home. Also insist that contractors don't enter contracts with their subcontractors which contain lien clauses.

Summary

Frequently projects are delayed and they increase in value. This is often a result of changes and delays caused by you or your team, or because the work and site conditions weren't fully described in the contract document.

There should be a binding contract between you and your contractor. This contract should clearly spell out the terms and conditions of the contract, the scope of work, and the obligations and duties of the contracting parties. The contract document provides the 'rules' governing the project and all parties must act in terms of these rules. The contract must be clear, enforceable and not have contradictory clauses and loopholes. There are many different forms of contract, but using a standard form, applicable to the project work, and regularly used by the building industry in your country is best.

All parties must understand the terms and provisions of the contract and must fulfil their obligations in terms of this contract.

It's essential that all insurances are in place, that they are of sufficient value and that you can comply with the conditions within the insurance contract.

The contractor usually has to supply a surety bond to cover you in the event that they don't fulfil their obligations, which could include them going bankrupt before the project is complete. These bonds must be from a reputable institution and must be for the value of the contract. In addition the contractor has to provide warranties and guarantees to cover defective work.

The contractor is entitled to claim for additional costs and delays for extra work, changes to the work, delays caused by you and for events that impacted their work which an experienced contractor could not have reasonably foreseen. Therefore it's important that you minimise changes after the contract is agreed and ensure that you timeously fulfil all your obligations in terms of the contract. The contractor can't claim for delays caused by them or for conditions that they should have expected. Nor can they claim the sum of two or more delays that occur concurrently, rather they can only claim for the overall impact of the delays.

The contractor could be entitled to claim standing time costs for their resources when they don't have access to work areas.

Disputes should be avoided as these are often costly and lengthy and inevitably there are no winners except the lawyers. Rather try and negotiate an equitable solution.

Even when a contractor isn't performing it can be difficult to terminate the contract. Termination procedures must be strictly followed and expert help should be sought.

The contractor, or their subcontractors, could enforce a lien on your property if there's a dispute or their bills haven't been paid. Where possible there should be no lien clauses in the contract.

If you're unable to move into your house on the day specified in the contract because of a fault of the contractor you may have the right to impose damages on them. The amount of damages are usually the costs that you suffer because the project is late.

It's vital that you understand your contractual rights and that you engage experts when you're uncertain. If all parties communicate regularly and act in a fair and reasonable matter then disputes can be avoided.

Chapter 10 – Financial – Money Matters

Nobody wants to overpay contractors, pay for something you didn't get, or have a contractor run off with your money. But, contractors also expect to be paid fairly for work that they've carried out. Payment terms for the contractor are usually spelled out in the contract documents or orders. It's important that you read these carefully and understand them. Sometimes, it's possible to negotiate some of these terms and conditions during the pricing process, and before signing and agreeing the contract. Once the contract is signed the terms and conditions are binding on all parties.

You must ensure that you will have funds available to pay the contractor when invoices are due. This means that you should have an accurate budget (see Chapter 3) and a forecast cash flow which is linked to the construction schedule.

Each invoice should be carefully checked as outlined below, to ensure that you're only paying what's due in terms of the contract.

Cash flow – don't run out of money

Cash flow is about ensuring that you have money available to pay bills when they're due. Money for your home project could come from different sources, such as bank accounts, bank term deposits, sale of investments, selling a property, investment earnings, salary, family loans, bank loans, and other income. Whatever the source, very few people have all the money for their new house sitting readily available in their bank account. Indeed, to do so may be foolish since it's normally a considerable amount of money that could be earning interest in a more favourable investment. Unfortunately some of the funds will only be available at particular times. Your paycheque arrives monthly, bank loans are often paid in tranches when the project reaches specific milestones and satisfies particular requirements, and of course the sale of investments and property can take time which will depend on market conditions and your asking price.

Apart from the costs of construction there'll be other costs to pay. Some, such as utility connection fees, permit costs and design fees are associated with the construction. But, there are your everyday costs, such as paying taxes, food, schools, medical costs etc. Then of course there are always unexpected costs, such as vehicle repairs and replacement of broken appliances that should be allowed for.

The bills that you have to pay for construction will vary depending on progress, the value of the work completed and the terms of the contractor's payments.

To work out your predicted cash flow you should take the construction schedule and based on the anticipated progress you can plot what amounts will be due when. If you have appointed one main contractor you can ask them for their anticipated invoice amounts and when they'll be required. If you're purchasing most of the materials, and have appointed subcontractors to execute different portions of the projects, you can put the costs of the materials and the various subcontract amounts on a timeline according to when the materials are required, and when the subcontractors will be finished and claiming for their work. Remembering that payments will be due at a set time after the receipt of invoice (which could be seven days, thirty days or at the end of the month).

Knowing when payments are due, you can schedule that you have the required money available to pay the bills, always allowing some slack for unexpected costs.

If you find that you won't have sufficient money available to pay accounts you may have to delay the start of the project, plan the project so that it takes longer, or arrange for bridging finance.

It's important to note that if your contractor works faster than planned, then you may find that you must pay bills sooner. Therefore, as discussed in Chapter 8 it's vital that you regularly monitor your contractor's progress. But, the contractor could also land you in trouble if your bank only releases loan finance on condition certain milestones and conditions are reached and your contractor delays reaching these milestones. In particular, if your contractor goes on to complete other work on the project which you must pay for, but which doesn't satisfy the milestones. This will leave you with contractor's bills to pay, but without the loan finance being released to pay the bills. You must ensure that the contractor meets the milestones that your bank has set for the release of funds, and that they satisfy all of the conditions required by the bank, such as having all test and inspection results and completing all the work associated with the milestone. In fact, if possible, you should ensure that the contractor's payment conditions are linked to the satisfactory release of funds from your bank.

You can improve your cash flow if you can negotiate better payment terms with your suppliers and contractors – that's where you pay them later after receipt of invoice. This needs to be done before agreeing and signing the contract, or when you order materials.

Even having materials delivered a few days later, rather at the beginning of the month than at the end of the previous month, could mean that you pay for them a month later.

It's important to continually track and manage your cash flow because your income streams and your costs can change.

See the next page for an example of a cash flow forecast.

CASH FLOW EXAMPLE

INCOME	PAYMENTS	ESTIMATE	DUE DATE	CASH POSITION AT END OF MONTH	
CASH ON HAND		50,000	31-Jan		
SALARY		5,000	31-Jan		
	MONTHLY COSTS	-4,000	31-Jan		
	DESIGN FEE - DEPOSIT	-5,000	31-Jan	46,000	
	DESIGN FEE - FINAL	-25,000	28-Feb		
	PERMITS	-2,000	28-Feb		
SALARY		5,000	28-Feb		
	MONTHLY COSTS	-3,000	28-Feb		
EX TERM DEPOSIT		50,000	28-Feb	71,000	
	CONTRACTOR DEPOSIT	-40,000	31-Mar		
SALARY		5,000	31-Mar		
	MONTHLY COSTS	-3,000	31-Mar	33,000	
SALE OF HOUSE		300,000	30-Apr		NOTE 1
SALARY		5,000	30-Apr		
	MONTHLY COSTS	-3,000	30-Apr		
	CONTRACTOR 2ND PAY	-40,000	30-Apr	295,000	
SALARY		5,000	31-May		
	MONTHLY COSTS	-3,000	31-May		
	CONTRACTOR 3RD PAY	-60,000	31-May	237,000	
SALARY		5,000	30-Jun		
	MONTHLY COSTS	-3,000	30-Jun		
	CONTRACTOR 4TH	-80,000	30-Jun	159,000	
SALARY		5,000	31-Jul		
	MONTHLY COSTS	-3,000	31-Jul		
	CONTRACTOR 5TH	-90,000	31-Jul	71,000	
SALARY		5,000	31-Aug		
	MONTHLY COSTS	-4,000	31-Aug		
	CONTRACTOR 6TH	-80,000	31-Aug		
BANK LOAN		80,000	31-Aug	72,000	NOTE 2
	UTILITY CONNECTIONS	-5,000	30-Sep		
	LANDSCAPING	-12,000	30-Sep		
	WINDOW TREATMENTS	-9,000	30-Sep		
SALARY		5,000	30-Sep		
	MONTHLY COSTS	-3,000	30-Sep		
	CONTRACTOR FINAL	-30,000	30-Sep	18,000	

NOTE 1: IN THIS EXAMPLE IF THE FUNDS FOR THE SALE OF THE HOUSE AREN'T RECEIVED IN TIME THEN YOU WON'T BE ABLE TO PAY THE CONTRACTOR'S 2ND INVOICE

NOTE 2: IF THE BANK LOAN IS NOT RECEIVED IN TIME YOU WON'T BE ABLE TO PAY THE CONTRACTOR'S 6TH INVOICE. IT MAY BE PRUDENT TO START THE PROJECT ONE MONTH LATER

Checking invoices – don't pay more than you should

Scrutinize invoices thoroughly before paying them, checking:
- ➢ That you received all the items on the invoice and broken items weren't charged.
- ➢ You haven't already paid for the items. Always keep delivery dockets and match them to the invoice. Staple them together. Then once the invoice has been paid mark the invoice clearly as 'paid' with the date of payment.
- ➢ That the rate charged is the same amount as on the order.
- ➢ That where applicable, discounts have been deducted.
- ➢ All arithmetic is correct.
- ➢ The taxes have been correctly applied.
- ➢ There are no additional charges.

Deposits – risky business when paying for work that's not done

Depending on the contract, the contractor may expect to be paid a deposit before they even start work. These deposits could vary from 6% to as high as 50%. Ostensibly this deposit is for the contractor to purchase materials for the project. Unfortunately, often the contractor uses the payment for other projects and you have no control over this. There's always the risk that the contractor could become bankrupt, or simply disappear with your money, or take an extended period before they start work on your project. In some jurisdictions the amount of deposit that the contractor can ask is limited by legislation. Paying a deposit is a risky business since there's often limited recourse to claiming the money back should the project go wrong. Even when the money is used to purchase materials for the project these materials don't belong to you unless the contractor has agreed and signed that they belong to you (ceded the materials to you) but even then, you don't have a guarantee that the materials have been paid for in full by the contractor, so the supplier could in any case lay claim to the materials.

Preferably deposits should be limited to a small amount, it should only be paid to reputable contractors, and not before the contractor has provided a surety bond, or guarantee for the project.

Interim payment valuations – paying for work done

For projects that extend over several months, and depending on the terms of the contract, the contractor will expect to be reimbursed for work that they've completed. This reimbursement could be monthly, or it could be when particular milestones are met (see below).

If the contractor has invoiced for an interim valuation you should ask for a breakdown of their invoice. It's important to check that they've actually done the work they've claimed and that the work is of the desired quality. It may be prudent to engage an expert to check the invoice since you don't want to pay for work which hasn't been completed, which could mean that you're out of pocket if the contractor becomes bankrupt or abandons the project before completing it.

With any invoice check that the amount is correct (including checking all arithmetic and calculations), that previous payments (including deposits) have been correctly deducted, that any retention (retainage money) is correctly deducted, that applicable discounts have been taken, and that the taxes are correct.

Milestone valuations – paying for what's complete

Often contract documents make provision for the contractor to be paid when they achieve specific milestones. For instance, they could specify payments for when the foundations are complete, when the walls are constructed, when the roof is on, and when the house is complete. Regularly these payments are specified in the contract as a percentage of the total contract value, so for instance, the contractor could be paid 20% of the project value when the foundations are complete.

Unfortunately, contractors often specify higher percentages than they're entitled to, so they actually get paid more than the value of work that they've really done. This is beneficial to their cash flow, but it's detrimental to your cash flow. Furthermore, you're at risk should anything go wrong and the contractor abandon the project or become bankrupt. Much of the cost of a new house comes in the finishes which are completed near the end. Sure it may look like your house is half complete after the walls are all up, but the contractor has probably only incurred about 25% of their costs. By the time the roof is on maybe they've incurred 40% of their costs.

Before signing the contract always check the amounts specified for milestone payments. If you're uncertain ask for expert opinion. Try to negotiate the quantum of these payments down. For amounts that seem excessive ask the contractor for a breakdown of the make-up of these payments.

Before making milestone payments always check that the contractor has completed all the work relating to the milestone, including supplying all test results and inspections where relevant.

Non-payment – be careful

You cannot withhold payment from a contractor (or designer, or project manager) without due reason, and such reason should always be in writing and given to the contractor ahead of when payment is due. Payment can be deducted for work claimed by the contractor which they haven't done, work that doesn't meet the required specifications or quality requirements and for back charges – see later.

Payment cannot be withheld for no reason, or because the contractor isn't performing, or they're behind schedule. This could place you in breach of the contract, which could allow the contractor to terminate the contract.

Late payments to contractors could impact the progress of your project since the contractor might not have money to pay their employees' wages, suppliers and subcontractors. In extreme cases, late or non-payment could result in the contractor becoming bankrupt, leaving you with a half completed project, worthless guarantees and additional costs to employ another contractor to complete the work.

Contractors could claim interest on late payments. These interest payments could be listed in the contract document, but at the very least would be at the prime bank lending rates.

From time to time contractors may not pay their suppliers or subcontractors. This usually causes problems to your project, including delays and sometimes even protesting workers which can impact your home and neighbourhood. As tempting as it could be, you should not pay these suppliers, employees and subcontractors and deduct these amounts from your contractor's account, unless you have written agreement from your contractor to do so and they've confirmed the amounts to be paid to these individuals and companies in writing and you get signed receipts from those paid. You have a contract only with your contractor and they're due the full monies they're entitled to, irrespective of what they owe to others for work done on your project.

Final payment valuations – when your house is complete

Final payments should only be released when the contractor has fulfilled all the requirements and their obligations in terms of the contract. See Chapter 11.

Retention (retainage) – your insurance

Retention money, or retainage, is a pre-agreed amount of money, usually expressed as a percentage of the amount due, that's withheld from the contractor's payment until they have satisfactorily completed their contractual obligations. This amount could be 10% for the duration of the contract, with half of this amount released when all the work is complete and the remainder at the end of the maintenance or warranty period. This percentage amount is deducted from every invoice presented by the contractor and applies to the value of work completed excluding sales or value added taxes.

The purpose of retention money is an insurance policy, which seeks to ensure that the contractor completes the project in accordance with the contract.

The norm is that you withhold the money, and any benefits and interest earned would accrue to you. However, in some cases the retention money could be deposited in a separate bank or escrow account and the interest earned in this account would be paid to the contractor when the retention is released.

Retention money must be released when the contractor has met all their obligations. Money can only be deducted from the retention if the contractor has failed to rectify defects within a reasonable time after being requested in writing. You must be able to justify all deductions from the retention money and these must always be reasonable and fair.

I would recommend that you negotiate holding retention money from all major contractors when you finalise the contract. A portion of this money should be kept until the end of the contractor's maintenance period (see Chapter 11).

What are overheads?

Contractors often include overheads in their price for the project. Overheads typically could include the contractor's profit, the contractor's direct project overheads (which may include the costs of their project manager and supervisor, project office, store and toilet rentals, project insurances and sureties, temporary fencing and some equipment costs) and the contractor's indirect management and running costs (such as a portion of their head office costs).

Overheads could be time related, which means that they could increase if the project is delayed for reasons beyond the control of the contractor. They could also be value related, which means that they'll increase if the project value increases. Or, they could be split between the two and even include a fixed portion.

Usually the contractor specifies how their overheads should be paid. They could be paid as a lump sum at the start of the project, or be paid in monthly instalments. You need to understand the amount of overheads and how they'll be paid, since they will impact your cash flow, or even add to your costs.

Generally, when extra work or items are added to the project the contractor will add an amount of overheads to their price for this work. This amount should be related to the overheads specified in the contract. So, if the contractor only has a time related overhead they shouldn't charge you overheads for additional work which will be completed within the contract period other than additional resources required.

Back-charges – when can I make the contractor pay me?

For certain reasons you could deduct monies from the contractor because:
➢ You supplied utilities (power or water), equipment or materials to the contractor which the contractor should have supplied.
➢ The contractor did not deliver a particular item.
➢ The contractor's work didn't meet the specifications or required quality, which the contractor failed to fix after they were issued written instruction, and you had to employ others to fix the work.
➢ The contractor damaged your property, or work done by others, which they failed to fix.

The contractor should always be notified in advance of these impending back-charges. It should be noted, that you can't unilaterally remove work from the contractor and do it yourself, or give the work to another contractor, even if the contractor isn't performing.

Back-charges should be the reasonable actual costs incurred for the item. Where another contractor fixed a problem then this contractor's costs for the repair must be reasonable, and the onus is on you to verify that these charges are sensible. You can't just pay the contractor for the repairs and assume that you can automatically back-charge the responsible contractor for this amount. Contractors will challenge any charges that they view as being unreasonable or excessive.

Cost-plus contracts – paying contractor's costs plus profit

Sometimes, contractors require to be paid their costs (which could include labour, equipment, materials and subcontractors) plus their overheads and profits on these costs (usually expressed as a percentage). They may do this when there's a job which is complex and where they can't quantify the costs (such as for difficult foundations, or when unexpected obstacles are uncovered while excavating on the project) or sometimes just because that's the way they want to charge for their work.

You should always be wary of accepting these arrangements since there's usually little incentive for the contractor to work efficiently and avoid poor productivity and waste of materials and equipment. After all, the more resources they use, the more you'll pay and the bigger profit they'll make. In addition, the onus is on you (or your project manager) to physically check that the people and equipment claimed by the contractor actually all worked the hours on your project, and that the materials were all used on your project. A cost-plus project means that you don't know what the final cost of your project will be and you may find that your budget is quickly blown.

You can always ask the contractor for an estimate of how much the work will cost, but if their eventual costs exceed this amount you'll have no recourse and will be stuck with the large bill. Be very wary of agreeing to the contractor doing work on a cost-plus basis and rather negotiate a fixed price.

Price increases – why did my house cost more than expected?

The prices of construction materials, equipment and labour frequently increases. In countries with a high inflation rate these changes can be significant. But sometimes prices are also affected by the current market conditions. So, if there's a lot of construction taking place in your locality you may experience a shortage of resources and materials which can often drive up prices more quickly than the rate of inflation. Obviously the opposite can occur when the volume of construction work decreases, causing prices to fall as contractors and suppliers become more desperate for work.

Some construction materials are imported and their price is impacted by the exchange rate variation between your country and the country where the product is supplied from.

Case study: A couple in the UK purchased their house as a complete prefabricated kit from Germany. In the time that it took to fabricate the components for the house and deliver them the Pound weakened against the Euro by 20%. Since they were paying in Pounds they had to pay an additional 20%, which was an extra unexpected and unbudgeted cost to their house. Of course there's always the small chance that the opposite could have happened and suddenly their house could have been 20% cheaper.

Some products such as copper, steel and oil are tied to the commodity markets. A sudden spike in the price of oil can add additional costs to many materials.

To guard against price increases you can:

➢ Insist that your contractor provides a fixed price for the duration of the project. Most contractors won't have a problem doing this for short duration projects.

➢ Order imported items as soon as possible and pay the full amount for them when they're ordered.

➢ Order materials ahead of when they're needed.

➢ For materials paid in another currency you can purchase forward cover from a bank. Basically you're guaranteeing the exchange rate for an agreed amount of money in that currency. This usually requires an additional fee.

It's always wise to have a contingency for price increases.

If your budget has been prepared some time before construction starts it's good practice to check that prices haven't increased in the interim.

Remeasurable contracts – the pitfalls

Sometimes contractors provide a schedule of tasks, or quantities, with rates against the items. These items could be cubic metres (yards) of concrete or earth, square metres (feet) of bricks, paving, roof, paint, flooring or walls, tons of steel, and numbers of windows, doors, sinks, bathtubs, etc. In fact they've measured all the quantities required to build the house. Or have they?

Their total price is the quantity of each item multiplied by the rate (price) against the item. Then the cost of all the items is added up to give a total price for the project. Although this appears to be the total that you will pay when the project is completed, this might not be the case. If the contractor has stated that the project is remeasurable then it means that at the end of the project the contractor will remeasure all the quantities and recalculate the revised price for the project. Should any of the quantities have increased from what was originally shown, then their price will increase. Obviously if quantities are reduced then their price will come down.

However, you will have to check the quantities, or employ someone to check them for you. The checking includes confirming that the original quantities the contractor has used to calculate their price are correct or reasonable, and then again at the end to also confirm that the final quantities are correct.

The problem is that you don't know what the final construction cost is until the contractor has measured the quantities of the finished house, which they normally only do at the end of the job. But the other problem is that the contractor's price at the start may appear lower than it actually is. You may think therefore that their price is lower than other contractors, but this could be an illusion if the quantities the contractor has used in their schedule are too low – which could in fact be a deliberate ploy to make you think their price is low, or maybe they just didn't complete an accurate measure. So always be wary of accepting a price that's subject to remeasurement.

Summary

- Contractors must be paid in terms of the contract.
- It's prudent to monitor your cash flow to ensure that you will have money available to pay invoices when they're due.
- Be careful when paying deposits. Paying large deposits can be very risky.
- Check all invoices thoroughly to ensure that they're correct and haven't already been paid.
- Contractors usually require payments monthly or when they reach particular milestones. Always check that the work has been satisfactorily completed and that it meets the specifications and quality requirements.
- Withholding payment from a contractor or a supplier should only be done as a last resort and after the contractor has been informed why payment is withheld. Not paying a contractor because they aren't performing may put you in breach of the contract allowing the contractor to terminate the contract. Alternatively they could exercise a lien over the property, see Chapter 9.
- Before releasing the final payment you must check that all the work is compliant with the specifications, that all paperwork has been received and all punch list items have been completed.
- It's good practice to ensure that the contract makes provision for withholding retention monies, which is an insurance to ensure that the contractor fulfils all their obligations in terms of the contract.
- Sometimes it's possible to charge the contractor for damages which they haven't repaired, or for items they didn't supply. These back-charges can be deducted from their payments, but you must notify the contractor why you've deducted money.
- Frequently contractors show their overheads separately in their price. These overheads could be value related, time related, fixed, or split between them. Overheads are the contractor's costs to oversee and manage the project.
- Care should be taken when the contractor wants to be paid for their costs incurred on the project plus a mark-up on these costs. It's usually difficult to

control the contractor's costs and the overall cost of your project can quickly spiral out of control.

➢ Frequently construction costs increase. These increases could be due to general price increases, a fall in the value of your country's currency against the country where the product is purchased, price increases for particular commodities, or they could be driven by the local demand for contractors and construction materials. These increases can disrupt your budget so you need to be aware of them and take steps to minimise them where possible.

Chapter 11 – Completing Your House

Your new house is almost complete and you think you'll be moving into it in a couple of weeks! You'll finally be rid of the contractors! Hang-on, not so fast. You've reached the critical stage of your project and there are a few things that still need to be done. Overlooking one item could delay your move by weeks.

Equally important is to understand the processes and your rights to ensure that the contractor fulfils all their obligations and that you aren't left with items that don't work, or are incomplete.

Planning ahead of time can avoid missteps, ensuring the successful completion of your project on time.

Punch listing or snags – where you get to check the work

When the contractor has completed all the works, attended to and rectified all defects, they must ask you to check the work. You should note all defects and prepare a snag or punch list. This is your opportunity to note all visible defects. It's your opportunity to check that everything is completed and working. When checking:

➢ You could employ a specialist to check all, or part, of the work.

➢ Put all the lights on and do the check in daylight, with all curtains, shutters or blinds open so there's maximum light in the rooms.

➢ Look inside cupboards and behind doors.

➢ Don't be rushed by the contractor. Ignore them if they keep looking at their watch. If they have another appointment to attend, then reschedule the inspection, or continue the inspection without them.

➢ Look behind where the contractor is standing. Contractors may deliberately stand in a particular spot to conceal a defect that they know is there.

➢ Make a note of each defect. Don't rely on the contractor to keep notes. List the defects per room. Give the contractor a copy of your list when it's completed. Keep a copy for you.

➢ Take photos so you are reminded of what the defect is.

➢ Do a full inspection room by room.

➢ View the outside walls at different times of the day. Depending on the angle of the sun imperfections could appear obvious at times, and then hidden when the wall is in shadow, or the sun is shining full on the wall.

➢ It's essential that you take care to carry out the inspection thoroughly.

➢ Note that where you, or one of your contractors, has damaged an item, either you must fix the item, or the contractor will charge you to fix it.

➢ If there're things in the room (furniture, ladders, tools, coverings) move them aside. Again contractors are adept at concealing things.

Particular items to check could include:

➢ That all items on the drawings are fitted. Walk the project with the drawings and check that everything is where it should be. Contractors could easily have left out a light or electrical socket.

➢ That everything is clean.

➢ Doors – check that:

- They have the correct handles and locks.
- The colour of the hinges, locks, handles and latches are the same on each door.
- The door opens the correct away as shown on the drawing.
- The door opens and closes freely, without catching on the frame or floor.
- There's an even and constant gap all around the door and frame when the door's closed.
- The door doesn't rattle when it's closed.
- There is a door stopper where required that prevents the door from bashing the wall when it's opened.
- The door handles are firmly attached.
- All the screws are in the hinges and that they're screwed in flush with the hinge. Note that the screws should all be the same colour as the hinge and all have the same head.
- External doors have seals to stop rain and drafts coming through the gaps.
- Painted doors are painted all around the edge. Use a mirror to check the tops and the underside of the door.
- There are no cracks between the door frame and the wall. Even give the door a slam to see that the frame is firmly fixed.
- There are two keys for all lockable doors.
- The locks on bathroom doors are fitted with latches on the inside.
- The handles and locks aren't scratched or covered in paint.
- The paint or varnish finish is even and smooth.

➢ Windows – check:

- The glass is clean with no paint, and it has no scratches or chips.
- Opening windows open and close freely and that when closed they seal and there's no rattling.
- There aren't gaps around the windows.
- The glass is firmly in position and that all glazing beads are secured.

- The glass fits the frame – sometimes glass is fitted and there's a gap between the edge of the frame and the glass on one side.
- That safety glass is fixed in all doors.
- If windows are tinted that this is uniform with no bubbles or marks.
- That sills don't slope towards the window frame where water could form a pool.

➢ Electrics – check:
- The lights work.
- That the light switches are in the correct position and set square and at the correct height with no gaps around the edge of the switch, that they work easily and aren't loose and that they're the correct colour which match others in the room.
- That the electrical outlets (sockets) work easily (test them with a hairdryer or lamp), are installed in the correct position at the correct height and are fitted square, they aren't loose, they're the correct colour (matching others in the room), they don't have gaps around the outside edge and they aren't scratched or covered in paint.
- Lights are in the correct place and there are no gaps or holes around the edges.
- Electrical boards are clearly labelled.
- Ceiling fans work, including at variable speeds.
- Smoke alarms are installed and working.
- That all television, telephone and data points are where they should be.

➢ Ceilings – check:
- They are uniformly painted.
- There are no obvious undulations, marks or holes.
- The cornices are installed uniformly with no gaps between the cornice and the wall, and all joints are neatly filled and sanded.
- There aren't damp patches, or water stains, which would indicate a water leak.

➢ Walls – check:
- They are uniformly painted.
- The texture is consistent and even.
- There are no damp patches or water stains.
- There are no cracks, chips or blemishes. Particularly check that external corners haven't been chipped.

➢ Floors – check:
- They are flat (other than in bathrooms and laundries where they should slope towards a drain) with no small steps between the

different rooms.

- Wall to wall carpets are laid correctly with no visible joints and fixed so there is no unevenness. Walk barefoot over the carpet to check there aren't sharp nails sticking through. Where the carpet meets other floor finishes the carpet should be fixed so that it can't come loose or fray at the edge.
- Timber floors should be free of dents and scratches and should be properly sealed.
- Skirtings are firmly attached, with no visible nails (or nail holes are filled) and that they're painted or varnished uniformly and evenly.

➢ Tiles (wall and floor) – check:
- For cracked and chipped tiles.
- That tiles are a uniform colour.
- That grout between the tiles is smooth, with no cracks or holes.
- Grout and adhesives have been cleaned from the tiles.
- That the tiles don't obviously sound hollow, which could mean there's inadequate adhesive.
- That the edge of tiles where they meet carpets have a metal strip to protect the tile edges from being chipped.
- That porous tiles (such as unglazed clay tiles) have been sealed.

➢ Stairs – check:
- The size of the steps (both the tread width and the height) are uniform. They should be comfortable for the average person to walk up and down.
- There's a handrail on at least one side and it's firmly fixed in place.
- Balustrades are firmly fixed and don't have gaps where small children could squeeze through.
- They are well lit.

➢ Bathrooms – Check:
- That taps work and are marked hot and cold correctly. Ensure they direct water into the bathtubs and basins without excessive splashes.
- Fill basins and bathtubs and check they hold water and don't leak. Open the drains and see that water drains easily.
- That there's hot water.
- Toilets drain and refill easily. Flush them several times to ensure that there aren't blockages.
- For leaks under the basins after you have run the taps and drained the water.
- That all bathroom fittings are firmly attached. Sit on the toilet. Try move towel rails and toilet roll holders.
- Everything is as per the drawing.

- That there aren't scratches or stains in the baths and basins. Carefully check that the contractor hasn't tried to hide scratches with paint or nail varnish.
- That where basins fit into vanities that the junction has been neatly sealed. Check that where bathtubs meet walls and tiles that the gap has been sealed. Ensure that the junction between shower glass and walls and floors has been sealed. Check the quality of the sealing that it's smooth and neat, that it hasn't been spread across the tiles or glass.
- For cracked and chipped tiles, including ensuring the contractor hasn't tried to hide the defects with paint or silicon.   .
- The mirror isn't scratched, cracked, or marked, and that it's securely fixed to the wall.
- The quality of the grout in the tiles that it's uniform and smooth and the tiles are clean of adhesive and grout.
- That the shower drains easily and that no ponds are left after the water has drained away. Check that the tiles on the step around the shower are sloped away from the door into the shower so that water doesn't collect against the door.
- That the shower door works easily and freely and that it seals when it's closed.
- The extractor fan works.
- Heaters work.
- For damp spots on the other side of the shower walls, particularly in adjoining rooms.
- The height of basins.
- That all cabinet and cupboard doors close.
- That the ceiling has been painted and is uniform.

➢ Kitchens – check:
- All appliances work and are the brand specified.
- The sink that the taps work and discharge into the basin and are marked correctly hot and cold, there aren't leaks under the sink, the sink isn't scratched or marked, and that the sink is sealed around the edges with the counter.
- Drawers work and that they can't pull out completely.
- Handles on cupboards and drawers are correct and aren't loose.
- That the extractor fan works.
- The stove functions correctly.
- Counter tops aren't chipped or scratched. Look for any attempt by the contractor to hide defects.
- Check cupboards that the inside of the cupboards aren't damaged (particularly with screws and nails sticking through), that doors close

properly and there aren't missing screws on the hinges and catches, that the doors all sit square with even gaps between cupboards, all shelves are in place and are level and can't tip, that they are firmly fixed to the walls, and that gaps for dishwashers and fridges are correct.

- Counter tops are sealed where they meet the walls.
- Electrical outlets and water supply points are provided for fridges, dishwashers and clothes washers as required.

➤ Outside – check:
- All lights work.
- Taps work.
- The irrigation system works and covers the garden evenly without spraying areas it shouldn't.
- Paving and verandas drain – use a hose to flood them.
- That external paving and tiles are clean of mortar.
- That the area around the house generally drains away from the house and that water won't dam in places, or even flood into the house. The floor levels inside must always be higher than the outside ground levels.
- That drains are clear of debris.
- The external walls are uniform in colour and texture. That mortar has been cleaned off face bricks, stone cladding or other claddings.
- That garden walls and fences are complete, the correct height, in the correct place, as per detail, secure, painted and clean.
- That garden gates work freely and shut securely.
- That ground isn't heaped up against the side of the house.
- Check that balconies drain and that there are no leaks below.
- That water shut-off valves are easily visible and accessible.
- Swimming pools and water features don't leak and pumps work correctly.
- Movement joints in the walls have been sealed.
- For cracks or unevenness in paving.
- Switch off all taps in the house and check that the water meter isn't moving. If the water meter is showing there is water consumption while all taps are closed it's an indication that there's a leaking pipe somewhere.
- If the contractor was responsible for landscaping then check for dying or dead plants.

➤ Roof – obviously it would be best to get on the roof, but usually this isn't practical or safe. (Of course there's no better test for leaks than a good rainstorm.) Look up under the eaves and also stand back from a distance where you can see the roof surface. Even consider using a drone with a camera, providing this is permitted in your area. Using a camera on a long selfie stick may allow you to take pictures in the gutters and of the roof. Check:

- That the roof follows an even plane with no dips or bows.
- The colour of the roof is uniform.
- That all penetrations, such as vent pipes, skylights and chimneys have been correctly flashed and sealed to prevent leaks.
- That gutters slope towards the outlets so water doesn't collect in them. Even use a hosepipe to test them.
- That gutters and downpipes are clear of blockages and are sealed so there are no leaks.
- That the edge of the roof covering ends within the gutter, but doesn't hang over more than half of the gutter.
- The roof is clean of debris.
- That the roof coverings appear to be securely fixed.
- That all barge boards and facias are installed.
- That exposed timbers in the eaves have been painted.
- That the gaps between the walls and the underside of the roof have been closed off neatly.
- That roof valleys are clear of rubble and appear to be correctly flashed and sealed.

➢ Check above ceilings that insulation is installed and there isn't obvious light shining through holes in the roof.

➢ Check air-conditioning and heating systems work and that the temperature can be regulated. This may mean leaving the items on overnight.

➢ Check that fireplaces work by setting and lighting a small fire.

➢ Check all security systems are working.

➢ Garage – check:

- That the garage doors operate smoothly and easily. That the doors aren't damaged, that the door rails (guides) are firmly attached to the walls and the roof. That the door is painted as necessary.
- Cars can drive into the garage and that the access ramp isn't impossibly steep.
- That the floor isn't cracked and that the exposed concrete isn't soft or powdery.
- That water from the road or property won't flood the garage.

When the contractor has attended to the snag list items they should call you to reinspect the work. Work through your list and check that the items have been fixed. Check that the contractor hasn't damaged other items while fixing the item, which can easily happen, especially when chipped tiles are replaced. Ensure that the area has been cleaned again. Cross off the items that have been fixed. Note, this shouldn't be an opportunity to look for additional defects that you missed on your first inspection.

Beneficial access – moving in but the contractor isn't finished

Before the contractor has completed all their work it may be possible to negotiate beneficial, or part access, so that your other contractors such as television cable installers, telephone and data connections, flooring contractors and curtain people can complete installations. This beneficial access could be spelled out in the contract document, or it will have to be negotiated with the contractor. It should not interfere with the contractor's work and should not damage any of their completed work.

It's good practice before taking beneficial access to prepare a preliminary punch or snag list to record the defects so that the contractor can't blame you or your contractors for damage that was already there.

Substantial completion – all work is complete

Substantial completion is when the work is sufficiently complete so that you can use the building for its intended purpose. The contractor may still have minor punch list items to attend to which don't negatively impact your use of the facility.

You should sign acceptance of substantial completion and this document should have a list of all the outstanding and defective items attached, preferably with a time by when they must be completed.

The project warranty period starts on acceptance of substantial completion. You accept responsibility for the work and are responsible for ensuring the completed work and for securing it. The contractor is not liable for liquidated damages beyond the date of acceptance of practical completion.

Know what's in the contractor's scope of work

It's important to remind yourself of what's included in the contractor's scope of work and confirm that they've completed all their work. Even when the project manager or supervisor assures you that they've done all the work, or that an item isn't part of their contract, go and reread the contract to check for yourself.

Work generally excluded by building contractors

So you think when the contractor has completed building the house it will be 100% ready to move into! Unfortunately this is usually not the case and you'll have to engage some specialist contractors. Make sure you:

➢ Have allowed money in your budget for this work.

➢ That you've allowed time for them to complete their work.

➢ That you have engaged them early in the construction process to ensure that you've included all their requirements in the design.

➢ That they're notified well ahead of the time when they'll be required so that they can complete their work as soon as you're ready for them.

Items that could fall outside the contractor's scope of work include:

➤ Installation of cable and satellite television.

➤ Installation of telephone and data points and cables.

➤ Window treatments, which could include curtains, blinds or shutters.

➤ Security installations.

➤ Fencing of the property, including installing a post-box and house number.

➤ Landscaping.

➤ Garden irrigation (sprinkler) systems.

➤ Installing appliances such as dishwashers, clothes washers and dryers.

➤ Connections of utilities.

➤ Construction of the driveway.

Check the contract document to understand what's in the contractor's scope and what you must arrange.

Connection of utilities – power, water & gas

When the building's plumbing, gas and electrical installations are complete and have been tested, and the necessary inspections and paperwork such as compliance certificates have been issued, then these can be connected to the town systems or grid. The connections may have to be done by the utility providers. Depending on the contract, either you or the contractor will be responsible for arranging these connections. It should be noted that sometimes these connections must be arranged several weeks in advance and they usually require a fee to be paid.

Marking and labelling

The contract document and specifications should have stipulated what needs to be labelled and marked by the contractors. This would include labelling of electrical and data cables, electrical distribution boards and air-conditioning panels.

Often buried utility pipes and cables require visible markers above ground. In addition they may require marker tape and/or protective covers installed in the ground above them.

Hot and cold water taps must be correctly marked as well as all on and off switches.

Is your house safe?

Safety is critical since you wouldn't want you, your family, or anyone else being injured on your property. In the world we live in where everyone seems quick to sue for damages it's important that every care is taken to ensure that your house is safe. Safety includes ensuring:

➤ That exits are functioning and can easily be opened from inside in an emergency.

> Specified fire-fighting equipment is available and working.
> The house has adequate ventilation.
> The edges of stairs, balconies and elevated areas have balustrades and railings which small children can't squeeze through or easily climb over.
> All equipment is safe and moving parts are covered.
> Electrical equipment is correctly earthed and electrical switchboards have the correct trip or safety switches.
> All electrical wiring is certified by registered electricians.
> Large areas of glass, particularly at doors, are made visible to avoid people accidently walking into the glass.
> Safety glass is used in areas where people could accidently break the glass.
> Components and equipment have been correctly connected and commissioned.
> All areas have sufficient lighting.
> Finished floors aren't excessively slippery, even when wet.
> Emergency alarms are functioning.
> Pools are correctly fenced so they can't be easily accessed by the public or small children. That gates lock firmly and can't be opened by children.
> There aren't loose items that could topple over should small children pull on them or climb on them.
> Fireplaces and heaters have the correct protection to prevent people or items being burnt.

Occupation certificates – red tape required before moving in

Some projects require that the contractor, or owner, obtain the certificate of occupancy from local authorities and fire departments before moving in. These permits could include fire authority permits, storage of hazardous and flammable materials for gas or fuel tanks, occupation permits, compliance with heritage requirements, and permits to operate some items of equipment such as lifts.

Some of these permits could take several weeks to organise.

Keys – locking up and more

The contractor must hand over all keys to you. These keys should be clearly labelled with the room name. Keys must be checked to ensure that they work and that all duplicates as required in the contract are included. Where 'master keying' is specified the master keys must be checked to see they open the doors they should.

Often contractors still require access to some areas to complete punch list items. Keys for these areas should be issued back to the contractor and they should sign receipt for them and return them at the end of the shift, or when they've completed their work. This ensures that keys are returned, and it provides a record of who had access to the areas in case theft or damage occurs after you accepted the keys.

To facilitate this process it's useful to keep keys in lockable key cabinets. Duplicate keys should be stored separately so they're available if the original key is lost.

For security, you may elect to install new locks to external doors and doors to secure areas before moving in, since the contractor's personnel would have had access to the keys for the locks the contractor installed. Sometimes, depending what's specified in the contract, a 'builders lock' or temporary lock is installed in these doors during construction, and the specified lock is only installed when the construction work is complete and the keys for the specified locks are handed over to you immediately the final lock is installed.

Some doors may have key codes and these must be provided to you and you should then change the codes.

Other doors could be operated by biometrics, such as fingerprints, and the previously accepted biometrics should be cancelled and you and your family's biometrics added.

Warranties – what you need when things go wrong

The contract normally specifies the warranties (guarantees) required. The contractor should hand these to you on completion of the project.

A check list of the warranties should be prepared to ensure that all the warranties are received. When warranties are received they should be checked that they are for the specific item installed, be valid for the period specified in the contract documents, specify the process to be followed and who to contact if the item breaks down (usually the warranty is voided if a non-authorised workman attempts to repair the item), and be filed with the operating manual.

It's important to understand when the guarantee or warranty starts. For most items the period starts from when they're purchased. However, the contractor may keep the item in storage for several months before installing it, and it could be a further few months before your project is completed and you take occupation of the house, by which time the guarantee from the original supplier has almost expired. You need warranties that start from when you occupy the house and which are valid for the specified period from that date.

Manuals – the book of your house

Normally the contractor should hand a full manual to you when work is complete. Manuals should include:
- Equipment guarantees and warranties.
- Operating instructions for equipment.
- Maintenance procedures for specific items of equipment and materials.

> ➢ As-built drawings.
> ➢ The list of attic stock (spare stock).
> ➢ Paint colours and tile codes.
> ➢ Locations of all master switches, cut-off valves and inspection points.
> ➢ Compliance certificates.
> ➢ Permits.
> ➢ Test results.

Insurance – protecting your new house

During construction the contractor often has insurances in place covering the facility. Once they hand the house over to you it's your responsibility to insure the house. Since the contractor may still be completing punch list items you should check that your insurance covers this work.

If you've arranged insurance for the works you should notify the insurer that the work is complete. Some policies may need to be stopped, while others may have their premiums reduced.

In particular, if security systems and precautions have been upgraded it may be possible to negotiate lower premiums on the existing policies. However, renovations of an existing house will probably have added to the value of the building so it's essential to ensure that the insurance policies reflect the new value of the house.

Unused materials – what's left over

Materials which the contractor has purchased should be cleared from the property. However, it's good practice for you to retain some boxes of floor and wall tiles as spares in case you need to repair and replace some later. Usually the contractor will supply these for no charge, otherwise you will have to negotiate a reasonable price for them. It's often tempting to keep left over materials, but some of these such as paint and glues have a limited shelf life. Much of the material often clutters your property unless you have an immediate use for it.

Materials that you purchased belong to you and excess must be removed by you.

Clearing the site – converting a building site into a home

At the end of the project the project site should be tidied and evidence of construction cleared. Clearing of the construction site includes:

> ➢ Contractors clearing all their offices, stores, temporary facilities, temporary fencing and all other items used for construction.
> ➢ Material that belongs to you should be stored in an allocated area if you intend to keep it. Unused unwanted material should be removed from site by the relevant contractors that procured it. Other material could be sold for scrap, donated to organisations which can use it, be advertised for free

➢ for people willing to remove it, or simply taken to the rubbish tip.
➢ The laydown areas used by the contractors must be restored to its original condition, or landscaped, or included in the final works as per the design and project requirements.
➢ Damages to the local roads, kerbs, sidewalks and neighbouring properties must be repaired by those responsible for the damage.
➢ All temporary service and utility lines must be disconnected, made safe and removed.
➢ Areas should be clean, which includes cleaning cement and paint splashes and oil and solvent spills from walls, paving, drains and gardens.

Final account – what's the final cost?

In most contracts the final statement of account must be prepared within a specified time after project completion. It's in the interest of all parties that the final account is resolved as soon as possible, while most of the contractor's personnel are still available and the project is fresh in everyone's minds.

You usually need the statement of final account as soon as possible so that you know the total project costs. You may need to arrange additional finance if the project budget has been exceeded, or if the project has come in under budget notify lending institutions that the full portion of the loan isn't required or return excess funds to the lender (always ensure all accounts are settled before reducing loan amounts).

On conclusion of the final account it should be signed by the contracting parties, acknowledging that there are no further costs or claims from any of the parties. You wouldn't want any surprises from suppliers or contractors for additional claims or outstanding amounts long after the project has been completed.

Final payments – settling the bills

Final payments should only be released once the contractor has fulfilled all the requirements of the contract. Items that the contractor should complete before final payment is made may include:
➢ Completing all work.
➢ Submitting the project documentation, which could include occupation permits, certificates of compliance, and inspection certificates.
➢ Handing over all guarantees and warranties.
➢ Completing all punch lists or snag items.
➢ Receipt of all drawings prepared by the contractor. These include architectural plans and engineering drawings.
➢ Handing over all equipment manuals such as for air-conditioning, cooking appliances, pool pumps, gate and garage door motors, etc.
➢ Resolving and agreeing all variations.

➢   A formal final account document, or 'deed of final release', is signed by the
       contractor which states that there are no outstanding claims and variations.
➢   Clearing and tidying the project site.

It should be noted that many standard contract documents state that the
contractor is entitled to receive their final payment once they have received the
certificate of practical completion. However, this leaves you exposed to risk since the
contractor may still have to complete outstanding punch list items and clear the site.
Once the contractor has received their final payment there often isn't incentive for
them to complete the outstanding items as quickly as you would like. Therefore,
when drafting the contract document consideration should be given to amending the
clause such that final payment is only released when all of the above items have been
satisfactorily completed. However, unreasonable excessive monies shouldn't be
withheld. It should also be noted that the release of retention (retainage) monies and
bonds could depend on the satisfactory completion of these items.

The final payment must take account of:
➢   All previous payments, including deposits.
➢   All the agreed variations, which could be positive or negative.
➢   Deductions for utilities and materials supplied by you which the contractor
       was responsible for supplying, or paying for.
➢   Deductions for non-compliant work. These deductions should have been
       previously agreed in writing with the contractor.
➢   Discounts agreed with the contractor.
➢   All taxes due, but ensure that taxes haven't been applied twice to variations.
➢   Credits due to you where provisional sums and provisional costs allowed
       were more than the actual cost of the items used.

Always check the arithmetic of invoices.

It's important to keep a record of all payments and obtain receipts for payments.

Changing rates and taxes

Once the project is completed, all permits are in place and the facility is occupied
the usage of the property may have changed. This change may affect the council rates
and taxes. In some cases for instance the rates charged for water and electricity may
be less for a residential house than for a construction site.

There may be other tax rebates for changing the land use, or for upgrading the
property.

Return of deposits and guarantees – getting money back

Sometimes you have paid deposits which could include:
➢   To utility providers, for temporary power and water connections.
➢   For the rental of alternative accommodation or storage facilities.
➢   To banking institutions for providing payment guarantees.

➤   To the local authorities as a deposit for the repair of infrastructure (such as roads, kerbs, stormwater drains and sidewalks) that may have been damaged during construction.

These deposits should be claimed back. It's good practice to maintain a register, or log, of all deposits paid so that they can be tracked and recovered.

Construction defects – problems after you've moved in

Defects could be patent which means that they're visible, or they could be latent meaning they're a construction defect which isn't visible at first, but may manifest itself as a visible problem later. For example, a pipe in a wall, or underground, is leaking because it was damaged when it was installed, but the leak isn't detected until the water becomes visible on the surface of the ground or wall. The leak is a latent defect, which then becomes a patent defect when it finally becomes visible.

Defects are items:

➤   That impact the structural integrity of the building.

➤   That lead to another problem, such as allowing water ingress into the house causing damage to the structure.

➤   Which mar the appearance of the building and which aren't aesthetically pleasing.

➤   Which impact the proper use of the building, such as a blocked pipe or lights or equipment that don't work.

➤   That don't meet the codes or specifications.

➤   Which are a safety hazard.

You need to understand the cause of the defect and then take action to fix the cause, as well as remedying the defect. So for example, the ceiling in a room could show a wet mark. It's easy to paint over the wet mark and tick off the item as being fixed. The cause of the wet patch, which could be a leaking roof hasn't been fixed and the wet mark will reappear and possibly other damage will occur.

Aesthetics is often in the eye of the beholder and can be difficult to quantify. You should be very specific with what you expect from the start, but this should be reasonable and the contractor must be able to meet these expectations. There are obvious aesthetic defects, such as chipped tiles and scratched and damaged surfaces and products. The flatness and smoothness of floors and walls are often regulated by specifications. Yet, even when the flatness is within the specified tolerances the wall can look unsightly under certain lighting. There'll always be some minor defects that owners may have to expect. Obviously, an owner of a multimillion dollar house should expect a much higher standard of quality with fewer aesthetic defects, while mass produced houses and houses for the low end of the market might not have such rigorous aesthetic standards. (It should be noted that structurally the standards should be similar between a high-end product and a low-end product and in all cases the product must meet the specifications and standards).

It's sometimes better to accept an aesthetic blemish than to create a potentially weak spot when rectifying the blemish – a weak spot that could ultimately fail causing an unsightlier problem. Some defects, such as a minor chip to a tile may be obvious to you once you've noticed it, but could go unnoticed by most other people. Replacing the tile probably requires the damaged tile, plus surrounding tiles be removed, with the risk that damage could be done to other tiles and fittings, and further, that the replacement tiles won't match the existing tiles exactly. In the meantime, you have suffered noise, dust and inconvenience of being unable to use the room for a couple of days. Is it really worth it?

I'm certainly not advocating you should ignore defects, but wherever possible insist on early interventions to ensure that defects are avoided during construction, and that when they occur that they are detected and repaired during the construction process. It doesn't help to come when the house is complete and complain about the quality of the products and finishes. Often by this stage rectifying the defects causes problems elsewhere and could even weaken the structure of the house creating future problems. Rather, ensure that you regularly inspect the work with a critical eye and point out problems as work proceeds. (See Chapter 8.)

Rectifying defects can delay you occupying the building. Where you've already occupied your home, then rectifying defects can disrupt your and your family's lives, causing inconvenience and additional expense, with the possibility that other items are damaged and security is compromised.

Sometimes you have to take a pragmatic approach and accept the defect. This acceptance is not recommended where the defect is a manifestation of an underlying problem, such as rising damp or leaking roofs and pipes, if the defect jeopardises the integrity of the building, or cause structural decay, it negatively impacts your use of the facility, or it compromises the appearance of the building and impacts its value.

In some cases, when repairing defects will cause damage to the building, or impinge on your use of your home, then you could agree a price discount with the contractor for your acceptance of the defective work, however you shouldn't accept a lesser warranty.

Sometimes the defect isn't a result of the contractor's work but is a result of a faulty design. In these cases, where you appointed the designer then you'll have to claim from the designer who will have to pay for the repairs. This is where design indemnity insurance is vital and provides a method for owners to be recompensed for repairs resulting from a faulty design if the designer can't pay. If the contractor was responsible for the design then it's the contractor's responsibility to rectify the issue and claim from their designer.

If the defect is the result of you, or the family misusing the property, then the problem must be fixed at your cost. So for instance, if a door is left open to bang in the wind and eventually the door comes away from its hinges, then the problem is almost certainly yours.

Materials or equipment supplied by you which are faulty will be your responsibility to repair, unless you can prove that the contractor installed the product incorrectly. So, if you purchased a light fixture which the contractor installed and the light 'blows' or doesn't work after a few months, you'll have to contact the supplier and hope they'll accept liability and supply a new light. You'll then have to pay a contractor to replace the faulty light with the new one.

When a defect is noticed the contractor should be advised in writing. In some cases the defect could be creating a danger, such as a loose balustrade, or it could be creating further damage, such as a leaking pipe or roof, or it could be disrupting your use of the building, for instance if lights aren't working. In these cases you could take immediate action to make the area safe and stop further disruptions and damages. These costs (which must be justifiable and reasonable) could be for the contractor's account if the defect is a result of their defective work. The contractor should be provided an opportunity to rectify the defect. If after a follow-up notification and a deadline to repair the work has passed without the contractor fixing it then you can engage another party to rectify the work and these costs can be charged to the contractor. Always ensure that all correspondence is in writing.

Where it's difficult to apportion blame then the designers, project manager, or another expert could be engaged to allocate responsibility.

When damage is detected it's important to notify your insurers. Often damage caused by leaking pipes and roofs are covered by insurance, although seldom will they cover repairing the actual fault.

Defects liability period – who fixes problems

The defects liability period is a time specified in the contract which starts at the date recorded on the certificate of practical completion. It's usually three months, six, twelve or twenty-four months. In this period the contractor is responsible for rectifying all patent defects. At the end of the defects liability period a certificate of final completion is issued and all remaining retention monies and sureties are released to the contractor.

It's good practice for you to walk through the new building before the end of the defects liability period and prepare a list of all defects that the contractor must fix. It's important to note that these items must be construction defects and shouldn't include items which have been damaged by you or your family, or items which are normal wear and tear issues. A 'blown' light bulb isn't a construction defect unless the light frequently requires the bulb to be replaced.

Major defects may have a further defect liability period which begins from when they are repaired.

If defects are detected during the defect liability period the contractor must be immediately notified in writing. The contractor should repair the defect in a reasonable time.

It should be noted that in many countries there's no time limit for uncovering latent defects, or the period for uncovering latent defects is much longer than the defects liability period – often seven or ten years. So for instance, even if the defects liability period has elapsed and you discovers a wet patch on a wall which wasn't obvious during the defects liability period, and the wet patch can be attributed to defective waterproofing or faulty plumbing installed by the contractor, then the contractor is liable for the repairs.

Warranty periods – when things break

Specific items of equipment, such as air-conditioners, may have their own warranty periods which are often longer than the project defects liability period. Should an item under warranty fail during the defects liability period you should notify the contractor and the contractor should arrange for the item to be repaired. If the item breaks after the defects liability period, but within the equipment warranty period then you should notify the supplier in writing to fix or replace the item. If you repair, or attempts to repair, the item, or asks another contractor to repair the item, this will void the warranty.

Maintenance – looking after your house

Maintenance of any building is ongoing. Failure to carry out regular maintenance, such as painting and cleaning can lead to bigger problems later.

Maintenance includes:

➢ Scheduled inspections which are required by law, such as for lifts and firefighting equipment.

➢ Recommended maintenance as required by the manufacturers, such as cleaning and inspecting air-conditioning units. Failure to do routine recommended maintenance can void warranties.

➢ Replacements and repairs, which could be as simple as replacing a light bulb. It's always wise to understand why the item failed, which could be due to lack of maintenance, or because the item wasn't suitable for where and how it's used.

➢ Fixing wear and tear caused by constant use. This could include carpets, paint and equipment. If the item is wearing more quickly than expected it could be advisable to replace it with a tougher and more durable item.

➢ Repairing damages, such as bumps, scratches, cracks and broken items. This is often due to carelessness. In some cases remedial action could be taken to prevent further damage so that the repairs don't become a continual job. This could for instance entail installing bump rails or rubber protection. Damage which isn't repaired is unsightly, but it may also lead to further damage of the structure, particularly for example when water can now enter the element causing other damage.

➤ Routine maintenance. Exposed timber may require regular treatment otherwise it could look unsightly and eventually rot, affecting the integrity of the building. Often painting helps protect the exterior of the house. The amount of maintenance will depend on the products used in construction, the design, the quality of the construction, the volume of traffic and the amount of use, and the environment where the house is located. Houses situated at the coast often require far more maintenance than similar houses elsewhere.

Summary

Before your house is finished there are a number of items that need to be attended to, which includes:

➤ Preparing a punch list or snag list, which is a list of all the defects that the contractor must fix before they can consider their work complete.

➤ Arranging to complete items which weren't included in the contractor's scope of work.

➤ Connecting all utilities.

➤ Ensuring that all items are correctly marked and labelled.

➤ Ensuring the house is safe.

➤ Obtaining occupation certificates and other paperwork so you can move in.

➤ Getting a full set of keys.

➤ Obtaining all warranties from the contractor.

➤ Getting a construction manual for the house from the contractor.

➤ Ensuring that your house is fully and adequately covered by insurance.

➤ Clearing and cleaning the site so it doesn't look like a building site anymore.

➤ Issuing the contractor with the certificate of completion when all work is complete.

➤ Keeping spare stock.

➤ Settling all accounts and paying outstanding bills.

➤ Calculating the final cost of the house. Obtaining additional finance if necessary, or returning unused finance.

➤ Returning sureties (bonds) and retention money (retainage).

➤ Obtaining deposit monies back.

➤ At the end of the defects liability period reinspecting the house and preparing a list of defects for the contractor to fix.

➤ Maintaining the house in a good condition, including repairing damages, conducting routine servicing and cleaning and fixing wear and tear.

It's vital that you understand your rights when things go wrong and what the contractor must fix at their cost and what's your responsibility.

Chapter 12 – Prevent Common Problems from Occurring

Frequently problems occur in houses which could easily have been prevented if proper care was taken during construction. Once the problems become apparent they're often costly to repair. Not repairing the problem could lead to it worsening and damaging other parts of the house, and in some cases even impacting your health and that of your family.

Below I discuss some of the common problems, possible causes and how you can avoid the problem from occurring.

Cracks in walls – unsightly, but could they be more?

Cracks on walls can be unsightly. However, larger cracks could be an indication of more serious structural problems. Severe cracks could eventually allow the weather to penetrate the house. Often cracks are minor and no more than crazing of the exterior render or plaster that has been poorly applied, or hasn't been cured properly. Sometimes newly built houses settle slightly on their foundations and cracks appear, but then remain static. These cracks can often be painted over and then remain hidden for years.

Generally walls are constructed of a variety of materials and utilise different methods. A common construction method is to use bricks (cement or clay) and leave the exterior exposed, or plaster (render) the exterior and interior to create smooth walls. Many houses are timber framed, covered in a variety of timber, gypsum or other boards, or even metal sheeting. Walls are typically created in layers, with a gap that's insulated and waterproofed.

There are a number of reasons for walls cracking and these depend on the type of materials and construction.

> ➤ Often cracks are caused by poor foundations. Either the foundations are constructed poorly, or they are inadequately designed for the soil conditions. Foundations are the most important part of the house and should be designed by an engineer. Poor ground, such as clay, or collapsing sands can cause foundations to settle, or even move upwards. Building on

uncompacted ground, land that was previously a rubbish tip, or over a swamp often results in foundations settling. Movement of the foundations causes the walls to move and crack.

➤ When the walls on the ground floor of a two floor house are supporting the upper floor level they must be strong enough to support the load from the upper floors. Higher strength bricks (load bearing bricks) should be used for these walls.

➤ Poor quality brickwork results in cracks. See the next section.

➤ Houses which have large windows require additional beams (lintels) over the windows to support the walls above the windows. The walls on either side of the windows may need additional strengthening, or columns, to support the beams.

➤ In some cases the render may not have stuck properly to the brick or concrete underneath because of poor preparation. This means the render eventually flakes off, looking unsightly and allowing water to weather the wall further.

➤ Water entering walls can be particularly damaging.

➤ The roots from big trees can move foundations and cause walls to crack.

Poor brickwork and blockwork

Often brick walls crack because of poor construction. Sometimes parts of the house are designed so that the brickwork isn't covered by render, plaster or timber cladding. This brickwork is often termed face brick, or exposed brick. Face brick which is done professionally with an attractive brick can be an architectural statement and it also reduces the maintenance since the walls don't have to be painted. Unfortunately, often brickwork is done poorly so it's unsightly and it also impacts the structural integrity of the house, even resulting in leaks and bigger problems.

Some causes of poor brickwork are:

➤ Poor quality bricks. These could be weak, or not baked sufficiently. This results in them cracking or weathering away in heavy rains.

➤ Using the incorrect bricks. Some bricks aren't meant to be exposed to the elements where they could deteriorate. Usually harder or engineering bricks must be used in structures where they are required as supports, such as on lower floor structures supporting upper storeys, and in foundations.

➤ Using mortar which isn't of sufficient strength. This could be because there's insufficient cement in the mortar.

Recently a large building contractor in the UK has been forced to spend millions on fixing hundreds of houses where it was found that the mortar used was too weak. The mortar was washing out in every rainstorm. Walls were cracking and the buildings were unsafe to live in. In the worst cases houses had to be demolished and rebuilt again.

➤ Using mortar which has 'gone off'. Frequently mortar is mixed in the morning and then it's used only several hours later (sometimes even only late in the afternoon). Water is added to the mortar when it dries out to refresh it. But in this process the mortar losses it's strength until eventually it's almost useless. Mortar shouldn't be used more than four hours after it's mixed.

➤ The incorrect mortar is used. Some cement is better for certain types of bricks and sands.

➤ The mortar beds between the bricks isn't solid and has gaps or holes. This impacts the wall's strengths and it makes it more permeable to water ingress.

➤ The sand used for the mortar is contaminated. The sand should be free of stones, vegetation, timber, seeds, etc. Timber, seeds and vegetation can rot weakening the structure. Some seeds and vegetation may later spout, resulting in trees growing out the wall. Stones could weaken the mortar, or cause the bricks to not bed down properly into the mortar.

➤ Building up walls too quickly. Mortar takes at least twenty four hours to gain strength. If the wall is built up more than one metre (three feet) in this time it could cause the bottom layers to buckle and sag under the load above. This can weaken the wall and also cause it to go out of plumb.

➤ The skins of the wall aren't adequately tied together. The individual skins of the brick wall should be joined by ties or bricks, so they form a combined stronger component.

➤ Broken, cracked and damaged bricks are used in the wall. A wall of whole bricks is stronger and the interlinking bonds of the bricks create structural integrity.

➤ Face brick walls aren't cleaned as work progresses. Mortar is easier to clean from brick surfaces when it is relatively soft.

➤ Work above is allowed to dirty the face bricks below. This is particularly a problem when mortar or concrete is allowed to spill on the completed bricks and isn't cleaned. Covering the completed work with plastic can help protect it from being dirtied by the falling mortar and concrete from above.

➤ Where a wall is designed to have a cavity this isn't cleaned out before the top of the wall is closed off. A clean cavity prevents water build-up.

➤ The top of windows and doors aren't set to be a constant level.

➤ The brick courses aren't set such that there is constant height between each row of bricks, or the lines of bricks aren't straight and level. Before building the walls work out what thickness, or height, each brick course should be so that the top of the layer of bricks at the level of the top of doors is the same as the top of the door. All good bricklayers will set a line for the top of each line (course) of bricks.

➤ Bricks are placed such that the vertical joints between adjacent layers or courses line up so there isn't a good bond between layers. The alternating layers should always overlap by half a brick length (or one third if the architect specifies a specific pattern). With exposed brickwork it is important to ensure that the vertical joints between alternate layers or courses lines up so that they form a vertical line.

➤ Brick walls are built so that one side has ground against it and the other side is exposed, and the face in contact with the ground isn't properly waterproofed. Water is able to penetrate the brick walls damaging the wall and marking the exposed face of the wall. Walls in contact with the ground must be properly waterproofed and the water in the ground should also have a way to escape, usually via drains installed behind or through the wall.

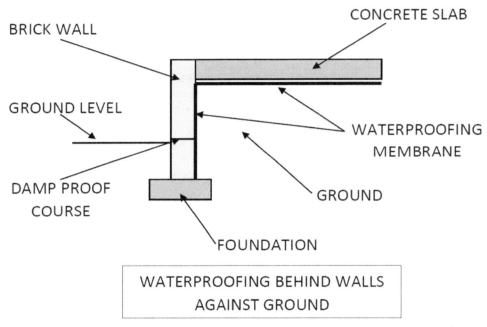

WATERPROOFING BEHIND WALLS AGAINST GROUND

➤ Reinforcing isn't installed in the walls in accordance with the designer's requirements or according to best practice. Walls usually require brick reinforcing and wall ties at specific levels, and in particular over window openings.

➤ Doors and windows aren't built in properly. They could later shake loose when slammed. In addition the openings aren't constructed straight, square or level. Always check openings. It could be costly to rectify openings which aren't square or plumb when the house is almost complete.

➤ Different bricks are used. Never mix clay and cement bricks because they shrink and contract at different rates. Also, use bricks of the same size.

➤ The supports (lintels or beams) over windows and doors don't overlap the end of the opening sufficiently, so aren't adequately supported.

> ➤ The lintels, or beams, over openings aren't adequately propped until they gain sufficient strength, causing them to sag or bend.

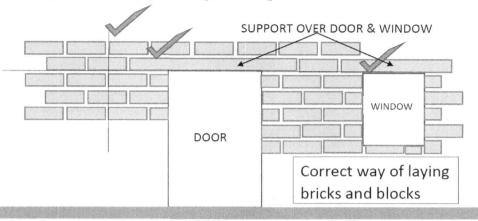

SUPPORT OVER DOOR & WINDOW

WINDOW

DOOR

Correct way of laying bricks and blocks

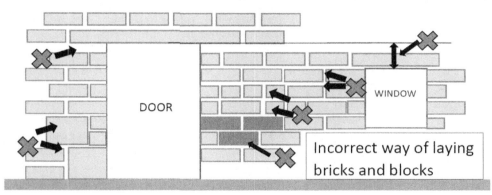

DOOR

WINDOW

Incorrect way of laying bricks and blocks

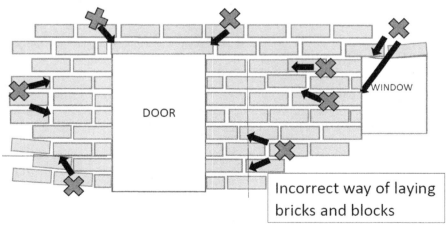

DOOR

WINDOW

Incorrect way of laying bricks and blocks

Cracks in floors – will the earth swallow your house?

Frequently concrete floors have minor cracks which aren't necessarily a problem. This cacking could be a result of inadequate curing of the wet concrete, a lack of movement joints in the concrete, or the concrete could be cracking at a designated movement joint.

Cracks can be a problem when:

➤   They're wide (say wider than 0.5 millimetres (1/50 inch)).

➤   There's a difference in elevations of the floor on either side of the crack, with one part of the floor being higher than the other.

➤   The crack appears through floor tiles which are now unsightly, even causing a sharp edge.

➤   Water from under the floor penetrates the room – this's particularly a problem in basements.

➤   The crack is increasing in size.

➤   The floor frequently gets wet and the water enters the crack where it can damage the reinforcing steel and the soil under the floor.

Severe cracking of floors could be a result of:

➤   The ground under the floor being inadequately compacted. The ground must be compacted properly and the compaction should be tested to ensure that it's compliant.

➤   The contractor using concrete that was under strength, they didn't put in the correct steel reinforcing or placed it in the incorrect position, they failed to compact the concrete adequately, or poured the concrete thinner than it should be.

➤   There being inadequate or insufficient movement joints in the floor. As concrete sets and gets hard it shrinks. This causes cracks. Concrete slabs and paving should have regular movement joints between three metres and six metres (nine to eighteen feet) apart to allow for this movement. These joints should be sealed with a joint sealant which allows movement but prevents water entering the joint.

➤   The ground under the floor is not being retained on the sides, allowing it to escape, falling out, leaving a void under the slab which means the floor is unsupported and will crack. Ground shouldn't be able to fall out or be washed out from under foundations, floor slabs, paving and driveways.

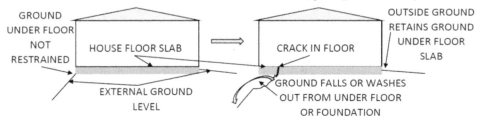

> ➤ A poor design.
> ➤ Tree roots growing under the floor getting so big that they force the floor up, cracking it. Large trees and trees with invasive roots shouldn't be planted near buildings.
> ➤ The soil under the floor slab being unsuitable. This is particularly a problem with clay, which could swell when wet and shrink when dry causing movement under the concrete slab which eventually causes cracks. Collapsing sands can also be a problem causing settlement. It's important to understand the founding conditions of your house.

Leaking roofs – do you need an umbrella inside your house?

There are a wide variety of roof covering materials and styles of roof, from flat roofs to steeply pitched roofs. But no matter the material or appearance of a roof a badly designed and constructed roof will invariably leak.

Causes of roof leaks could be because:

> ➤ Roof materials haven't been secured properly allowing rain to penetrate. This may be because the incorrect fixings have been used which aren't watertight, the fixings are too short so they pull loose, or because the fixings have allowed the roof tiles or sheeting to move thus creating gaps for water.
> ➤ The roof is inadequately designed for the weight of the material. The roof supports may be too far apart, which results in sagging of the roof causing gaps in the roof covering materials.
> ➤ Some materials require the roof not to be flatter than a particular minimum pitch or slope. If the roof is too flat rainwater will be able to penetrate. Always consult the suppliers to understand the requirements and roof design suitable for their products.
> ➤ The roof covering materials haven't been lapped sufficiently. Roof tiles and roof sheeting (tin, aluminium) must be lapped over the adjoining tiles and sheets in accordance with the suppliers recommendations.
> ➤ The roof covering materials are damaged during installation or by other contractors working on the finished roof. They may have holes, cracks, dips and bows.
> ➤ People walked on the roof in the wrong places damaging the roof.
> ➤ Water doesn't drain from the roof. Flat roofs shouldn't be perfectly flat but should allow water to run to a drain. Standing water can eventually result in leaks on the roof.
> ➤ The roof wasn't waterproofed properly. Flat roofs need to be properly waterproofed by a professional. The waterproof material must be able to withstand the impacts of the sun and extreme cold, and may need to be protected in some manner. Care should be taken that the waterproofing isn't damaged by heavy equipment or workmen installing other building

finishes. Equipment should never be bolted through the waterproofing, unless the bolt assembly is properly waterproofed over afterwards.

➢ Vent pipes, skylights, chimney flumes and other penetrations aren't properly flashed and sealed.

Case study: One house we lived in developed leaks inside the study when it rained hard. The first time we had a torrential storm the carpets and cupboards inside were soaked and had to be replaced. We summoned the builder who made several attempts to fix the roof, with no success. Every time it rained we had to place buckets in the room to catch the water dripping from the ceiling. Eventually I climbed on the roof and found that the builder hadn't installed the flashing around the chimney correctly, meaning that rain running on the roof tiles easily penetrated the gap between the chimney and the tiles, especially during heavy rain. Once we rectified the flashing we never had a problem again.

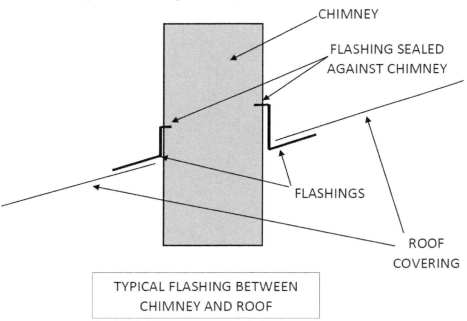

TYPICAL FLASHING BETWEEN
CHIMNEY AND ROOF

➢ Extensions are poorly designed and the new roof doesn't connect to the existing roof properly to form a watertight connection.

➢ The roof is damaged by severe weather events such as hailstorms. Ensure the materials you use are suitable for the normal expected weather conditions.

➢ The gutters are blocked causing rainwater to back up and overflow into the roof. Providing emergency overflow pipes in the gutters can prevent the water backing up to a point where it causes flooding. Having guards on the roof can help keep leaves and fruit out of the gutter.

➢ Gutters and downpipes are too small and can't cope with the volume of rainwater so they overflow, possibly into the house.

➢ Hale or snow has created dams which trap the rainwater causing it to flow into the roof.

➢ The roof valleys (where two pitched roofs at an angle to each other meet) are too flat to cope with the volume of rainwater flowing off the two roofs, or they haven't been flashed properly. Or, sometimes building rubble (broken tiles, etc) is left in the valley causing an obstruction. It's important to note that the slope of a valley formed between two pitched roofs is 30% flatter than the slope of the roofs. So, if the roofs have a 10% slope the valley only slopes at 7% which may be too flat.

With time most roofs require maintenance, re-waterproofing and even replacement. The type of materials used will dictate the lifespan of the roof.

As illustrated above and in the example below the problem with any water leak is tracing the origin of the leak. Water travels around until it finds an outlet, and often the source of the leak can be several metres (feet) away from where you see the water. Water leaks cause significant damage, which costs time and causes inconvenience to repair, often far more money than to repair the actual leak.

Leaking pipes – where's our water going?

There are various pipes in our houses which include water, wastewater (sewer), stormwater pipes, gutters and downpipes. Unfortunately any of them could have leaks. Sometimes these leaks remain hidden for months, or even years, and are only noticed when the water finally reaches the surface of the floor, wall or ceiling, normally only after it's caused damages to the various finishes in the house (such as ceilings, cupboards, paint and flooring). Common causes of leaks include:

➢ Pipes aren't installed properly. This could include pipes which aren't joined together using the appropriate fittings and adhesives. Only use licensed reputable plumbers and check pipes before they're closed up in concrete or with ground. Water pipes should be pressure tested before the house is accepted by you.

Case study: In one house we lived in we discovered that water was leaking from the covered veranda ceiling where it joined the house. We couldn't understand where the water was coming from so poked holes in the ceiling to try and trace the source of the water. Eventually we isolated the source to a brick column which was four metres (twelve feet) from where the original leak was detected. There was no obvious place for the water to get into the column. The builder tried various solutions which failed, so they eventually cut the column open where it was discovered that the plumber had not correctly connected the drainpipe from the floor above with the appropriate pipe joints. This meant that water in the drainpipe was escaping the pipe, running into the column and eventually finding its way into the ceiling, where it flowed until it found a point to escape.

➢ Pipes are damaged during construction. Plastic pipes can become crushed when concrete or earth is placed around them. Pipes should be protected during concreting and backfilling operations.

Case study: In one house that had been built fifteen years earlier the paving in the driveway suddenly collapsed. On investigation we found that the soil under the paving had eroded away and there was a cavity connecting to a broken drainpipe. The pipe had obviously been broken when it was installed and the workers had made a poor attempt to patch the hole. With time the ground surrounding the pipe had been eroded away, washing into the pipe forming a cavity, eventually causing the paving to collapse.

➢ Holes are accidently drilled through pipes, either during construction, or later when fixtures and fittings are added to the house. Always check that there aren't any pipes or electrical cables where you're drilling holes in walls, ceilings and floors.

➢ Pipes corrode. This could happen when pipes with the wrong specification are installed. Also, using harsh drain cleaners can prematurely corrode some pipes.

Blocked drains – don't drown in sewage

Blocked drains can result in flooding in the house, leaks, foul smells and inconvenience. Blocked drains are often caused by poor designs and poor installation. Some causes of blocked drains include:

➢ Pipes have insufficient falls, or even slope uphill. Drainage pipes must slope in the direction the water must flow. See Chapter 5.

➢ Building materials and rubbish were allowed to enter the pipe during construction. Exposed ends of drainage pipes should always be temporarily sealed with plastic or special covers to avoid concrete, sand, or other materials entering the pipes before the next section is added. Unfortunately there have also been cases of workmen deliberately dropping materials into pipes, which include beverage cans and bottles. This may be done as a joke, or because they are unhappy with their employer for some reason.

Case study: In one new house we had a bathroom which we seldom used. It was several weeks after moving in that we discovered that the toilet was blocked. One toilet flush and it all seemed to work fine, but after flushing it a few times, or adding solids it quickly backed up. We called the builder and they arranged specialists to clear the blocked pipes. Their attempts failed. The only way was to access the pipe from another point, but the pipe was built into the brick walls. Since the bathroom was tiled they attempted to get to the pipe from the outside by cutting the exterior wall. They still couldn't reach the blockage, so had to remove the bathtub to get to the pipe and finally locate the problem. The waste pipe from the toilet was three quarters full of concrete. Obviously someone had deliberately put concrete in the pipe, or it had accidently got into the pipe because the end wasn't protected. What a big mess, inconvenience and cost! The lessons here are to always keep the exposed ends of pipes covered until the plumber is ready to connect the next section of pipe. In addition, when testing toilets in a new house always flush them several times because sometimes the blockage is only partial and water can slowly drain away between flushes.

➤ Pipes installed in concrete aren't connected properly and they come loose when the concrete is poured, allowing concrete to enter the pipes, blocking them.

➤ Pipes are damaged when they're installed and wet concrete or ground enters the pipe causing a blockage.

➤ Bends in the pipes are too sharp and solid materials build up at the bend.

➤ The pipes are too narrow to handle the volume of material, this causes temporary back-ups which eventually causes the deposition of solids which results in blockages.

➤ There are a number of side branches that all meet the main pipe at the same point. This can cause back-ups and blockages.

➤ Side branches enter the main pipes at right angles. Joins should preferably come in at an angle that's aimed in the direction of the flow.

➤ Tree roots enter the pipes causing blockages, or tree roots growing under or over the pipe force the pipe from its proper alignment. Always avoid planting large trees, or trees with vigorous root systems near sewer and stormwater pipes.

➤ Pipes are damaged by vehicular traffic. Sewer and stormwater pipes should be installed well below where vehicles will be driving over them. Shallow pipes could be protected by encasing them in concrete. Pipes also come in various strengths, or grades, and a heavy duty grade should be used under roads and driveways.

All plumbing pipes should be installed by reputable plumbers and care must be taken that construction works don't damage the pipes. Damage caused to pipes should be properly repaired so that a leak doesn't later appear.

Damp – slowly ruining your house

Damp is a problem in many houses and manifests itself in a number of ways, including bubbling and peeling paint, plaster flaking from walls, staining of walls, rotting timber, mould and damage to carpets and furniture.

Damp is caused by:

➤ Leaking pipes.

- ➤ Leaking roofs.
- ➤ Rising damp from the ground coming up through the walls.
- ➤ Leaking windows.
- ➤ Rainwater penetrating the walls from the outside.
- ➤ When walls are built below ground level, then the water in the ground penetrating the walls.
- ➤ Leaking showers.
- ➤ Water leaking around the edge of baths, basins and sinks where they are fitted into counters and tiles.

Proper construction can prevent damp occurring. Unfortunately, when work hasn't been performed correctly and damp occurs it's often difficult and costly to fix. Preventative actions during construction to stop damp occurring include ensuring that:

- ➤ There's a waterproof barrier under floors in contact with the ground.
- ➤ Brick walls have a dampproof course (waterproof membrane) installed in the correct place, above the ground and below the floor.
- ➤ Ground isn't piled up against the walls above the position of the dampproof course.
- ➤ Walls are constructed properly preventing ingress of water. Normally in areas subject to lots of rain, applying a waterproof membrane to the outer face of the inner skin of the external walls is good practice. Often a cavity is formed between the inside skin (layer) and the outside skin of external walls and this cavity has drain holes where the cavity is interrupted by a floor slab which allows moisture in the walls to escape to the outside.
- ➤ Walls which have earth fill material against them on the outside are waterproofed so that water in the ground can't penetrate the wall.
- ➤ All plumbing pipes are installed correctly so that no leaks occur.
- ➤ A waterproof coating is applied to the inside of showers on the walls and floor, under the tiles. This waterproofing must be sealed around the waste (outlet) drainpipes in the floor and around taps and plumbing fittings. Even the tiniest hole can render the waterproofing useless.
- ➤ Baths, basins and sinks are sealed around joints with tiles and counters to ensure that water splashes can't seep through to cupboards and voids below.
- ➤ Windows are built into walls correctly. Seal around the windows. External windowsills must slope outwards so water doesn't pool against the window.
- ➤ Roofs are installed correctly.
- ➤ You conduct regular maintenance. This includes checking silicon sealant around windows, baths, showers, basins and sinks and replacing it when it becomes old and is pulling away.
- ➤ Gutters are regularly cleaned. Blocked gutters can overflow, or rust, causing water to leak into the roof.

When damp is discovered after construction is complete the source of the problem must be found and fixed.

Poor waterproofing – it happens so often

Frequently waterproofing isn't applied correctly, or it's damaged by follow on activities. This leads to leaks, damp, mould and damage to fittings and fixtures. Poor waterproofing often manifests itself several months, even years, after construction is completed. The actual cause of the problem is often difficult to find and fix. Never take chances with waterproofing. Waterproofing is usually applied to:

> ➢ Shower walls and the walls immediately above baths where splashes can wet the walls.
> ➢ Bathroom floors where there's a room below the bathroom.
> ➢ Upper storey balcony floors which could become wet with rain.
> ➢ On flat, or near flat, concrete and timber roofs.
> ➢ On walls which have ground against them. This could include areas of the house below finished ground level, such as basements and sunken areas.
> ➢ In planted areas, such as permanent raised planters.
> ➢ Walls that retain ground on one side.

Generally waterproofing looks ugly so we hide it with a permanent finish (covering), which could include painting or covering it with tiles or paving.

Frequently waterproofing fails because:

> ➢ It isn't installed by an expert. It's applied incorrectly.
> ➢ It's applied to surfaces which are wet. In particular concrete must be dry. Newly poured concrete requires time to cure, as does new brickwork and plaster. The use of dehumidifiers and hot air blowers can assist with drying.
> ➢ It has faults and holes.
> ➢ The waterproofing doesn't tie in (join) correctly to outlet pipes, meaning there's a gap for water to penetrate.
> ➢ Waterproofing is damaged by the following contractors. This could include walking on the waterproofing before it's cured, tramping sharp objects into the waterproofing, or scuffing the waterproofing with barrows and tools.
> ➢ The finish applied over the waterproofing causes damage to the waterproofing because of protruding steel or stones.
> ➢ Waterproofing which isn't flexible is applied over a joint that's designed to move.
> ➢ Holes are punched or drilled through the waterproofing to install fixtures and fittings.
> ➢ The waterproofing isn't protected from the sun or extreme cold and isn't designed to withstand the elements.
> ➢ Waterproofing is applied to surfaces which it isn't designed to stick to.
> ➢ The surface or substrate that the waterproofing is applied to fails and breaks, which inevitably will cause the waterproofing to fail.

Ensure the correct waterproofing is used and that it's applied by experts. Preferably get a warranty from the applicator. Check waterproofing to ensure there aren't obvious problems. Then ensure workers doing the following trades don't damage the waterproofing.

The best prevention method to avoid water problems and leaks is to ensure that water isn't allowed to build up and that it can drain away easily. Shape floors with good falls (slopes) towards the drain outlets, allowing no low points for water to stand.

Dark interiors – bringing light into your home

Some houses appear dark, gloomy and uninviting. Not only can this impact your health, mood and wellbeing, but it impacts the house's resale value. Dark interiors also don't suit particular décor. Dark interiors are caused by some of the following:

➤ Insufficient windows, or windows that are too small.

➤ Windows which are shaded on the outside by trees and shrubs, or that are too close to neighbouring houses or garden walls.

➤ Dark floor tiles, carpets or timber flooring.

➤ Insufficient lights, or lights that are dim, or which have opaque shades reducing the light emanating from them.

➤ Walls that are painted dark colours, have dark patterned wallpaper, dark tiles, or that have wooden panelling.

➤ Dark wooden furniture, or furniture covered in dark fabrics. Large bulky furniture and rooms that are cluttered can also make rooms appear dark.

➤ Heavy dark window drapes, curtains and blinds.

Always keep rooms as light as possible. Walls in a shade of white can appear boring, but with the right choice of furniture, pictures and floor finishes they can be a blank canvas, allowing you to create an inviting interior with accents of colour.

Consider adding skylights to let more light into dark rooms.

Mould – black stuff on your walls and more

Mould is a fungi which can be a serious problem. It's not only unsightly, it also permanently marks materials, it spreads around the house and even affects furniture and clothing, but more importantly it's a health issue for those living in the house.

Mould usually grows indoors in damp areas with poor ventilation. It can be found on walls, in insulation materials, on ceilings, on tiles, in fact anywhere that's damp.

To prevent mould it's important:

➤ To ensure that damp rooms, such as bathrooms and laundries, are properly ventilated by installing ventilation fans and providing windows that open.

➤ That building timbers and other materials which are wet aren't used where they won't be able to dry out. Preferably only dry materials should be used.

➤ That all plumbing pipes are installed correctly so there're no leaks.

➤ That partly completed work is protected from rain to prevent it becoming wet. When construction work does become wet that it's allowed to adequately dry out before being closed up.

➢ That the roof doesn't leak and that any leaks are repaired immediately.

➢ That walls have the correct dampproof membranes installed to prevent rising damp. Walls and floors in contact with the ground should have adequate waterproofing membranes installed under them.

➢ That moist air from bathrooms isn't vented into roof spaces where it creates humid conditions attractive to mould growth.

➢ Carpets and wooden flooring aren't laid on concrete that's still moist. New concrete requires time to completely dry, particularly in cool damp weather. The use of heaters can accelerate the drying process.

➢ To have good stormwater drainage, since flooding into the house introduces damp in walls and behind cupboards.

➢ To ensure that clothes dryers vent externally.

➢ When rooms get flooded that the water is removed as quickly as possible and dryers and heaters are used to dry the area.

Mould should be cleaned as soon as it appears, before it spreads further and results in a bigger problem. If mould continues to reappear it's important to find the underlying cause and rectify it. For large mould infections it may be necessary to employ professional cleaners to eliminate it.

High energy consumption means high bills

Some houses have high energy consumption because:

➢ Air-conditioning and hot-water systems are inefficient.

➢ The systems need servicing.

➢ Hot-water systems are placed far from where the hot water is required, resulting in long pipe runs where the water can cool before it reaches where it's required. Lagging or insulating pipes help reduce the heat loss.

➢ There are air gaps (especially at doors, windows and ceilings) allowing hot or cold air to enter the house from outside, or to escape from the house.

➢ The house is poorly insulated.

➢ Appliances aren't energy efficient.

Reduce your energy bills by incorporating energy efficient appliances and equipment in your house. Ensure walls, ceilings and roofs are properly insulated. Doors and windows should seal properly. Orientating the house correctly, together with good placement of windows, will help to shade the house from the hottest summer sun while making maximum use of the winter sun.

Small steps in the floor – aren't they annoying!

Steps in floors are a trip hazard. Unfortunately steps occur when:

➢ Renovations are done and the floor level on the new section of the house isn't the same as in the existing house.

➤ Concrete floors aren't cast level and they could end higher at doorways where they meet the floor of the adjoining room.

➤ The height of the floor structure doesn't take cognisance of the finish that will be applied to the floor. Floors have different finishes, which could include no added finish, floor tiles, carpets, vinyl tiles, timber veneers, sprung timber (timber on battens with a gap between the underside of the timber floor and the floor slab) and solid timber laid directly on the floor slab. These floor finishes have different thicknesses from zero millimetres to twenty five millimetres (one inch) or thicker. Frequently various rooms in the house have different floor finishes and we don't want a step (even of a few millimetres (an eighth of an inch)) between the rooms. It's therefore important before deciding the level (height) of the concrete or timber floor that goes under the final finish that you understand what type and thickness floor finish will be installed. The concrete or timber substrate level should be constructed to take account of the thickness of the floor finishes.

➤ The underlying floor doesn't take account of the requirement to install waterproofing under the floor finish, or that the finished floor should slope towards a drain. It's good practice for the structural floor under bathrooms, laundries and kitchens to be installed up to fifty millimetres (two inches) below the floor of the rest of the house. This allows waterproofing to be installed, ensuring it's protected, and then for the top of the finished floor to be graded to fall to the drains as required.

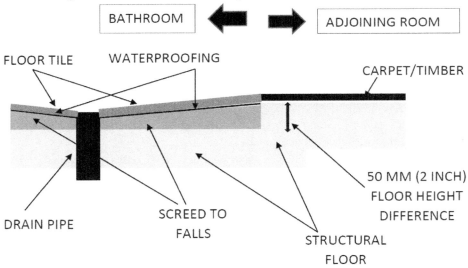

TYPICAL DETAIL OF FLOOR UNDER BATHROOMS, KITCHENS AND LAUNDRIES

Floors which aren't level – rocking furniture and more

Generally floors in your home should be level, unless they're designed to fall to a drain outlet, such as in a bathroom. Floors which aren't level can result in doors not opening properly because the underside of the door scrapes on the floor which is higher than at the door, the gap under the door being too big because the underside of the door has to be cut higher so it can pass over the higher floor, furniture not sitting level on the floor, and awkward and untidy gaps between wall tiles which are level and the uneven floor.

Floor are often out of level because:

➤ The concrete floor slab isn't poured level, which could be due to poor workmanship, or the incorrect levels being inserted.

➤ The battens under a timber floor being spaced to wide, causing the floor to sag.

➤ There are level differences between the rooms in the house so contractors try and taper floors up or down to tie into the adjoining rooms.

➤ The floor is sinking unevenly.

Often these problems are only detected when the house is nearly complete. It's important to check the levels of the underlying concrete or timber floors when they are installed, certainly well before the finishes are installed, so that rectifying actions can be taken.

Poor tiling – why do my expensive tiles look horrible?

Well laid floor and wall tiles that match the architectural style of your home can be an asset adding to the value of the house, as well as enjoyment of your home. Unfortunately, sometimes tiling choices are poor and workmanship shoddy. Some of the pitfalls include:

➤ Selecting floor tiles which have a very smooth finish and become slippery when wet. These tiles aren't suitable for wet areas such as kitchens, bathrooms and external areas. They also aren't good for stairs.

➤ Choosing tiles which don't fit the architectural style of the house.

➤ Picking tiles which are difficult to clean. This could include using porous tiles in kitchens. Porous tiles should be sealed to prevent marking and staining.

➤ Sticking tiles to a substrate that's flexible. Movement of the material under the tiles will cause the tiles to crack and come loose.

➤ Applying the tiles to a weak substrate (base layer), for instance render or screeds that are substandard. Inevitably the substrate material will break, which will cause the tiles to crack and come loose.

➤ Using the incorrect adhesive.

➤ Not thoroughly cleaning the tiles and the joints (gaps between tiles) before applying the grout. Dirt could contaminate the grout resulting in discolouration and roughness of the grout. It could also result in the grout coming loose later.

➤ Not applying the adhesive uniformly to the back of the tiles. Tiles which have hollow places behind them (because adhesive didn't fill the area) could crack.

➤ Walking on floor tiles before the adhesive has fully set. This can cause tiles to sink down in places resulting in uneven surfaces. Movement of the tiles in partly set adhesive will also weaken the bond, causing the tiles to come loose.

➤ Not properly cleaning the substrate before sticking the tiles. Dirt will create a weak bond and tiles could pull loose.

➤ Placing tiles over expansion joints in the substrate. Expansion or movement joints are designed to move. Tiles are rigid and don't move so they'll crack if the structure they are attached to moves. If the structure beneath the tiles has a movement joint then the tiles must have a joint in the same position. (I do mean exactly above the structure's joint, not a half inch away.) This movement joint in tiles can be created in a number of ways, including using silicon sealant or specialised movement joint fillers.

➤ Using tiles from two different batches. Often the colour of tiles can vary slightly between batches. While in the box this can be difficult to see but once the tiles are laid the floor will appear to have a patchwork pattern. Always order sufficient tiles to complete the floor or walls, allowing extra tiles for cutting and breakages. Beware when buying end of range products, or tiles which are on sale. Sometimes these lots can be an assortment of leftover stock from various projects or stores which have come from different batches.

➤ Applying tiles to areas where walls are skew and out of plumb, or window and door openings aren't square and straight. Before tiling check that walls are square, plumb and level, that window and door openings are square and that the surfaces are level. Far too often tiles are stuck to poor quality work. Tiles follow the surface profile they are stuck to. Because tiles have lines running in two directions they actually accentuate the faults of the surface below. So for instance, the fact that a wall is skew might not be obvious until the floor is tiled when it becomes obvious when the tile joint lines don't run parallel to the wall. It's expensive and time consuming to rip out tiles so that walls can be straightened and built plumb.

➤ Not keeping the joints (gaps) between the tiles straight. Always string a line along the edge of the tiles to keep the joints in a straight line.

➤ Not keeping the tile joints an even spacing. When laying tiles use spacers to ensure the gaps between tiles are constant – even professional tilers use them. Tiles that are too close together makes it difficult to get grout between the tiles resulting in grout falling out later. In addition, tiles which are placed too close together can't move and they could press together so hard when movement occurs that they actually pop loose from the wall or floor. Joints between tiles which aren't a uniform size look terrible.

➢ Using the wrong grade of tiles. Some tiles are too thin, or too weak, to use on floors.

➢ Selecting second grade tiles, or poor quality tiles. Tiles can vary slightly in size, but some tiles, particularly clay tiles or second grade tiles can be several millimetres (one sixteenth of an inch) different in size. This causes joint thicknesses to vary and looks unsightly. It also causes problems if the smaller tiles are laid first, then later the larger tiles won't fit into the rows formed by the smaller tiles. When you know there might be a variance in tile size use bigger joints (or gaps) between the tiles. Also, mix tiles from different boxes, blending them so there's variation from when you start laying tiles. Larger joints make the variance in the joint size less obvious (a one millimetre (one twentieth of an inch) change in tile size is relatively small when the joint is ten millimetres (two fifths of an inch) wide, but it can appear large when the joint is only three millimetres (one eighth of an inch) wide).

➢ Not setting the tiles out correctly before starting. Usually floor tiles should be set out from the centre of the floor, so find the centre. Avoid having small cuts around the edge of the room as the narrower the tile is at the intersection of the wall and floor then the more likely it will show up walls which aren't straight. Dry pack the tiles on the floor to work out the best layout, with either the centre of a tile in the middle of the room, or the joint between two tiles lying over the centre point.

➢ Not taking account of the tiles flowing through to an adjoining room. When the same floor tile is used in an adjoining room it's essential that the joints flow through the doorway, forming straight lines and patterns from one room to the next. That means that the tiles must be set out taking account of the best layout which suites both rooms.

➢ A poor choice of layout for wall tiles. Generally if all the walls in a room are tiled then there're a number of ways to set the tiles out. We should aim to satisfy some of the criteria below:

▪ As with the floor, we want to avoid having narrow strips of tiles down the sides of the wall, where they meet windows, doors and the corners.

▪ If the tile is the same, or is of the same dimensions as the floor tiles, then consideration should be given to lining up the joints in the wall tiles with the joints in the floor tiles.

▪ Setting out wall tiles so they are in a symmetrical pattern with equal cuts at either ends of the wall. Again mark the centre of the wall and either place the centre of a tile on this mark, or the joint between two tiles. Choose the option that provides the largest amount of cut tile at the ends of the wall.

- Start applying the tiles in the corner opposite the door (or diagonally opposite) and use full tiles on each wall working away from the corner.

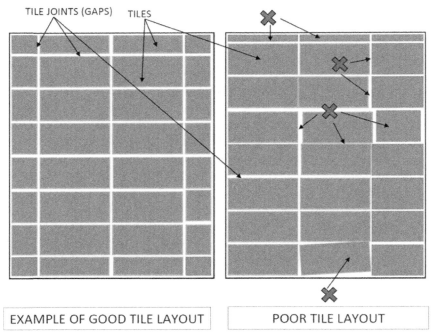

EXAMPLE OF GOOD TILE LAYOUT   POOR TILE LAYOUT

➢ Selecting the wrong size of tile – large tiles shouldn't be used in small spaces.

➢ Using a tile pattern that is too 'busy' – this includes using multicoloured tiles, tiles that are too small, laying tiles in complicated or frequently changing patterns, or mixing contrasting colours. This is particularly a problem in small spaces.

➢ Choosing a grout colour that doesn't fit the tile colour, type of tile and architectural style you're striving for. The whole effect of a tile floor or wall is a combination of the tile, the spacing of the tiles (thus the size of the joint and amount of grout) the tile grout colour, the pattern in which the tiles are laid and other features and colours in the room. Grout colours can complement or contrast with the colour of your tiles depending on the effect you're looking for. Using a light coloured grout on the floor may show up dirt more easily and require regular cleaning.

➢ Not protecting the edge of tiles where they meet another floor finish, such as carpets. The edges of tiles are susceptible to knocks and can become broken and chipped. Where a tile surface ends its good practice to install a metal angle. The depth of the angle is usually equal to the thickness of the tile. The one leg of the angle finishes flush with the top edge of the tiles, while the other leg is fixed in the adhesive under the tile – the metal upstand of the angle protects the edge of the tiles where they stop, so they aren't chipped or cracked.

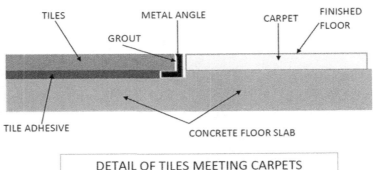

DETAIL OF TILES MEETING CARPETS

Using the incorrect timber (lumber)

The variety of different timbers is enormous, as is their price. Selecting the wrong type of timber could lead to structural or maintenance problems. Timbers come in various:

> Hardness, which is related to the type of tree. Generally these are classified as hard woods and soft woods. Soft woods are easier to cut and work with and are cheaper, but hard woods are stronger, heavier and more durable.

> Grades, with timber which has more knots and imperfections not being as strong as timbers without flaws.

> Treatments. Some timbers have been treated to be used in wet areas, while others are treated to withstand attack by pests. Using untreated timbers in your roof or in bathroom areas could result in problems.

> Lengths, widths and thicknesses. Make sure to order the correct sizes to minimise waste and work.

> Finishes, from being rough logs, cut timbers, and cut timbers which have been smoothed on one or all sides.

> Laminates, which are layers of timber glued together, or timber particles glued together in a sandwich. Laminated beams where pieces of wood are glued together can be very strong. But particle board, chip board and composite wood (super wood) often have little structural strength and can swell and deform when wet.

All timber should be suitably dried (cured) before use. The use of freshly cut timber could result in the timber shrinking, deforming (twisting and warping) and splitting as it dries out.

Some timber requires less maintenance than others. Always be sure to understand what's the best treatment for timber that's exposed to the weather. In fact, some timber requires no painting at all and painting only creates additional work and maintenance.

Uneven steps – a trip hazard waiting for an accident

Steps should be of a constant height and depth. Unfortunately, sometimes stairs aren't uniform which is dangerous and could cause people to trip. It's also often unsightly. Even a height difference of ten millimetres (a half inch) between steps can be a problem.

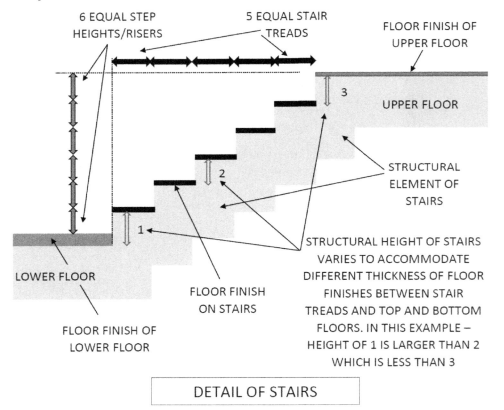

DETAIL OF STAIRS

Uneven steps are caused because:
  ➤ When the stairs are planned they don't take account of the type of finish that will be on the stairs, on the floor at the foot of the stairs and the landing at the top of the stairs. As discussed earlier these finishes can have various thicknesses which could vary from zero millimetres to twenty five millimetres (one inch) or more. So for instance, if the structure of the stairs is designed with the height of all steps being identical, and the stairs receive

a solid wooden tread which is fifteen millimetres (three fifths of an inch) thick, then the steps are each lifted by fifteen millimetres (three fifths of an inch). This isn't a problem between individual steps since they're each raised an equal fifteen millimetres (three fifths of an inch). But if the base of the steps and the landing of the steps receives timber veneer five millimetres (one fifth of an inch) thick, then the first step is ten millimetres (two fifths of an inch) higher (fifteen millimetres minus five, or three fifths of an inch minus one fifth) than the other step heights, while the top step is ten millimetres lower (five millimetres minus fifteen) (two fifths of an inch – one fifth minus three fifths) than the other steps.

> The steps are poorly constructed with uneven step heights and tread widths.
> The step heights haven't been worked out to fit exactly between the upper floor and the lower floor levels, resulting in the first or last step being a different height to the other stairs.

Sinking or cracking paving – looks untidy

Frequently paving in driveways, around the house, on footpaths or patios, cracks, sinks, or moves apart. This could be caused because:

> The ground under the paving hasn't been compacted properly so it settles beneath the paving. Proper ground preparation must be done before the paving is laid. Where the paving is under driveways and areas where vehicles will pass additional care must be taken to prepare the ground. Normally a proper base layer should be placed (using suitable material) and this must be compacted to the required specifications.
> Paving blocks aren't restrained. Paving blocks are usually placed loose on top of the ground. If there's no edge kerb, or if the paving along the edges isn't embedded in concrete, then the blocks on the edges will move away, opening the joints between the pavers. This results in an unsightly ragged edge and allows water into the paving.

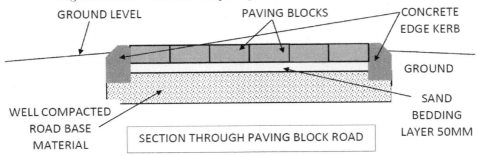

> Water sits in pools on the paving, or along the edge of the paving. Water can cause settlement of the ground under the paving so paving should be laid in an even sloping grade (slope) so the water runs off the paving.

> ➤ The bedding layer under paving blocks is too thick, too thin, or is not of a uniform texture or thickness. Usually paving blocks are bedded into a layer of river sand which is about 50mm (2 inch) thick. The paving is compacted or hit into the sand forming an even top surface. If the bedding material has stones or doesn't compact uniformly then the top surface of the paving won't be level, and the paving may also crack. It's therefore also essential to ensure that the subsurface ground is shaped and compacted to the correct height, with no depressions or unevenness before the paving is laid.

> ➤ Using paving stones which are too thin, or weak, under where vehicles will pass. Paving which isn't suitable for the weight of vehicles will crack.

> ➤ Not applying an adequate weed barrier. Vegetation under the paving will grow between the paving blocks causing it to deform.

> ➤ Not laying the paving blocks in straight lines. Always set the paving out to minimise cutting. Use stringlines to get the joints straight in all directions. If you aren't careful lines of paving can quickly get out of shape and the paving will look untidy and the blocks won't fit.

> ➤ Not maintaining the paving. Paving can deteriorate if it's not maintained. This means stopping grass and weeds from growing in the paving and destroying ant nests that form under the paving. It also means fixing severe depressions which cause water puddles and repairing the edge of the paving where the pavers come loose.

Measurement mistakes – walls in the wrong place and more

Regrettably often mistakes are made when measuring and setting out structures. Walls are built in the wrong place or they are out of plumb (vertical alignment), rooms, windows and doors aren't square, and doors, windows, steps and fixtures are installed at the incorrect level. Many of these issues can be prevented if proper checks are performed during construction, the right procedures are implemented, and if information is communicated properly with no chance for misunderstandings and misinterpretations.

What do the setting out lines and markings denote – are they to the inside, outside or centre of the wall? Is the outside, the outside of the bricks or frame, or the extremity of the render (plaster) or cladding? Does the inside measurement refer to the inside of the bricks or frame, or does it allow for the render, cladding and wall tiles? These differences can account for twenty millimetres (four-fifths of an inch) or more – which could be the difference between a bath, cabinet or fixture fitting the space or not. It could be the difference between your building being inside your property or building lines, or extending outside.

Where are you measuring heights from? Are they measured from the finished floor level (the top of floor tiles, carpet or timber) or is it from the top of the structural element (concrete or timber structure) before the floor finish is added? The difference could be twenty millimetres (four-fifths of an inch) or more and could mean the difference between your dishwasher fitting under the kitchen counter or not. If different subcontractors use different datum levels it could mean that fixtures aren't all at the correct levels.

Setting out building foundations, structures and walls is critical to ensure that the building is positioned in the correct place on the property. Indeed as I mentioned in an earlier example, that your house is constructed on the correct property, and that it's orientated facing the right direction. Unfortunately all too often structures have to be broken down because they're built in the wrong position. Using a land surveyor to set structures out is good practice - but then it's vital that those doing the work understand what the marks and lines denote, and that these points are protected on the ground so that they aren't damaged or moved until the structure is built.

If walls aren't built square it could mean that cupboards and furniture don't fit, it could result in unsightly unequal gaps where counters and cupboards meet the wall, and it will surely make floor tiles and wooden floors look untidy.

Door and window openings which aren't square may result in the doors and windows having to be specially made and fitted. Often there will be untidy gaps.

Walls that aren't straight, that are bowed, and aren't vertical will look unsightly and it will mean that fitted furniture and counters won't fit, or will have awkward gaps that have to be filled.

Never assume that render, tiles, cladding or other finishes will hide the wall or floor structure that's not level, that isn't flat and that's not straight. Sometimes it is possible to hide this poor workmanship, but then it often comes at a price, an extra cost and a smaller room. Unfortunately all too often these finishes only amplify the poor workmanship underneath!

It's therefore critical that measurements on drawings clearly show precisely where the dimension is measured from.

But, even when marking out structures on the site, whether it's on the ground, on a newly constructed concrete foundation, floor slab or a wall, it's vital that it's clear what the line and dimension indicates. Frequently those doing the work don't know and make the wrong assumption, constructing the wall or foundation out of position.

Datum levels, where height measurements are taken from should be clearly marked on the ground - an immovable level point that can't be damaged or have its height changed. Points that should be used for setting out purposes must also be clearly marked and protected so that they can't be damaged or moved by construction equipment. Unfortunately mistakes often occur because these points are unknowingly damaged and moved during construction, or because those measuring from these points don't know, or understand, what these points and marks signify.

It is essential that measuring equipment is in good condition. Damaged laser levels, tape measures, survey equipment, spirit levels and square measures will result in expensive mistakes. Remove them from the project.

Constant checking is essential to ensure that structures are being constructed in the correct location and that they are built square and vertical. Mistakes happen very easily, and they happen far too often.

Preventing damage during construction

All too often materials, partly completed work and completed installations are damaged during construction because adequate precautions aren't put in place, or because you or your contractors were careless. Damage results in additional costs to fix, could delay the project, may lead to a weakened element and often results in a blemish which mars the appearance of the house. Damage is often caused by:

➢ The weather.

- ▪ Rain could flood excavations causing them to collapse, even making them unsafe. Always fill excavations as soon as possible. If rain is expected, form an earth wall around the sides of the excavation to keep stormwater out and ensure there's a path for the stormwater to pass around the outside of the excavation without flooding it.

- ▪ Rain will damage newly poured concrete, or freshly laid bricks. Don't pour concrete when rain is expected before it will gain sufficient strength. Have waterproof coverings available to cover fresh work.

- ▪ Rain can damage internal finishes so always ensure the building is weathertight before items and materials are installed which could be damaged by water. Check that roofs are watertight.

- ▪ Extreme cold (below freezing) will damage wet concrete and mortar. Ensure that the concrete and mortar will be set before the onset of extreme cold and then cover it for protection.

- ▪ Wet surfaces can't be waterproofed so ensure that these areas are kept dry and are waterproofed as soon as possible.

- ▪ Wind can damage partly completed structures, ripping off roof coverings and pushing over partly completed walls, or walls that haven't gained full strength.

➢ Poor handling of materials when they're offloaded, stored, moved or fixed in position. Some materials shouldn't be left in the hot sun or allowed to get wet. Frequently items like roof sheets are scratched when they're handled. Even a small scratch causes a blemish and can lead to the item rusting. Incorrectly stored items can bend and twist.

➢ Items are damaged after they've been installed.

- ▪ Items are walked on, touched, pushed or bashed before they've set and gained sufficient strength. Protect and clearly mark areas such as fresh waterproofing, newly laid tiles and wet paint. New concrete and mortar takes several days to gain strength.

- ▪ Things like bathtubs, hand basins, window frames, tiles, counters and timber floors are damaged by the following work. Even tools left carelessly on a surface can scratch it, and objects dropped or carelessly scraped on surfaces can crack, chip or scratch them. Protect items with layers of cardboards, old carpet and even cover surfaces with tape and plastic until all the following work is complete. Be vigilant to see workers aren't careless.

- ▪ Protect existing structures and ensure workers and suppliers take due care. Even splashes of paint and cement will cause damage.

- ▪ Sparks from grinders and welding can mark tiles and glass.

Summary

There are many things that can go wrong when building a house. Some of these problems are obvious since they're aesthetically displeasing, while many problems only manifest themselves long after construction is complete. If you're doing the construction yourself it's best to have adequate training so that your workmanship is of a good quality and you don't make simple mistakes which could cost you time, money and inconvenience to fix. Regrettably there are many shoddy contractors so you should only employ reputable ones. But, even with the best contractor it's essential to keep an eye on them to check that they have rigorous quality controls in place and only used skilled tradespeople. If you don't have the necessary skills and expertise to check the work you should consider employing a clerk of works to periodically check the quality of the work and ensure it complies with the standards and specifications.

Some faults emanate from poor detailing, so having a good architect or designer, who prepares and draws the details correctly can help avoid many faults.

Water is the leading cause of problems. Water problems are caused by leaking pipes, poor waterproofing, windows and doors which don't seal and poor roof construction and details. Finding the problem isn't always straightforward as some leaks can remain hidden for years, only becoming apparent after large storms or after the substrate has become totally saturated. Finding the source of the leak can be difficult since water often travels many metres (yards) from the leak source, seeking a weakness where it can eventually surface.

Other causes of problems include the wrong choice of materials, poor workmanship and failing to compact the ground under foundations, floors and paving.

Always take care when marking and setting out structures and items.

Protect all work and ensure that workers take due care not to damage items.

Good communication is essential. Many mistakes occur in construction because of misunderstandings. Ensure that the other person understands what you are asking them to do and what you are explaining. Written instructions are usually better than verbal ones. If you are unsure of something ask and never assume or guess the answer.

Knowing some of these problems enables you to keep an eye open for them and take steps to prevent them occurring, or certainly get them rectified in time. Definitely take action before the final finishes are installed.

Conclusion

Before starting on your construction project it's important to understand your limits – your financial limits, your physical limits, your time limits and limits regarding your construction knowledge and experience. Knowing these you will be better prepared to select the best options for designing and constructing your house. Getting in over your head will cost more money when you have to hire a professional to help out.

A successful house building and renovation project is one where:

> ➤ You are happy with the end result and wouldn't almost not change anything – essentially it's a project where the big stuff is right, and most of the small stuff is almost right.

> ➤ The project ended within budget – okay that also doesn't happen often, but, if there's overspend it's small and manageable.

> ➤ The quality of your house is good – aesthetically and structurally, and it meets all the local and national codes and specifications.

> ➤ You and your family are happy with the house for many years. It's functional and delivers the lifestyle you and your family desire.

> ➤ The house is safe and secure for you, your family and visitors.

> ➤ Nobody was seriously hurt during construction.

> ➤ None of the neighbours are unhappy – or they were only briefly unhappy.

> ➤ The contractor made money – but not extortionate profits. Obviously poor contractors and those that were inefficient and made frequent mistakes don't deserve to make money. But you shouldn't have saved money at someone else's expense.

> ➤ Your house will be easily sellable when the time comes to move on.

> ➤ The house is environmentally friendly.

> ➤ You are proud of the end result and your achievements.

> ➤ The house construction didn't cause you undue stress, or result in lengthy and acrimonious arguments and legal battles.

You can ensure the success of your home project by:

> ➤ Knowing what you want and need. This includes preparing a good house design – one preferably done by a good architect.

> ➤ Knowing what you can afford.

> ➤ Preparing a budget. This budget must be realistic and it should have a contingency. It must include all the costs. Regularly update the budget as

new information comes available and as costs are incurred.

➤ Being prepared to stop the project if you find your expectations can't be realised, or that you can't afford the project.

➤ Educating yourself on the construction processes.

➤ Getting advice and employing experts when necessary.

➤ Understanding the property restrictions such as zoning, access, heritage and setbacks, and ensure that you know what impact local and the estate regulations will have on your house construction. (See Volume 2 for more information on this topic.)

➤ Ensuring that you have reasonable and attainable expectations in terms of the time, costs, aesthetics and the finished result.

➤ If you're doing the construction work yourself, work safely, have a master plan of what you want to achieve, understand how you're going to do things and know the order that everything must be done. Be willing to call for expert advice and help. Never take shortcuts.

➤ Not selecting your contractor based on price alone. Investigate your contractor, checking that they're reliable and can produce the quality home you're looking for.

➤ Providing contractors all the information you have that may be relevant to their price.

➤ Reviewing and carefully checking prices. Understand what's included and excluded. Read the terms and conditions, ensuring that they're acceptable.

➤ Always appointing contractors using a proper contract document, preferably one that is the industry standard for the type of project.

➤ Before starting the project ensuring that you have sufficient finance for the project, that all permits and permissions are in place, that there's adequate insurance and that the design is complete.

➤ Checking that the property boundaries are clearly marked, that items that must be retained and not damaged are protected and that existing services and utilities are marked and protected.

➤ Checking that all insurances and surety bonds are in place and are valid before construction begins.

➤ Understanding how your decisions, or lack of decisions can impact the progress and cost of the project. Resist the temptation to make changes as construction progresses.

➤ If required, appointing a clerk of works to check the quality.

➤ Always ensuring that the required inspections and tests are carried out.

➤ Regularly checking the works to ensure that the contractor is working safely, they're keeping the site tidy, the quality is acceptable, nothing has been left out, and that they're progressing according to the construction schedule.

➤ Ensuring that all communications with the contractor of a contractual nature are in writing. If you have any concerns raise these in writing. Always ensure that you communicate with the contractor's nominated representative.

➤ Ensuring that you provide all access to the work areas and all information timeously, and that materials supplied by you arrive according to the construction schedule so that you don't delay the contractor.

➤ Understanding your obligations and rights in terms of the contract.

➤ Encouraging the contractor to submit any variation costs as soon as they're aware of them so that you can update your budget.

➤ Keeping accurate records. Keep a daily diary. Take photographs regularly. Maintain a good filing system.

➤ Carefully checking all invoices and paying them in accordance with the contract. Only withhold money for legitimate reasons, informing the supplier or contractor in writing why money has been deducted from their payment.

➤ Knowing what needs to be done before you can move into the house.

➤ Ensuring that the contractor has completed all items in their scope.

➤ Preparing a snag or punch list of all the defects and unfinished items when the contractor is ready. Once the contractor has completed all the remedial work check that it has been completed satisfactorily. Check that the worksite has been cleaned and returned to the condition it should be.

➤ Settling and agreeing all accounts as soon as possible after the work is completed.

➤ Obtaining copies of all warranties, operating manuals and as-built drawings.

➤ Maintaining your house once it's completed.

Building or renovating a house can be daunting, but I hope that I've armed you with the knowledge to dodge most of the pitfalls and dangers of the construction process. It's important to acknowledge that no construction project will be perfect. There will be delays, frustrations and additional costs. Some of these are within your control and they can be limited by thorough planning, selecting the right contractor and you not making changes to the project during construction. Some of the problems are a result of the contractor's actions and failures – but actively managing the contractor to ensure they deliver a quality project on time will mitigate many of the potential problems. Unfortunately there will be problems which aren't due to you or your contractor. Inevitably there will be bad weather, suppliers and subcontractors will let you down, the authorities will move slower than anticipated and the project may hit snags. It's important to work with your contractor to limit the impacts of these events. But equally important is not to become frustrated by the additional challenges. You need to be flexible and ensure that you have time and money in reserve to deal with the unexpected.

Even the most experienced project manager, with a meticulously planned project will encounter snags and problems. There will be red tape and delays in obtaining permits. However, being properly prepared you can pre-empt many of these, putting in place contingency arrangements and quickly solving problems. Take a steady and logical approach, ticking off items as you proceed. Don't underestimate the processes.

Knowledge is power, so ensure that you research your project, ask questions, read, and even attend courses - at the end of the day it will save you money and avoid many potential problems, and invariably they will be interesting. It's important that you understand what you don't know, so that you can employ an expert, or undertake more research to fill in the missing knowledge. I know this book is packed with information, and some may now feel totally overwhelmed. Pick out the items that are pertinent to you and reread sections relevant to the different stages of your project as you progress.

Always employ a reliable team that you can trust to deliver their scope of work to the required quality, on time and with minimal fuss. Never be swayed by price alone. Don't sacrifice quality.

Good communication is essential between you, the designer, the authorities and your contractors. There should be a clear understanding of who is managing the various processes and their limits of authority, otherwise confusion will reign. Realise that you can't micromanage every detail - sure you can ask questions, but never let your interference hold the project back unnecessarily, delaying it and adding costs.

Building or renovating a house should be an exciting time. You can make it a success, whether you do everything yourself, outsource some of the work to experts, or leave everything to the experts. But, even experts need to be managed - and of course, make sure that they really are experts! How much you do and how much work you leave to experts will depend on your expertise, confidence, means and time.

Good luck with your project. May you and your family enjoy many happy years in your new home.

In my book *'An Introduction to Building and Renovating Houses - Finding Your Ideal Property and Designing Your Dream Home'* I discuss what you should consider when choosing a property, factors that should influence your planning and design decisions, important design considerations, and then a few simple changes which you can make to most houses which can often transform them with relative ease and modest costs to a new, more comfortable and valuable home.

Visit www.pn-projectmanagement.com **for more home building advice.**

Other books by Paul Netscher

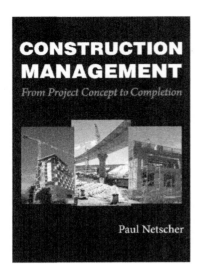

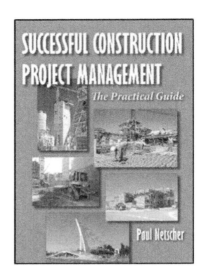

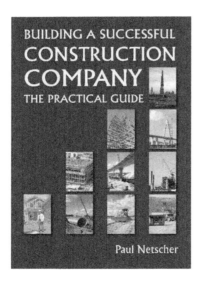

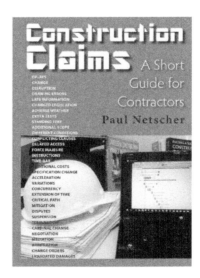

'This is a fantastic book to get a realistic and detailed idea of construction management. It seems like it would be useful to people with experience, and it is very accessible to people like me that want to learn more about the field.' (Review of Successful Construction Project Management: The Practical Guide on Amazon)

Glossary

Terminologies vary between different construction fields, countries and even companies. The descriptions below relate more to their meaning within the book and aren't necessarily their official descriptions.

Access – how you get to your house and how your vehicle goes from the road to the garage. Also, the contractor needs to reach the work areas and be able to work there. Access to the work area must be provided to the contractor in the condition specified in the contract document so they can do their work.

Aesthetics – what the finished house looks like. Could be interpreted as beauty versus ugly. Something that is aesthetically pleasing to one person may not be aesthetically pleasing to another. This is particularly a problem with modern architecture which some could object to, while others think the building is beautiful. Some estates and cities may restrict buildings that don't fit particular aesthetic guidelines. Blemishes on the finished product, such as mismatched tiles, colour variations, poor workmanship and visible patches can mar the aesthetics (look) of the finished product.

Air-conditioning (HVAC) – is equipment used to cool air down and then circulate the cool air into a room. Reverse cycle air-conditioning can also heat rooms.

Appliances – could be dishwashers, clothes washers and dryers, fridges, freezers, etc.

Approval (permission) – constructing a new house, or renovating an existing house, usually require approvals from various authorities. These approvals could include approving the drawings as well as the stages of the completed work.

Architect – a person that plans and designs a building, including preparing construction drawings. They could also be employed to manage the construction process. Usually architects require a qualification and a license to operate in the region.

As-built drawings – are drawings showing the exact location and size of the finished structures and positions of utility lines. Where the construction drawings haven't been deviated from then these drawings could be used for the as-built drawings.

Attic stock – are spare materials retained by you to make good damages after the project is completed. Typically attic stock could include boxes of floor and wall tiles. It's useful to have stock of items which may not be available in a few years' time, or where the item could later vary in colour.

Authorities – used generally to define city, town, county, or state and country government agencies.

Back-charges – money charged to a contractor for costs you incurred to rectify the contractor's work, or for items supplied to the contractor which they were responsible for supplying.

Backfill (filling) – ground (soil or earth) used to fill a hole, trench, against a building, or to create a level earth platform.

Basement (cellar) – that part of the house below ground level. Usually the ground is at least threequarters (usually more) the height of the rooms on all sides of a basement.

Balustrade – a railing supported by columns to prevent people falling from a terrace, balcony of staircase. The area beneath the railing is filled with decorative panels, glass, railings, etc, which have spacing small enough to prevent children from squeezing through gaps. Children shouldn't be able to easily climb over balustrades.

Bathroom – room in the house specifically for toilets, showers and/or bathtubs.

Bay window – a window that projects outwards from the walls of the house.

Bearing wall (loadbearing wall) – wall that supports a load above in addition to its own weight – usually an upper floor or roof.

Beneficial access (early use) – allows you to take access of part of the work so that you or your contractors can complete work (such as fit-outs or specialist installations). The contractor is still working in the area and is responsible for their work until they attain practical completion.

Bid (tender, price, quotation) – the price and supporting documents to carry out the project work which the contractor submits to you, the owner.

Bonds (surety) – a form of guarantee issued by a bank or insurance company to insure you (up to a specified value) should the contractor fail to fulfil their obligations as detailed in the contract.

Bricks – small rectangular blocks used to construct walls. These could be clay or cement and could be solid or hollow. They come in various sizes depending on the manufacturing process and are also in different strengths. So an engineering brick is typically stronger and can be used in foundations and to support an upper storey. Face bricks are clay bricks which are designed to be exposed. Face brick walls can be decorative and they require no painting or render.

Budget – an estimate of income and expenditure (costs).

Build (construct) – complete any portion of your house.

Builder (contractor) – company appointed by you to construct or renovate your house.

Building lines (setbacks) – a portion of your property, measured from the boundary, where you cannot construct your house. Usually measured as the horizontal distance from the front, rear and sides of the property boundary. These are stipulated in building codes, property zoning regulations, property title deeds or in housing estate rules.

Building plans (drawings, blueprints) – schematic representation of the house and property.

Bylaws – regulation made by a local authority or housing estate.

Cash flow – calculating the money that you have, including money or income you'll receive over the time of the project and balancing this with the money that has to be paid when bills (invoices) are due. If you have surplus cash after each bill is paid then you're cash positive. Negative cash flow is when you haven't received money and don't have money available to pay a bill when it's due.

Ceilings – the upper interior portion of a room, usually constructed of gypsum board or timber. It could be level, or follow the profile of a sloping roof – like a church. It generally hides the roof structure and the utilities fixed in the roof space.

Cement – is a powder which can be mixed with stone and sand. When water is added the cement undergoes a chemical reaction causing it to set hard when dry.

Circuit breaker (breaker) – an automatic electric switch designed to turn power off when a fault is detected or when the circuit is overloaded (the circuit is being forced to carry more electrical current than it's designed for).

Codes – are a uniform set of mandatory technical provisions for the design and construction of buildings and other structures. These can be national codes, state codes, or even codes applicable to a city or region, and usually the structure must comply with the most stringent applicable code.

Completion date – the date specified in the contract and the approved construction schedule when the project must be completed.

Concrete – the mixture of cement, sand, stone and water that sets hard when it dries.

Construction drawings – the drawings required by the contractor to enable them to construct the project.

Construction – the physical work of building, renovating or constructing a house.

Construction schedule (construction program/programme) – the depiction of the activities required to construct a house, showing their duration, the inter-relationship with other activities, their order, and when the activities are planned to start and be complete. It's used to measure progress, adjudicate any extension of time claims, and if necessary, to quantify the amount of the liquidated damages.

Contract – is the agreement between you and the contractor setting out the scope of the project, the price, milestone dates, the terms and conditions of the agreement as well as the obligations and rights of the contracting parties.

Contract document – are all the documents that form the basis of the contract between the parties.

Contractor (builder) – a company that renovates or constructs a house or building, or a portion of the house.

Cost-Plus (cost-plus a fee) – when the contractor is reimbursed their actual costs incurred in carrying out the contract, or variation, as well as a mark-up on these costs, which is proportional to the costs and is normally expressed as a percentage.

Critical path – is a sequence of activities in the construction schedule which are linked, and whose delay will affect the overall project completion.

Cupboard (closet, cabinet) – usually a piece of furniture with shelves (and sometimes rails) for storing clothes, crockery, etc. For this purpose I've used it to define cupboards built into the house. These may have doors.

Curing compound – is a liquid (a resin, wax or synthetic compound) that's applied to fresh concrete (by spray or rolling) immediately the concrete is set and has been worked smooth. The compound forms a barrier or seal to retard water loss from the concrete so that it can cure (harden) developing its full strength without excessive cracking. Rapid water loss will inhibit concrete strength gain.

Damages – are the costs or losses that one party suffers, often because of the actions of another party. These costs could be recovered in a claim for damages.

Defects – work that doesn't meet the specifications or acceptable quality standards. An item that has failed, such as a leaking pipe or cracked walls.

Delay claim – claim from the contractor for a delay that has impacted project progress as measured against the critical path, where that delay is not due to the contractor and couldn't have been reasonably foreseen or anticipated by the contractor when they priced the project.

Demobilisation – the process of moving off site when the project is complete.

Demolition – the act of breaking down part or all of the structure. It could involve breaking an opening in a wall for a window, chopping up floor tiles, removing part of the roof or bashing down walls.

Designer – architect or engineer that designs the structures and house.

Dispute Resolution – the process whereby a dispute is resolved.

Disputes – when a difference between the contractor and the owner, or other parties to a contract, cannot be resolved amicably and it has to be referred to third parties for resolution. The dispute could arise because the parties cannot agree that a variation claim submitted by one party has a legitimate basis, or they cannot agree the quantum of the claim.

Drawings (plans, blueprints) – are the graphic representations of the structures and facilities.

Driveway – the road or paving that connects the house to the public road. Designed for vehicles and constructed of compacted ground, concrete, surfaced with asphalt or various paving blocks.

Earthworks (ground works) – includes all work involving excavating, filling and levelling the ground (earth or soil) on the project.

Engineer – designer of elements of the building, such as the structure, air-conditioning and stormwater.

Estate (housing estate) – is an area of land set aside for a specific use, often with specific guidelines and rules, sometimes with their own governing body or authority.

Extension of time – is the additional time required to complete the project because a delay not caused by the contractor impacted the project's completion date, or because additional scope or work was added.

Flashing – thin pieces of material, usually metal, designed to seal the gap where the roof joins to chimneys and walls, where pipes penetrate the roof and to join two pieces of roof together that intersect at an angle. The flashing often takes an L-shape, with one leg of the angle sliding under the roof covering and the other leg being securely fixed to the chimney or wall above the surface of the roof, thus forming a channel for the water to flow away. Flashings can be cut and bent to suit specific roof junctions and shapes.

Fill (backfill, filling) – ground, soil, earth, used to fill holes, trenches, under buildings and to level an area. The ground usually has to be compacted in layers so that it is firm and doesn't settle when it's wet or loads are placed on it.

Finishes – generally taken to mean the non-structural elements of the building that provides the building it's finished aesthetics. The finishes may include carpets, floor and wall tiles, the render (plaster) on the walls and the type of ceiling. It could include the type of fixtures, such as bathtubs, washbasins, tapware and lights. A garage could have minimal finishes with bare concrete floors and walls and industrial lights, while a bathroom could have expensive finishes, which could include marble floor and wall tiles. The type of finishes can add hugely to the cost of a building.

Fixtures – light fixtures, built in cupboards (cabinets), sinks, taps, basins, toilets, bathtubs, etc.

Formwork (forms) – the temporary forms or moulds used to shape and contain the wet concrete used in structures until it has gained sufficient strength to support itself.

Foundation – the lower portion of the building that connects the building to the ground, supporting the weight of the house and anchoring it to the ground.

Garage – secured covered area where vehicles are stored.

Garden – used to describe the portion of your property outside the house. This could consist of patios, driveways and swimming pool, but generally is the area covered by plants, trees and lawn (grass).

Green buildings – are buildings specifically designed and constructed to be sustainable and environmentally friendly. This is achieved by them being resource efficient (which is limiting the amount of energy and water required to operate and construct the facility), using recycled materials and materials which can be recycled, and limiting the impact of the building on the environment during operation as well as in the construction phase.

Ground (soil, earth, dirt) – material which can easily be excavated, usually consisting of sand and sometimes including stones and small rocks. This material can also be levelled and compacted to fill holes and trenches, or to create level areas where the house can be constructed.

GST (in some countries VAT) – taxes that are added onto the price of products and services.

Heaving clay – some clay will expand when it's wet and then shrink when it dries out. This causes the ground to move, which can break pipes in the ground and cause house foundations to move, often unevenly, resulting in cracking of the building.

Heritage buildings – are buildings that have been declared to have cultural or historical importance. Sometimes whole precincts are declared to be heritage protected. Heritage buildings are usually protected (listed), often meaning that they can't be changed, and when any work is done on the building the new materials and workmanship must match the existing building, or comply with strict guidelines. There are often different levels of heritage protection which dictate what can and can't be done to the building.

Hoardings - a temporary fence, often of wood, tin or iron, normally of solid construction, erected around construction sites or work areas. Hoardings can serve several purposes depending on construction and could keep people out of the construction area, retain the construction work in the enclosed area, make the construction work less visible to the public, secure the project work area and reduce the impacts of noise and dust to you, your family, or the public.

Inspections – records that work meets the specifications and quality requirements. Inspections could be done by the contractor, you or your representative, or by representatives of local authorities, utility providers or banks.

Instruction (Site Instruction) – is a contractual request made by you or your representative directed at the contractor. Instructions often cause the project to be varied and may result in a variation claim.

Insurance – cover for potential losses.

Interim valuation claims (progress valuation claims) – are interim payments paid to the contractor for work that's complete, but the project hasn't been completely finished. These payments could be for reaching specified milestones, completing sections of work, or be calculated on work completed in a specified time period, normally per month. Interim valuation claims should be in accordance with the terms and conditions in the contract.

Joint – The junction of adjacent surfaces. In some cases a joint is specially formed in walls or floors to allow independent movement without causing cracking.

Landscaping – the process of making a garden, including shaping the ground.

Land survey – checking the physical position and elevations on the property and plotting these on a drawing. It could also be the act of marking out what's on drawings physically on the ground. So for instance, marking the position of the property boundary and the position of where structures must be constructed.

Laydown areas – the temporary areas to store materials and equipment and to place offices, stores and toilets required for construction.

Lead time – the amount of time taken for an item to be delivered to the project once it has been ordered. This time includes the time to design, manufacture and transport it to the project.

Levelling the site – flattening the area so that the house can be constructed, usually by excavating high areas to remove material and filling lower areas. This could involve making areas perfectly level and even compacting the ground.

Lights (light fixture, luminaire) – an assembly that contains the light.

Liquidated damages (penalty) – are a specified amount of money which the contractor will pay the owner (you) should the contractor fail to meet the agreed contract completion dates, or other specified targets.

Lump sum (fixed sum) – the contractor provides a total price for the work, which is fixed, only changing when there is a variation to what the contractor priced.

Maintenance – to repair damages and faults as well as undertaking preventative maintenance, such as servicing equipment, and painting and cleaning the building.

Main contractor (prime contractor) – the contractor that executes the bulk of the work. They may employ subcontractors to do some, or all of the work.

Manuals (operating manuals) – contains information required for the operation and maintenance of the building, such as construction drawings, warranties, operating instructions, servicing advice and types of materials.

Master key – locks that have their own key design which only opens that lock, but, these locks are also able to be opened by a master key which opens several other locks. So an individual will have a key only for that lock, but you may have a master key that unlocks that lock and other locks in the house. Often utility providers will have a master key, say to open all the electrical meter boxes in the town, but you will only have a key to open your box.

Mark-up – the profit margin the contractor adds, although in some cases it may include the profit plus the contractor's overheads.

Materials – all items permanently incorporated into the works. This may include concrete, reinforcing, timber, bricks, glass, etc.

Milestone – an important event, such as granting access, or a completion date.

Mortar – a mixture of cement, sand and water and sometimes lime that's used to connect bricks, blocks and masonry together. The mortar sets hard when dry.

Mould (mold) – fungal growth on walls, timber, tiles, etc. Usually black.

Negotiate – to try and reach an equitable agreement through discussion.

Neighbours – could be people or companies located immediately adjacent to your house, as well as those in the vicinity who are in the immediate area.

Orientation – the direction your house faces.

Overheads (overhead costs, indirect costs, preliminaries) – overhead project costs are costs the contractor incurs to run the project which cannot be directly related to specific tasks. This usually includes the provision of management, supervision, site facilities, insurances and bonds. Company overheads are the costs a contractor incurs which are not directly attributable to a specific project, but are related to running the company and include costs such as head office rental, management and various support departments, such as finance and tendering.

Owner – the party who will own the project. You.

Paving – referring to an outdoor hard surface to driveways and patios. Paving may be bricks (clay or concrete), concrete paving stones, asphalt or natural stone.

Permits – are documents that officially allow the receiver of the permit to carry out the action stated on the permit, often subject to conditions and constraints attached to the permit. There may be a number of permits required for a construction project and these may be issued by different departments and agencies.

Piles – steel, timber or concrete posts which are driven or drilled into the ground to create the building foundations. Usually used when the soil conditions are poor, or when the building is on the edge of a steep slope or hole. Sometimes piles can be placed right next to each other, or sheet piles (steel piles that look similar to roofing materials) are used, to form a continuous wall in the ground – this helps retain the ground on one side of the wall while the ground is excavated from the other side.

Preconstruction survey (dilapidation survey) – a record made before construction starts of the condition of existing structures on the project site and neighbouring structures that could be damaged by the construction work.

Preliminaries (overheads) – this is the contractor's price for complying with the general obligations of the contract. These costs cannot be allocated to a specific task or portion of the project, but are rather the costs associated with managing the project as a whole. These costs could include the contractor's project offices, management and supervision, insurance and bonds.

Prime cost – a monetary amount in the contract price, normally inserted by the contractor, for an item or material. The final cost that you pay will be the actual amount that the item costs, which could be more or less than the amount allowed and depends on the product that you select.

Principle agent – is a person delegated the responsibility of representing your interests. Often the architect, or engineer, is appointed the principle agent and their duties usually include project managing the construction work, assessing the contractor's variation claims and payment claims, and ensuring that the construction work is delivered on time, safely and meets the quality standards and specifications.

Progress valuation (interim valuation) – is an interim payment to the contractor for work that has been satisfactorily completed on the project. The contractor usually invoices monthly or when specified milestones have been reached.

Project – any construction work.

Project manager – is the person (or company) appointed to manage the project for the owner. Often the contractor's person responsible for managing their portion of the construction work is also called the project manager (or construction manager, site manager or site agent). However, these two project managers fill two distinct roles in the project, with the one representing you and the other the contractor.

Property (lot, block, land) – the land that you own where your house is, or where your new house will be constructed.

Provisional sums (allowances) - A provisional sum is an amount of money included in the contract sum to cover work or materials, or both, which could not be specifically detailed when the project was priced by the contractor or when the contract was signed. The amount of the provisional sum is usually an estimate inserted by the contractor or you. The final amount will be priced by the contractor once sufficient information is available, or you've decided what you want.

Punch list (snag list, defects list) – is a list of outstanding items or repairs (defects) that must be completed so that the house complies with your requirements.

Quality – the properties of the product supplied to you, defined by the requirements in the contract document, specifications and drawings, which may include the visual appearance, as well as the strength and durability.

Rates (prices, cost) – on some projects the contractor provides costs for various tasks or items, and these are included in the contract document. The total contract price is calculated by multiplying the rate by the number of units in the task and adding all these amounts together.

Reinforcing (re-bar) – the steel bars incorporated into concrete structures for strength.

Render (plaster) – a composition of sand, water and cement, or of lime or gypsum and water, which is spread over walls or ceilings to create a smooth, or a textured, finish that's uniform and even and covers the underlying surface, which could be bricks or gypsum boards.

Renovations (remodelling) – the act of changing an existing house or structure to increase its size, change its use, or improve it to better suit your needs. Renovations could be as simple as repainting the house or involve partly demolishing and extending the house.

Resources – people, materials and equipment required to construct the house.

Retention (retainage)– a portion of money that is owed to the contractor but is withheld by you as insurance until the contractor has fulfilled all their contractual obligations. This amount must be specified in the contract document.

Riser – the vertical height between steps.

Rock – ground that is hard and can only be excavated using mechanical means or with explosives. The rock may be solid or could be fractured (cracked).

Running costs (ongoing costs) – the costs incurred to keep the house going. These costs could include the utility bills, property taxes, loan repayments and maintenance costs.

Scaffold (staging) – a temporary structure to access high areas of the house during construction.

Schedule (often referred to as a programme, program, bar chart or Gantt chart) – a graphic representation of the timetable needed to complete the project, showing the sequencing, inter relationship and duration of the various project tasks and activities.

Schedule of rates – is a list of items which could include different categories of labour, tradespeople, and equipment, that the contractor fills in a hourly, daily or weekly rate against. The contractor is paid the actual hours worked for each category multiplied by the relevant rate. A schedule of rates may also be a list of tasks, which could be placing cubic metres (yards) of concrete, tons of steel, square metre (feet) of bricks, etc. The item would have an exact description which could include the strength and other details and the unit of measurement.

Scope of work – the work which the contractor is contracted to do. The scope normally takes the form of a written description of the work contained within the contract document.

Screed – usually a sand and cement mixture placed onto a concrete slab to make it level, to raise a floor to a desired height, or to create a slope towards a drain or low point.

Septic tank – are underground chambers of PVC, concrete or other materials. Household sewage flows into the tank where it's broken down by bacteria. The treated effluent fluid flows from the tank into a French drain where it is allowed to seep into the ground. Periodically the sludge that accumulates in the tank must be pumped out and disposed by specialist contractors. Usually licenses are required to install septic tanks.

Services (utilities) – water, power, gas, telephones, sewer and data cables, ducts and pipes.

Servitudes (easement) – a portion of the property which can be used by others, such as for installing utility cables and pipes. The easement or servitude should be in the title deeds or on the property plans.

Set-back (building line) – A prescribed distance that a building must not be closer to the property boundary. This amount is usually dictated by the local authorities and the zoning of the property. In some instances it's part of the conditions of building on the property dictated by estate rules. The set-back could vary depending on the height of the building and the set-back could vary for different floor levels of the building.

Setting-out information – information to position a structure in the horizontal plan and the vertical plane. Often given as X and Y coordinates and an elevation or Z coordinate. Could also be a measurement, height and direction from an existing structure or known fixed point.

Sewer pipes (wastewater pipes) – pipes that take the wastewater from toilets, sinks, bathtubs, basins and showers to the town wastewater (sewage) system, or to a septic tank.

Shop drawings – drawings produced (normally by the contractor, their suppliers or subcontractors) to show the details of an item that they have to fabricate.

Site (project site) – the area where construction takes place.

Slabs (concrete slab) – concrete structural element forming the floor on the ground level, and the floor between the different levels in the house.

Soil (ground, earth, dirt) – material used to fill holes and against foundations and under floor slabs.

Specifications – definitions and requirements of the materials, processes, quality, products and systems to be used in the house.

Storey (story, floor, level) – the number of floor levels above the lowest level. A house that has a ground floor and an upstairs level is two storeys, while a house with three floors or levels would be three storeys high.

Subcontractor – a contractor employed by a contractor to do a portion of their works.

Supervisor (foreman) – is the person who supervises the contractor's workers, or a section of work.

Supplier – a company which supplies materials which are incorporated in the project.

Surety (bond) – a form of insurance supplied by a bank or insurance company to ensure that the contractor complies with their contractual obligations.

Survey (construction survey) – used here to set out structures and to plot the position of structures, site boundaries and other relevant items, locating them on plan and elevation. However, preconstruction survey is used to record the condition of existing structures.

Tender (bid, estimate or quote) – a price, or quotation, to carry out work which is submitted by the contractor.

Tender document (Request for price (RFP), request for quotation (RFQ)) – are the documents issued to the contractor to enable them to price the project. These documents could include the scope of work, the terms and conditions of the contract, specifications, drawings and ancillary project information.

Testing – the act of confirming the properties of a material, or ensuring that a system is operating as it should.

Tiles – a manufactured hard waring product of ceramic, cement, stone (such as granite, marble) and glass used to cover floors and walls. They can be square or rectangular and range in size from mosaics to tiles of six hundred by three hundred millimetres (two feet by one foot). Roofs are often covered by cement, clay or wood tiles.

Topography – the slope of the property.

Topsoil – uppermost layer of soil which usually contains vegetation and nutrients. Topsoil is a valuable commodity for plants to grow.

Tradespeople (craftspeople) – skilled construction workers, which could include; carpenters, plumbers, electricians, bricklayers and tilers.

Tread (going) – horizontal part of a step.

Utilities (services) – water, gas, electricity, telecommunications cables. Also used here to include sewer pipes.

Vanity (bathroom vanity)– the combination of the bathroom handbasin and the surrounds, which is normally a shelf holding the basin plus creating storage around and often under the basin. The top surface, or slab, is usually made of natural stone, concrete, timber, or tiles. It must be water resistant to withstand regular splashing.

Variation claim – is a claim to vary the contract. The claim could be for additional time and (or) for additional monetary compensation.

Warranty (guarantee) – a guarantee that the product will function as it should.

Waterproofing – the process of making a wall, floor or roof impermeable to water. Waterproofing can be an impermeable material, such as, PVC sheeting, tar paper, or a bituminous paint applied to the surface.

Water table – the level of water in the ground below the surface.

Window dressings – curtains, blinds or shutters.

Zoning – areas of land are divided by authorities into zones within which various uses are permitted. These zones may also dictate the minimum size of the property. So for instance, we could have land zoned for industrial use, commercial use, residential and apartments. From time to time the authorities may revise the zoning, changing the land use and revising the property density. Zoning laws may also dictate the size and height of the house, the type of structure and how close the buildings can be from the property boundaries.

Bibliography

Cambridge, David. *Manage Your Home Build & Renovation Project: How to Create Your Dream Home on Time, in Budget and Without Stress.* Live It.

Cauldwell, Rex. *Wiring a House, 5ᵗ ed. For pros by Pros.* Taunton Press.

Daum, Kevin, Brewster, Janice, Economy, Peter. *Building Your Own Home for Dummies.* For Dummies.

Editors of Cool springs Press. *Black & Decker the Complete Guide to Wiring, Updated 7th Edition: Current with 2017-2020 Electrical Codes.* Cool Springs Press.

Editors of Cool Springs Press. *Black & Decker the Complete Guide to Plumbing Updated 6th Edition.* Cool Springs Press.

Elis, Angela. *Design & Construction of Stairs & Staircases.* Home Design Directory.

Gelavis, John. *Tips to Avoid Overcapitalising.* New Homes. The Weekend West April 7-8 2018.

Gelavis, John. *Renovating Your Home – Think First Before You Act.* New Homes. The Weekend West June 23-24 2018.

Gelavis, John. *What's the Price?* New Homes. The Weekend West June 9-10 2018.

Government of Western Australia, The Department of Health. *Healthy WA. Mould and Dampness.*

Johnston, Amy. *What Your Contractor Can't Tell You: The Essential Guide to Building and Renovating.* Shube Publishing.

Kohlstedt, Kurt. *What Style is That House? Visual Guides to Domestic Architectural Designs.* 99% Invisible.

Lester, Kent and McGuerty, Dave. *The Complete Guide to Contracting Your Home: A Step-by-Step Method for Managing Home Construction. Fifth ed.* Betterway Home.

Litchfield, Michael. *Renovation 4th Edition: Completely Revised and Updated.* Taunton Press; 4th ed. Edition.

Molinelli, Jim. *Remodel: Without Going Bonkers or Broke.* Publisher Jim Molinelli

Netscher, Paul. *Construction Claims: A Short Guide for Contractors.* Panet Publications.

Netscher, Paul. *Construction Management: From Project Concept to Completion.* Panet Publications.

Netscher, Paul. *Construction Project Management: Tips and Insights.* Panet Publications.

Pages-Ruiz, Fernando. *Building an Affordable House: Trade Secrets to High-Value, Low-Cost Construction.* Taunton Press.

The Chubby Builder. *How to Build Your Dream Home Without Getting Nailed!: Save Your Time, Money, Sanity and Relationships.* Chubby Builder Publishing

United States Department of Labour. *Excavations, Sloping and Benching.* Occupational Safety and Health Administration.

Wing, Charlie. *The Visual Handbook of Building and Remodeling.* Taunton Press.

Wulfinghoff, *Donald R. Super House: Design Your Dream Home for Super Energy Efficiency, Total Comfort, Dazzling Beauty, Awesome Strength, and Economy.* Energy Inst Pr.

An Introduction to

Building and
Renovating Houses

Volume 2
finding your ideal
property and designing
your dream home

Paul Netscher

For more valuable information on building and renovating houses read 'Volume 2 – finding your ideal property and designing your dream home'.

Printed in Great Britain
by Amazon

72776509R00140